Understanding and Implementing Trauma-Informed Practice in Schools

This book bridges the research-to-practice gap by providing clear, evidence-based strategies to enable and advance trauma-informed practices for teachers, school leaders, and student support professionals.

Drawing on innovative research, this book explores key trauma-informed practice principles and their practical application. Core topics include a deep dive into the latest research about how trauma and stress impact children and young people in the education setting, including observable and invisible physical responses, relationships and attachment, learning and executive function, and interventions such as supportive policies, routine, music, and movement. Each chapter combines research insights with practical recommendations and real-world case studies, supporting educators in translating theory into effective practice. By explaining the *what, why*, and *how* of trauma-informed practices and policies in schools, this book makes the science and practice of trauma-informed education accessible, actionable, and meaningful.

Comprehensive, evidence-informed, and deeply practical, this is an essential guide for school leaders, educators, and preservice students committed to building safe, supportive, and trauma-responsive school communities.

Emily Berger (she/her), PhD, MAPS, FCEDP, is an Associate Professor and Registered Psychologist with the School of Educational Psychology and Counselling, Monash University, Australia. She is also an adjunct Associate Professor with the School of Rural Health and Monash Gender and Family Violence Prevention Centre, Monash University. Associate Professor Berger is a nationally and internationally recognized trauma-informed researcher. Her research focuses on transforming organizations and schools to incorporate trauma-informed practice.

Shantel D. Crosby (she/her), PhD, LCSW, is an Associate Professor in the School of Social Work and Family Science at the University of Louisville, USA. She is also a clinical therapist, with experience working with youth and adults from marginalized backgrounds. Her research focuses on trauma and racial trauma among racial/ethnic minority youth, and equity-centered, trauma-informed practice in schools and organizations.

Karen E. Martin (she/her), PhD, is an Adjunct Professor in the School of Health and Clinical Sciences at The University of Western Australia and the School of Education at the University of Tasmania, Australia. With health research experience spanning three decades, Professor Martin is driven by her passion to help create socially just and compassionate environments for children and young people. Supported by a dedicated team of colleagues and university students, Professor Martin led the creation and publishing of the International Trauma-Informed Practice Principles for Schools (ITIPPS) and the Thoughtful Schools Program.

Understanding and Implementing Trauma-Informed Practice in Schools

An Evidence-Based Guide

Edited by
Emily Berger, Shantel D. Crosby,
and Karen E. Martin

Routledge
Taylor & Francis Group
LONDON AND NEW YORK

Designed cover image: Getty Images

First published 2026
by Routledge
4 Park Square, Milton Park, Abingdon, Oxon OX14 4RN

and by Routledge
605 Third Avenue, New York, NY 10158

Routledge is an imprint of the Taylor & Francis Group, an informa business

British Library Cataloguing-in-Publication Data
A catalogue record for this book is available from the British Library

ISBN: 9781032565446 (hbk)
ISBN: 9781032565439 (pbk)
ISBN: 9781003436034 (ebk)

DOI: 10.4324/9781003436034

Typeset in Optima
by codeMantra

The editors would like to dedicate this book to our families and friends who show unwavering support for our drive to build trauma-informed schools and communities for students, families, and school staff worldwide.

Contents

Contributors

Kelly-Ann Allen (she/her), PhD, FAPS, is an endorsed Educational and Developmental Psychologist and Associate Professor in the School of Educational Psychology and Counselling in the Faculty of Education at Monash University, as well as Honorary Principal Fellow at the Centre for Wellbeing Science, Melbourne Graduate School of Education at the University of Melbourne.

Courtney N. Baker (she/her), PhD, is an Associate Professor in the Department of Psychology at Tulane University and a licensed child clinical psychologist. She is a violence prevention researcher and an implementation scientist, and one area of her work focuses on measuring, implementing, and evaluating trauma-informed approaches in schools.

Jaime Barratt (she/her) is Assistant Professor in Early Childhood Education at Brock University. Jaime is Registered Early Childhood Educator with a multidisciplinary, cross-cultural background in Health and Education. Her primary focus is on fostering physical literacy in Early Childhood Educators, recognizing the pivotal role they play in promoting young children's movement valuation and holistic wellbeing. Jaime developed a conceptual model of The Effective Early Childhood Physical Literacy Pedagogue, elucidating the essential competencies and traits that contribute to the successful advancement of physical literacy in young children. Subsequently, she developed a comprehensive self-report instrument to assess Early Childhood Educators' capabilities, knowledge, and practices related to physical literacy.

India Bryce (she/her), PhD, BEd, MGuiCous, MSW (Forensic), is an Academic, Researcher, Practitioner, and Senior Lecturer (Counselling) in the School of Psychology and Wellbeing. India's expertise and experience span education, child protection and family law, and other forensic settings, and her research focuses on trauma and lifespan outcomes.

John Cairney, PhD, is Professor and Head of the School of Human Movement and Nutrition Sciences at the University of Queensland. He is an academic leader in the field of pediatric exercise medicine and child health research.

Sandra Chafouleas, PhD, is a Board of Trustees Distinguished Professor and Neag Endowed Professor in the Department of Educational Psychology within the Neag School of Education. She also serves as the founder and Co-Director of the UConn Collaboratory on School and Child Health (CSCH). She has authored over 150 publications and regularly serves as a national presenter and invited speaker. She is a fellow in both the American Psychological Association and Association for Psychological Science and is Invited Member and Past-President of the Society for the Study of School Psychology. Professor Chafouleas's work on trauma-informed education is among the most highly cited scholarly works in the field.

Vicki C. Dallinger (she/her) is a Clinical Psychologist in private practice. She is a Researcher and Lecturer for the University of Southern Queensland and Director of the Psychology and Wellbeing Clinic at the Toowoomba University campus. Vicki has worked in community mental health and private practice for a number of years. Her research and clinical practice focus on recovery and resilience building for youth and adults in both community and private settings. Her latest research includes the development of a youth recovery measure and the exploration of trauma-informed practice within schools supporting young people recovering from trauma.

Kate Fitzgerald (she/her) is a PhD Candidate in the School of Allied Health at The University of Western Australia. Her research is focused on teacher-student relationships and trauma-informed practice in schools.

Emma Gawthorne (she/her) is Clinical Registrar with 12 years of experience as a psychologist, having worked in diverse settings such as community and non-government organizations, hospitals, and private practice. She has worked extensively across the lifespan and is currently a psychologist at a grade 5–12 all-boys school. Emma's clinical practice adopts a holistic approach, emphasizing the improvement of mental health and educational outcomes for both individuals and the systems within which they co-exist. She collaborates closely with a multidisciplinary team, including teachers, nurses, and other allied health professionals.

Angela Gazey (she/her) is a PhD Candidate in the School of Allied Health at The University of Western Australia. Angela's research is focused on parenting practices in the context of trauma-informed practice.

Emily Hall is a proud Wiradjuri woman and PhD Candidate in the School of Human Movement and Nutrition Sciences at the University of Queensland. Hall specializes in the cultural determinants of Aboriginal and Torres Strait Islander health and wellbeing.

Louise Jenkins (she/her), PhD, MEd Studies, GradDipEd, BArts is the Deputy Dean (Education) and Associate Professor in the Faculty of Education at Monash University. Louise's research focuses on Music Education and inclusive educational practices.

Amanda Kasten-Lee (she/her) is an Evaluation Consultant currently evaluating programs for the Stephen Michael Foundation, a not-for-profit service providing support and programs for young people across Western Australia. Mandi is also Education Consultant for the Thoughtful Schools Program. A qualified teacher, Mandi is highly experienced in working with young people who have experienced adversity and is passionate about supporting and fostering learning for those most vulnerable.

Jessica Koslouski (she/her), PhD, is an Assistant Research Professor in the Neag School of Education at the University of Connecticut. Her research focuses on the implementation of trauma-informed and whole child approaches in schools. Dr Koslouski facilitates professional development for schools working to implement trauma-informed policies and practices. She has published several articles describing implementation of these approaches as well as guidance for those leading this professional development. Dr Koslouski previously worked as an elementary special education teacher.

Alysha Kramer (she/her), MEDP, GDipPsych(Adv), GDipPsych, BMus, is a registered Psychologist and Educational and Developmental Psychologist Registrar. Alysha has over 15 years' experience working as an instrumental music teacher in both primary and secondary schools. Alysha recently completed her thesis exploring trauma-informed music interventions within educational settings.

Govind Krishnamoorthy (he/him), PhD, is a Clinical Psychologist and Senior Lecturer at the University of Southern Queensland, Australia. Dr Krishnamoorthy's research and clinical practice focuses on improving mental health and educational outcomes for children, youth, and families from priority populations. He has collaborated extensively with schools and a number of health and child welfare services in implementing systems approaches for trauma-informed and recovery-oriented practices.

Ellie Lawson (she/her) is an Accredited Exercise Physiologist. Ellie graduated with a Bachelor of Clinical Exercise Physiology (Honors) from the University of Queensland. Ellie's research at the University of Queensland examined the key features of trauma-informed, movement-based learning programs for early learners from the perspective of exercise professionals.

Sophie Lea (she/her), PhD, MACA, is a Counsellor, Clinical Supervisor, and Lecturer in the School of Educational Psychology and Counselling in the Faculty of Education at Monash University. Sophie is a former School Counsellor, Primary and Secondary Educator. She is the co-founder and research lead of Kind Schools Ltd, an educational not-for-profit.

Cassandra Lobley (she/her) is a Researcher and Practitioner in trauma-informed educational practices. She is a PhD Candidate and is completing her master's degree in Clinical Psychology. Cassandra serves as Provisional Psychologist at Windsor Allied Health, where she provides compassionate guidance. With over two decades of educational leadership, Cassandra has experience in implementing trauma-informed practice with rural and remote Indigenous communities in Australia.

Sharon Louth, PhD, is a Senior Lecturer in Education in the School of Education and Tertiary Access at the University of the Sunshine Coast. Dr Louth specializes in embedding trauma-informed culturally responsive pedagogies, focusing on Aboriginal and Torres Strait Islander ways of knowing, being, and doing.

Katrina Skewes Ferran (she/they), PhD, RMT, RGIMT, is Professor and Head of Creative Arts Therapist at the University of Melbourne, as well as Director of the central professional development unit for researchers across the university. She has published six books, 32 book chapters, 123 journal articles, a TedX Talk, and a Massive Open Online Course.

Theodore McGlynn-Wright (he/they) is a Belonging-Based Facilitator, Politicized Healer, aspiring Tea Farmer, and former Director of the Coalition for Compassionate Schools, a trauma-informed schools project in New Orleans, LA. He now works with organizations and individuals committed to transforming the systems that break people through his company, Belonging Based.

Michelle Munyun (she/her) is a senior Primary School Teacher with 23 years' experience in Australian classrooms. She now specializes in Visual Arts and has the pleasure of teaching all year levels across her school from Foundation to Year 6.

Andrew Orapallo (he/him), PhD, is Research Psychologist in the Department of Child and Adolescent Psychiatry and Behavioral Sciences at the Children's Hospital of Philadelphia. His research broadly focuses on the integration of evidence-based mental health programming into schools and community settings, with a particular emphasis on prevention and early intervention for high-risk infants, toddlers, and young children. His work leverages principles inherent to dissemination and implementation science, trauma-informed approaches to care, and community-engaged research.

Murray Phillips, PhD, is a Professor of First Nations Health and Sport in the School of Human Movement and Nutrition Sciences at the University of Queensland. Professor Phillips specializes in the historical perspectives of sport and assimilation policies imposed on Aboriginal and Torres Strait Islander peoples.

Andrea Reupert (she/her), PhD, is Professor and School Lead in the School of Educational Psychology and Counseling at Monash University. She has published over 250 research articles and is a nationally and internationally recognized expert in the area of childhood adversity, family mental illness, and school and home-based interventions.

Liska Schramm (she/her) is an Educational and Developmental Psychologist currently working within Student Support Services Team as part of the Department of Education. She has also previously worked as Student Wellbeing and Inclusion Leader at a Secondary School in Melbourne, Australia.

Allisyn L. Swift (she/her), PhD, is a School Psychologist in New Orleans, Louisiana. She is currently the Executive Director of the Coalition for Safe and Compassionate Schools (CforCS), a program of Tulane University that seeks to engage schools and youth-facing organizations in anti-racist, trauma-informed, healing practices for the communities they serve.

Kai Wheeler, PhD, is a Ngarabal person and Lecturer at the School of Human Movement and Nutrition Sciences at the University of Queensland. Dr Wheeler was the first Aboriginal PhD recipient from the University of Sunshine Coast. Dr Wheeler was awarded the 2020 Accredited Exercise Scientist of the Year Award by Exercise and Sport Science Australia.

Michelle Wilson-Ching, PhD, MPsych, MAPS, is a Registered Psychologist and an Educational and Developmental Psychology registrar currently working in private practice. Michelle's research has focused on pediatric neuropsychology as well as trauma-informed practice within schools.

Foreword

Recent decades have brought the science on trauma, including adverse childhood experiences, and its connection to negative outcomes across the life course. Childhood trauma can disrupt neurodevelopment and challenge healthy development, creating a cascade of intractable neurobiological dysfunction followed by adoption of risk behaviors, disease, disability, social problems, and even early death. We have witnessed a proliferation in knowledge about trauma, beginning with what it is, and extending to documenting high prevalence rates and root causes. There is growing understanding that trauma is not something that fits solely within a diagnostic checkbox (e.g., posttraumatic stress disorder), but also must be viewed as a systemic problem rooted in adversities and injustices that often begin at birth. The alarms have been sounded, and conversations have moved out of therapeutic settings and into the general public. Our challenge now is how to disseminate, implement, and sustain the trauma-informed practices that have potential to not only reduce adversities and the effects of exposure but also to advance wellbeing. Collectively, the chapters in this book offer a tremendous push toward this goal, pulling together a valuable roadmap to trauma-informed practices in a primary system of care for children – schools.

Schools are a critical setting for addressing the vulnerabilities that children bring through their doors. These vulnerabilities – such as community violence, emotional neglect, food insecurity, and household instability – challenge healthy development and the work of schools. Schools, however, can also serve to contribute to child vulnerabilities through exclusionary practices such as school discipline, bullying, or unsupportive adult interactions. Schools play a role, therefore, in either perpetuating or interrupting the pattern of vulnerabilities that can be transmitted intergenerationally (Chafouleas & Iovino, 2021; Osher et al., 2020).

The interruption of vulnerabilities happens when school caregivers work together, and with caregivers across home and community settings, to build knowledge about trauma and its impact as well as their role in contributing assets to reduce net vulnerability. This knowledge must include understanding of the critical role of nurturing relationships toward enabling pathways to positive, whole child development. Nurturing relationships also helps avoid the missteps in adult practices that can trigger patterns of re-traumatization when handling challenging student behavior. Given that these missteps can occur at individual, classroom, school, or district levels, a whole-school approach is therefore necessary.

Together, a whole child and school approach to trauma-informed practices wrap together the many different gears to a positive school environment in which students can thrive. This approach focuses on nurturing across developmental pathways, including academic, social, emotional, behavioral, and physical. Nurturing practices also embrace tiered systems of support, bringing universal implementation of trauma-informed practices for all students as well as flexibility to intensify supports for those students who require more assistance. This flexibility meets children where they are at – in every moment. Such flexibility also includes understanding that progress can sometimes feel painfully slow and is rarely linear. Doing all of this can sometimes feel like an impossible juggling act and most certainly requires adults who can draw strength from their own wellbeing. It is therefore particularly helpful to have a book such as this one that extends content to the wellbeing of the adult caregivers who are tasked with implementation of trauma-informed practices. All too often, childhood trauma conversations engage blame toward adults without sufficient attention to the structures that may be preventing the adult from using trauma-informed practices. Interrupting trauma pathways to pathology for children means adults are equipped with the knowledge and skills as well as the system supports that can advance pathways to wellbeing for both themselves and the children they care for. It is refreshing to find this attention woven throughout the chapters in this book.

Taken together, this book provides an essential roadmap to trauma-informed practices for schools. But it is important to note that we know schools alone are not the answer. Even the most supportive school environment may have limited effectiveness in the absence of context, and thus, this book embraces an ecological perspective within the presented roadmap. We know that now is our time to collectively tackle the "what to do" in addressing childhood trauma. These collective efforts demand a public health perspective that makes information widely accessible to readers without the resources to secure an advanced graduate degree in related human services. This book offers just that, bringing a wide range of interrelated topics into focus in usable ways for diverse audiences. The content offers predictable structures with an eye toward usability. Each chapter is chock-full of practical information and examples with cross-cultural applicability. Practitioners, policymakers, and researchers alike will find the information that they need to advance a cross-sector agenda aligned with a trauma-informed whole child approach.

Professor Sandra M. Chafouleas

References

Chafouleas, S. M., & Iovino, E. A. (2021). Engaging a whole child, school, and community lens in positive education to advance equity in schools. *Frontiers in Psychology, 12*. https://doi.org/10.3389/fpsyg.2021.758788

Osher, D., Cantor, P., Berg, J., Steyer, L., & Rose, T. (2020). Drivers of human development: How relationships and context shape learning and development. *Applied Developmental Science, 24*, 6–36. https://doi.org/10.1080/10888691.2017.1398650

1

Introduction and Background

Karen E. Martin, Emily Berger, and Shantel D. Crosby

There is strong and ever-expanding evidence that childhood trauma can create significant immediate and long-term challenges for individuals, subsequently impacting broader society. Increasingly, organizations working with children are adapting their practices in response to this knowledge and attempting to become 'trauma-informed'. Such an endeavor, however, can be complex, takes time, and currently lacks clear guidance about 'what works'. This is particularly relevant for schools, which often experience limited resources and a workforce who have minimal (if any) education about trauma. With research suggesting that school staff will decide what constitutes trauma for a student, even with minimal information (Sonsteng-Person, 2022), there is an urgent need to share research with school educators and leaders and the education sector overall.

Trauma can be defined as a lasting response to a deeply disturbing, overwhelming event/s for an individual, which greatly threatens their sense of safety. However, many other definitions exist, and the concept of trauma has shifted. Initially, the term trauma, in relation to psychology, was associated with the diagnosis of Posttraumatic Stress Disorder (PTSD) (Friedman et al., 2007). However, over time the concept of trauma has expanded both in relation to severity and causes (Baes et al., 2023), and the term is now also used to describe ongoing distress experienced due to adversity and injustices, such as inequity, poverty, and racism (Baes et al., 2023). In this book, use of the term trauma includes distress caused by adversity and chronically stressful environments.

Extensive evidence indicates that those who experience trauma during childhood face more challenges in their lives and are at far higher risk of

DOI: 10.4324/9781003436034-1

Trauma can be defined as a lasting response to a deeply disturbing, overwhelming event/s for an individual, which greatly threatens their sense of safety.

poorer health and wellbeing outcomes than children who do not experience trauma (Houtepen et al., 2020; Kerker et al., 2015; Romano et al., 2014). Children and young people experiencing trauma often encounter a large range of difficulties within the school environment. Challenges experienced by these children and young people range from emotional dysregulation (Samson et al., 2024), maintaining attention (Korgaonkar et al., 2023), memory impairment (Vaillancourt et al., 2011), hypervigilance (Pollak et al., 2005), to gastrointestinal problems (Konturek et al., 2011), and more.

Trauma-informed practice incorporates behaviors and communication which are empathetic and responsive to knowledge about the causes and impact of trauma on individuals and groups (Substance Abuse and Mental Health Services Administration (SAMHSA), 2014). Trauma-informed environments are places which incorporate physical spaces, policies, protocols, and practices which respond to the needs of those who have experienced trauma and benefit all members of the community. Practices and environments which are trauma-informed are also adapted to avoid potential triggers of past trauma to help prevent re-traumatization (the re-experiencing of the initial event due to unconscious or conscious reminders) (SAMHSA, 2014). Increasingly, trauma-informed practice is being identified as a necessary requirement for reducing health and societal issues and inequities experienced worldwide (Venet, 2023). Evidence indicates environments which create or exacerbate distress, or uphold structural inequity, need to be identified and adapted to reflect principles of equity-centered, trauma-informed practice (Venet, 2023).

Rationale

Schools in regions such as Canada, the United States (US), the United Kingdom (UK), and Australia have been relatively early adopters of trauma-informed practice. This shift toward trauma-informed approaches has led to critical, positive changes in learning environments (Fondren et al., 2020). However, support from the education sector as a whole has lagged. Few regions appear to provide overarching trauma-informed pedagogy policies, education, curriculum or adequate resources. Fortunately, burgeoning awareness has led to increased research and work in this field, with many new publications and resources available for practitioners, academics, and other stakeholders. Lacking, though, is a resource which brings together evidence direct from primary peer-reviewed research applicable to early childhood, primary (elementary), and secondary (high) schools. Further, there appears to be a paucity of texts which approach trauma-informed practice education from a strengths-based approach, one in which stigmatizing is avoided. A focus on strengths is important, as the accomplishments of those who have experienced trauma are likely to be central in informing effective trauma-informed environments. This book aims to provide researchers, school leaders, educators, and other practitioners with evidence-based knowledge, examples, and explicit case studies to assist them in becoming trauma-informed. The content also provides for advocacy in the development of sustainable trauma-informed education settings and sectors.

School leaders and educators lack specific evidence-based guidance on trauma-informed practice and policy generation. This book seeks to fill this gap.

Education about trauma and its impact is provided worldwide via professional learning presentations, workshops, or short courses for school staff. However, intervention research indicates that embedding trauma-informed practices and policies into a school does not result from trauma education alone, and that support from policymakers and leaders is necessary (Martin et al., 2024). Preferably, both 'top-down' and 'bottom-up' approaches are implemented, in which the overall education sector and school leaders adapt policies and provide resources to create trauma-informed environments, and students, parents/carers, and school educators contribute to the process. This is not only likely to assist schools to address the needs of all students, but will also help schools to work toward creating 'socially just' environments; ones that do not perpetuate oppressive practices and harmful systemic behaviors that further traumatize.

Aim and Audience

The aim of this book is to conceptualize and exemplify evidence-based school trauma-informed practice for researchers, research students, educators, school leaders, practitioners, and policymakers. Each chapter provides a review of the evidence for the respective trauma-informed topic, from relationships and attachment, physiology, and anatomy, to use of music and play with students impacted by trauma. In addition to incorporating the evidence-based underlying a trauma-informed approach, this book aspires to inform current and future education practices, policies, and research in this growing field of study. Although the focus of this book is framed around schools, there is relevance beyond these settings and sectors. For example, practitioners or carers of children in out-of-home care may benefit from reading Chapters 3 and 4. Child and mental health practitioners are likely to find Chapter 2 has valuable information to assist their work. This chapter may also benefit generalist nurses in pediatric hospitals, music therapists, occupational therapists, and people working with children in the community.

A challenge for trauma-informed practice educators and researchers is to ensure research shared with practitioners and policymakers is relevant and does not further stigmatize already disadvantaged individuals and groups.

Contents

Chapter 2

Following on from this Chapter 1, which provides this book's context and background, Chapter 2 provides further background and descriptions of trauma, potential traumatic events, trauma prevalence, and the physical, psychosocial, and cognitive impact of trauma. The physiological impact of trauma is described in relation to a single incident of stress and longer-term manifestations of trauma on the body. This knowledge assists in understanding how even the most supportive environments and intensive interventions may seem to have limited effectiveness.

Chapter 3

Chapter 3 explores the impact of childhood trauma on school functioning, at an individual and school level and classroom management practices. By noting that re-traumatization can result from current dominant behavior management approaches in schools, this chapter explains how trauma-informed practice provides a paradigm for assisting to address concerns related to student behavior challenges in schools. This chapter addresses the impact of trauma on children and young people in the classroom and school setting, teacher reflective practice, and the importance of educators and educational systems understanding the impact of trauma. This chapter further explores inclusive practice and policies, and how schools can apply a trauma-informed lens to avoid triggers, responses, and patterns of behavior that may increase a child's risk of school exclusion and disengagement. A whole-of-school perspective is applied in this chapter, addressing systematic, classroom, student, and teacher-led changes to assist with behavior support and social-emotional and learning needs of students experiencing trauma.

Chapter 4

Chapter 4 provides a narrative review of the effects of interpersonal trauma on children and the impact that this can have on students within the school context. Trauma-informed practices which encourage healthy connections between teachers, peers, and school environments, where students feel safe, supported, and have a sense of belonging, are discussed in this chapter.

Chapter 5

In Chapter 5, the authors explore the importance of trauma-informed practice to address the wellbeing and mental health needs of teachers and school staff. Evidence about teacher wellbeing, student learning outcomes, and the impact of exposure to students who have experienced trauma on teachers' mental health and professional outcomes is provided. Evidence-based programs and frameworks designed to improve outcomes for teachers exposed to students who have experienced trauma are discussed. The role of school leaders and education departments in addressing the wellbeing needs of teachers is also explained. This chapter concludes with a discussion about important recommendations for whole-school practices, policies, and processes to address the needs of students exposed to trauma and their teachers.

Chapter 6

Chapter 6 explores the impact of the school-built environment on students and the school community. In this chapter, the impact and importance of the school setting and how these spaces support all students' learning, specifically those requiring a trauma-informed approach, is discussed. This chapter also covers three major foundations of design: the physical, ambient, and aesthetic elements in a school setting. This chapter finalizes with recommendations for implementing a suitable trauma-informed school environment.

Chapter 7

Chapter 7 unpacks the concept of trauma-informed practice in relation to Black and other racially marginalized students, as well as the history of systemic oppression that has been pervasive in school settings. This chapter describes how schools have been complicit in upholding and perpetuating oppressive practices that have harmed Black youth. This chapter also highlights the concept of schools being a healing environment by embracing collective and systemic change, rather than individual intervention. Additionally, this chapter offers recommendations and examples of schools working toward this more collective, system-wide framework for trauma-informed practice.

Chapter 8

Chapter 8 describes parent/carers' awareness of trauma and how their involvement and interaction with schools is essential to enable trauma-informed policies and practices. The challenges associated with trauma arising from parent/carer behavior through child abuse are briefly covered. This chapter also discusses the potential for trauma-informed parenting approaches to be delivered in schools to support children impacted by trauma, leading to improved child outcomes and family functioning.

Chapter 9

Chapter 9 takes a strengths-based approach to the innovative solutions necessary to address the wide gap in the health, wellbeing, and education of Aboriginal and Torres Strait Islander[1] peoples when compared with non-Indigenous people. Evidence consistently places the life expectancy for Aboriginal and Torres Strait Islander peoples at around ten years shorter than their non-Indigenous counterparts, but there is considerable hope. A growing body of evidence now supports health, wellbeing, and education practitioners using the social determinants of health to better inform Aboriginal and Torres Strait Islander partnerships. This chapter explores the key health and wellbeing aspects that impact Aboriginal and Torres Strait Islander engagement within schools. Specifically, this chapter outlines the advantages of a trauma-informed care approach for Aboriginal and Torres Strait Islander children, and then continues with highlighting application of this approach for Aboriginal and Torres Strait Islander children in schools.

Chapter 10

Chapter 10 reviews the available literature and discusses the implications of music interventions for children in schools exposed to trauma. This chapter discusses what is currently known about music interventions for children and adolescents exposed to trauma, how music is used within educational settings, and how music interventions can be applied within a trauma-informed framework. A case study to demonstrate how trauma-informed music interventions can be applied with children and adolescents within educational settings has also been provided. Recommendations for schools implementing music therapy for students exposed to trauma are provided.

Chapter 11

Chapter 11 explores trauma-informed practice with specific reference to children participating in play as a physical activity (active play). This chapter outlines the important relationship between active play and increasing opportunities for children to process emotions, build resilience, and regain a sense of mastery of their bodies and surroundings. Finally, this chapter guides integration of trauma-informed active play within practices in the school setting to support positive student health and wellbeing and potentially assist with the healing of trauma.

Chapter 12

Chapter 12 provides practical considerations and guidance to measures available for exploring trauma-informed environments, attitudes, knowledge, and practices trauma-informed as well as school staff psychosocial health and trauma symptoms within students. Brief descriptions of several evidence-informed tools that are available for use by school leaders, educators, and other school staff are included. At the end of this chapter, a case example is provided to illustrate a real-world exemplar for how educators and school staff may use data-based decision-making processes to strengthen the entire school system and promote a culture that is healing for all students, staff, and families.

Chapter 13

This book's concluding Chapter 13 summarizes the main themes emerging from the literature, future research directions, and key recommendations for designing and delivering trauma-informed practice in schools and education sectors worldwide. The need for the additional focus on marginalized and high-risk and impacted groups, who have been largely excluded from the trauma-informed literature, is emphasized. This includes First Nations people (who are vulnerable to intergenerational trauma and school exclusion), students, and farming families from regional and rural settings (experiencing impact from drought, disasters, and significant loss), LGBTQIA+ people, and people with disability. The importance of a whole-school approach to trauma-informed practice is discussed to summarize literature presented in earlier chapters of this book.

Conclusion

Experiencing trauma can make attending, engaging, and learning at school very difficult for students. Emotional, behavioral, and learning challenges experienced by students may be perceived as disengagement, disrespect, disruption, and at times dangerous. Clearer knowledge about how trauma can create physiological and anatomical anomalies, and subsequently impact development, learning, and social-emotional wellbeing, whilst identifying student strengths, is likely to assist whole school. Understanding how children and young people may respond to trauma, how to avoid re-traumatization, and how long trauma often endures can benefit everyone. Supportive schools provide a positive sense of community for school staff as well as students and their families.

However, current societal norms and expectations, and thus school policies and practices, do not bode well for many children and young people impacted by trauma. Although many Governments, at an international level, pay lip service to implementing supportive policies, training, and resources for disadvantaged and vulnerable students, there are few regions which demonstrate truly supportive and effective approaches which change lives. Thus, it seems that creating safe, supportive, and healing school environments aligned with research evidence for all children and young people is ambitious. Change requires concerted advocacy by passionate innovators, as well as support by policymakers, leaders, and practitioners. Appropriate resourcing will aid transformation. However, by initiating and supporting networks and collaborations, trauma-informed champions can use the extensive evidence to advocate for change. It is hoped that this book provides advocates and champions with important and necessary information and evidence to help them on their path to change.

Note

1 Using Aboriginal and Torres Strait Islander peoples rather than Indigenous or First Nations in writing is important for specificity and respect. Aboriginal and Torres Strait Islander peoples directly refers to the distinct groups within Australia, acknowledging unique identities, cultures, and histories. This terminology ensures clarity and precision, avoids generalization that can occur with broader terms like Indigenous or First Nations, which encompass diverse peoples worldwide. Additionally, using the preferred terminology of the communities themselves demonstrates respect and recognition of autonomy in defining identities. It fosters a more accurate and respectful dialogue, essential for promoting understanding and reconciliation.

References

Baes, N., Vylomova, E., Zyphur, M., & Haslam, N. (2023). The semantic inflation of "trauma" in psychology. *Psychology of Language and Communication, 27*(1), 23–45.

Fondren, K., Lawson, M., Speidel, R., McDonnell, C. G., & Valentino, K. (2020). Buffering the effects of childhood trauma within the school setting: a systematic review of trauma-informed and trauma-responsive interventions among trauma-affected youth. *Children and Youth Services Review, 109*. https://doi.org/10.1016/j.childyouth.2019.104691

Friedman, M. J., Keane, T. M., & Resick, P. A. (2007). *Handbook of PTSD: science and practice*. Guilford Press.

Houtepen, L. C., Heron, J., Suderman, M. J., Fraser, A., Chittleborough, C. R., & Howe, L. D. (2020). Associations of adverse childhood experiences with educational attainment and adolescent health and the role of family and socioeconomic factors: a prospective cohort study in the UK. *PLoS Medicine, 17*(3), e1003031. https://doi.org/10.1371/journal.pmed.1003031

Kerker, B. D., Zhang, J., Nadeem, E., Stein, R. E. K., Hurlburt, M. S., Heneghan, A., Landsverk, J., & Horwitz, S. M. (2015). Adverse childhood experiences and mental health, chronic medical conditions, and development in young children. *Academic Pediatrics, 15*(5), 510–517. https://doi.org/10.1016/j.acap.2015.05.005

Konturek, P. C., Brzozowski, T., & Konturek, S. J. (2011). Stress and the gut: pathophysiology, clinical consequences, diagnostic approach and treatment options. *Journal of Physiology and Pharmacology, 62*(6), 591–599.

Korgaonkar, M. S., Breukelaar, I. A., Felmingham, K., Williams, L. M., & Bryant, R. A. (2023). Association of neural connectome with early experiences of abuse in adults. *JAMA Network Open, 6*(1), e2253082.

Martin, K., Kasten-Lee, A., Dobson, M., Fitzgerald, K., Lund, S., Egeberg, H., Walker, R., Wheeler, K., Gazey, A., Platell, M., & Berger, E. (2024). *Thoughtful Schools Program Pilot Study; Interim Report*. Perth: The University of Western Australia.

Pollak, S. D., Vardi, S., Putzer Bechner, A. M., & Curtin, J. J. (2005). Physically abused children's regulation of attention in response to hostility. *Child Development, 76*(5), 968–977.

Romano, E., Babchishin, L., Marquis, R., & Fréchette, S. (2014). Childhood maltreatment and educational outcomes. *Trauma, Violence & Abuse, 16*(4), 418–437. https://doi.org/10.1177/1524838014537908

Samson, J. A., Newkirk, T. R., & Teicher, M. H. (2024). Practitioner review: neurobiological consequences of childhood maltreatment–clinical and therapeutic implications for practitioners. *Journal of Child Psychology and Psychiatry, 65*(3), 369–380.

Sonsteng-Person, M. A. (2022). *The (re)production of violence and trauma in high schools: how institutional policies and practices influence teacher and staff decision making* (Publication Number 29211719) [Ph.D., University of

California, Los Angeles]. ProQuest Dissertations & Theses Global. United States – California. https://www.proquest.com/dissertations-theses/re-production-violence-trauma-high-schools-how/docview/2669094241/se-2?accountid=14681

Substance Abuse and Mental Health Services Administration (SAMHSA). (2014). *SAMHSA's concept of trauma and guidance for a trauma-informed approach* (HHS Publication No. (SMA) 14-4884). https://store.samhsa.gov/shin/content/SMA14-4884/SMA14-4884.pdf.

Vaillancourt, T., Duku, E., Becker, S., Schmidt, L. A., Nicol, J., Muir, C., & MacMillan, H. (2011). Peer victimization, depressive symptoms, and high salivary cortisol predict poorer memory in children. *Brain and Cognition*, *77*(2), 191–199.

Venet, A. S. (2023). *Equity-centered trauma-informed education*. Routledge.

2 Anatomy of Trauma

Karen E. Martin,
Amanda Kasten-Lee,
Kate Fitzgerald,
Angela Gazey, and
Emily Berger

Introduction

Research over the last few decades has provided a wealth of knowledge about the physical impacts of trauma and distress on children and young people. Extensive evidence demonstrates how children are particularly vulnerable to stressors and the subsequent impact this can have on their development, including brain physiology and anatomy, and other body systems (Cross et al., 2017). In turn, children and young people experiencing trauma often experience challenges to their immediate and longer-term psychological and physical health, social development and behavior, learning, and overall life outcomes (Houtepen et al., 2020; Kerker et al., 2015; Romano et al., 2014). This chapter initially defines trauma and outlines the complexities and changing understanding of the concept. The causes and prevalence of trauma are then discussed. The focus of this chapter is to demonstrate how trauma and distress can influence body structures and functions for children and young people, and the mechanisms underpinning noted differences. The ways in which trauma and distress may present in children and young people are then summarized. The final section of this chapter provides recommendations to assist whole-school communities in their approach to preventing and responding to trauma and distress.

Definitions and Context

What Is Trauma?

There is no single definition for 'trauma' which is used consistently in research and practice. Furthermore, changing concepts of trauma over the past three

DOI: 10.4324/9781003436034-2

decades has added to variation in the understanding of the concept of trauma. In psychiatry, the term trauma is generally used in relation to Posttraumatic Stress Disorder (PTSD) and Complex Posttraumatic Stress Disorder (CPTSD). Of interest, evidence indicates that the term 'trauma' is now used in fewer contexts in the research literature (Baes et al., 2023). To help with defining trauma, the internationally recognized Substance Abuse and Mental Health Services Administration (SAMHSA, 2014) describes trauma using the three 'Es': event, experience, and effect. The updated Diagnostic and Statistical Manual of Mental Disorders (DSM-5) (American Psychiatric Association, 2013) incorporates a new category of 'Trauma and Stressor Related Diseases'. This goes some way to expanding the definition of trauma, however disorders within this category have clear diagnostic and experience requirements related to trauma.

In addition to issues of definition and diagnostic clarity, the growing popularity of trauma discourse, particularly on social media, has led to the emergence of different trauma 'types' (such as little t and big T traumas, or Type 1 and Type 2 traumas, single and complex trauma), many of which often lack evidence or expert consensus. Except for the trauma disorders recognized by the World Health Organization (World Health Organisation, 2022b) and in the DSM-5 (American Psychiatric Association, 2013), there is a lack of consensus and evidence about other proposed trauma categories. Further, these arbitrary classifications and descriptions may oversimplify or overcomplicate the conceptualization of trauma and impede appropriate interventions and prevention needed and influence help-seeking behaviors.

With no clear definition of the term 'trauma' and consensus about its use, disseminating research and providing clear education in this field can be challenging. With recent research starting to distinguish physiological differences between experiences of childhood adversity, chronic distress, and trauma, increased research, and clearer definitions are likely to be useful for practitioners, researchers, and policymakers.

Re-traumatizing

Although there are multiple definitions for this term, re-traumatizing can be defined as the 're-experiencing' of trauma symptoms due to an event, interaction, or experiences which reminds someone (consciously or unconsciously) of a prior traumatic experience (Dallam, 2010).

This book's definition of trauma (adapted from multiple definitions) aligns with the broader understanding of trauma:

'Trauma is a lasting response to a deeply disturbing, overwhelming event/s for an individual which greatly threatened their sense of safety'.

Used in this context, 'trauma' is not considered a component of a disease or illness, but rather a response to a highly stressful event. This definition implies that unresolved or unhealed 'trauma' may lead to a 'trauma disorder' (such as CPTSD or PTSD).

Stress and Distress

Previously, the term 'stress' was used in relation to a negative or a maladaptive state in which the sympathetic nervous system is overactivated, causing acute or chronic physical, psychological, and behavioral impairment (Lu et al., 2021). However, with awareness that some stress is normal and necessary, and that insufficient stress can be detrimental, stress is now more commonly conceptualized in relation to a shift in the body's physiological resting state (called homeostasis). Thus stress can be defined as 'a state of homeostasis being challenged' (Lu et al., 2021). Chronic stress is a term which may be useful to distinguish the concept of healthy and unhealthy stress, with chronic stress signifying that the stress is heightened, ongoing, and thus likely to negatively impact an individual.

Distress can be defined as when a person's homeostasis has been strongly challenged by high levels of stressors, this may induce a severe stress response and endanger health (Lu et al., 2021).

Causes

Categorizing stressful events which cause trauma and/or trauma disorders is not simple. For people who experience the same event, not all will be 'traumatized' (experience trauma) and not all will end up with a diagnosis of PTSD or CPTSD (World Health Organisation, 2022b). Furthermore, single or multiple stressful events, adversity in living conditions, and other highly distressing experiences are difficult to exclude as a cause of trauma due to the subjective nature of experiences and recall about the events.

Traumatic Event and Potentially Traumatic Event

In line with the lack of a consistent definition of trauma, there is associated robust discourse about the types of events which can lead to trauma. Unless a specific event has led to one or more people experiencing trauma, the term 'potentially traumatic event' is more appropriate when listing causes of trauma. Table 2.1 summarizes the various definitions of potentially traumatic events from different sources.

Understanding and perceptions about what may lead to trauma have shifted over time. An expanded scope for the causes of trauma has been proposed by public health experts. Gradus and Galea (2022) argue that racism/racial discrimination, financial difficulties, and stress due to environmental (climatic) conditions can lead to trauma. They further recommend shifting from considering 'traumatic events' to 'traumatic experiences'

Table 2.1 Definition of potential traumatic events and potential outcomes by source

Source	Potential traumatic event	Stated possible health and other outcomes
DSM-5 (American Psychiatric Association, 2013)	*Include, but are not limited to:* Exposure to war as a combatant, or civilian Threatened, or actual physical assault (e.g., physical attack robbery, mugging, childhood physical abuse, threat, or actual sexual violence) (e.g., forced sexual penetration, alcohol/drug-facilitated sexual penetration, abusive sexual contact, non-contact sexual abuse) Sexual trafficking Being kidnapped Being taken hostage Terrorist attack, torture Incarceration as a prisoner of war Natural or human-made disasters Severe motor vehicle accidents.	• Reactive Attachment Disorder • Disinhibited Social Engagement Disorder • PTSD • Acute Stress Disorder • Adjustment Disorders • Other Specified Trauma- and Stressor-Related Disorder • Unspecified Trauma- and Stressor-Related Disorder

(Continued)

Table 2.1 (Continued)

Source	Potential traumatic event	Stated possible health and other outcomes
International Classification of Diseases (ICD-11) (World Health Organisation, 2022b)	*…event or situation (either short- or long-lasting) of an extremely threatening or horrific nature. Such events include, but are not limited to:* Directly experiencing natural or human-made disasters combat Serious accidents Torture Sexual violence Terrorism Assault Acute life-threatening illness (e.g., a heart attack); Witnessing the threatened or actual injury or death of others in a sudden unexpected or violent manner Learning about the sudden unexpected or violent death of a loved one.	PTSD
ICD-11 (World Health Organisation, 2022b)	*…event or series of events of an extremely threatening or horrific nature most commonly prolonged or repetitive events from which escape is difficult or impossible. Such events include, but are not limited to:* Torture Concentration camps Slavery Genocide campaigns and other forms of organized violence Prolonged domestic violence Repeated childhood sexual or physical abuse	CPTSD
APA website (https://www.apa.org/topics/trauma)	…event like an Accident Crime Natural disaster Physical or emotional abuse neglect Experiencing or witnessing violence Death of a loved one War, and more	Longer-term reactions include: Unpredictable emotions flashbacks Strained relationships Physical symptoms like headaches or nausea

(Gradus & Galea, 2023; Gradus & Galea, 2022). This is based on the premise that delineating traumatic events from distressing events is not useful, as all people experiencing distress and trauma reactions should be supported. In contrast, for the past two decades, concerns have been aired in psychiatry literature about 'bracket creep' of what can cause trauma-related diseases, such as PTSD, and the potential impact on diagnosis and treatment (Elhai et al., 2005; Dalenberg et al., 2017).

The broad definition of a potentially traumatic event by the American Psychiatric Association (2013) is:

> … event like an accident, crime, natural disaster, physical or emotional abuse, neglect, experiencing or witnessing violence, death of a loved one, war, and more. Immediately after the event, shock and denial are typical.
>
> (no pg)

Adversity/Adverse Childhood Experiences

Adversity or stressful living conditions, such as housing insecurity, poverty, and/or having an incarcerated parent, are somewhat distinct from a 'traumatic' experience in that they describe ongoing stressors which create a range of challenges. However, adversity caused by circumstances such as a parent being incarcerated, housing insecurity, and poverty is associated with increased risk of negative health outcomes later in life (Felitti et al., 1998). Felitti et al.'s (1998) seminal work, incorporating data from 13,494 adults, noted a relationship between specific experiences of adversity (related to child abuse or household dysfunction) and experiencing disease as an adult. Further work by the team (2002) identified that the number of specific adverse conditions experienced was directly related to the risk of a range of short- and long-term detrimental outcomes, including depression, drug and alcohol misuse, suicidality, and incarceration.

Childhood Abuse

Abuse during childhood is likely to be internationally the largest cause of trauma disorders and many other mental and physical disorders in children, young people, and adults. Although there is some indication that not all children from violent or severely violent families experience negative psychological outcomes (Grych et al., 2000), evidence indicates that abuse by the primary caregiver/s may create distinct outcomes for a child. Of relevance, trauma expert Judith Herman (2015) distinguishes traumatic experiences in relation to the 'betrayal in key relationships' by parents/caregivers from the outcomes for less personal events, such as natural disasters and war.

Multiple and Context-Relevant Stressors

When embedding trauma-informed practice into the education sector, it is imperative that concepts of social justice, equality, equity (Venet, 2023), and disability are considered. Children and young people experiencing multiple adversities are more likely to experience highly distressing events, such as those leading to chronic stress or trauma, than those who do not (Johnson et al., 2013). For example, living in a violent community in which there is limited social cohesion can place a child or young person at distinct disadvantage compared with those living in a comparatively safe and connected community. Experiences of adversity in addition to trauma can be even more debilitating. For instance, a child may be inexperienced in knowing how best to respond to stressful experiences, have few resources to assist them and yet also be living with one or more experiences they never should have encountered in the first place (such as physical, emotional, or sexual abuse from a caregiver).

It is important to note that experiences which some people may not perceive as 'extremely threatening or horrific in nature' (as per ICD-11 requirement for a trauma disorder) can also lead to distress and future negative outcomes. For example, school bullying can have a lasting negative impact on mental health (Sasaki et al., 2024), with some indication that it can lead to PTSD (Nielsen et al., 2015). However, the actual bullying event/s may not be considered 'extremely threatening or horrific in nature'. This research supports the notion of expanding events which may be considered traumatic.

Vulnerable Populations

Populations experiencing significantly higher rates of negative experiences, such as community violence (Fowler et al., 2009), genocide (Rieder & Elbert, 2013), prior and ongoing negative stereotyping (including racism) (Gradus & Galea, 2022), homelessness (Davies & Allen, 2017), unequal opportunities (Troutt, 2017), have much higher risk of experiencing trauma. This is particularly relevant for populations such as Indigenous/First Nations (e.g., Australian

Aboriginals and Torres Strait Islander, Canadian Aboriginal and American Indigenous) peoples (Treloar & Jackson, 2015), LGBTQIA+ community members (Craig et al., 2020), people with a disability or neurodiversity (Hoover, 2020), and asylum seekers/refugees (Gandham et al., 2023).

Cultural Considerations

Distress and trauma are especially relevant when a 'Westernized' education approach is almost exclusively mandated within invaded and colonized regions, for example, Australia, New Zealand, the United States of America, and Canada. Thus non-traditional education is imposed on Indigenous communities, regardless of their embracing or resistance to this. Government processes, representatives, and schooling overall have been experienced by many Indigenous peoples as traumatic (Treloar & Jackson, 2015). Whole communities have been impacted in the past through atrocities such as the Stolen Generations (e.g., Australia and North America) (Treloar & Jackson, 2015). With this in mind, understanding what may cause trauma and distress for different populations and individuals themselves is important. Failing to consider cultural and historical contexts when defining what constitutes a traumatic experience or what may cause distress can be considered inappropriate and potentially harmful.

In consideration of the cultural aspects of distress and trauma, the ICD-11 (World Health Organisation, 2022a), in relation to 'Disorders Specifically Associated with Stress' states:

> Culturally sanctioned and recognized concepts and means of expressing distress, such as local idioms of distress, explanations, and syndromes, may be a prominent part of the trauma response. Examples of these cultural concepts include possession states in many cultural groups, susto or espanto (fright) among Latin American populations, ohkumlang (tiredness) and bodily pain among tortured Bhutanese refugees, ihahamuka (lungs without breath) among Rwandan genocide survivors, and kit chraen (thinking too much) in Cambodia, among others. The symptoms of Disorders Specifically Associated with Stress may be described in terms of emotional, cognitive, behavioural and somatic elements of these cultural concepts. Idioms of distress may also influence the symptomatology and co-occurrence of other mental disorders.
>
> (no page number)

Genetics and Epigenetics

Human genetic background, environmental influence, DNA methylation (control of which genes are active), and gene expression are all thought to relate to how trauma may impact the body. Trauma which is 'passed on' through generations (often termed 'intergenerational trauma') is thought to be due to a combination of both environmental factors and gene expression (Agorastos et al., 2018). The combination of epigenetics, genes, and environmental interactions may influence the effects of trauma and impact long-term risk of disease development (Agorastos et al., 2018). Analysis of the literature suggests that childhood trauma may induce depression, anxiety, and PTSD through cell processes associated with gene expression and brain development (Nie et al., 2022). An example of an epigenetics process noted through research is that mothers' stress during pregnancy is associated with epigenetic 'hyper-methylation' (extra methyl groups are added to DNA) and higher cortisol stress reactivity in their children (Oberlander et al., 2008). This field of work is burgeoning however complex and thus a full description is out of scope for this book (see Zhou and Ryan's (2023) review for further information).

Prevalence

> An estimated one-half of the world's children (approximately 1 billion children) are affected by physical, sexual, or psychological violence (World Health Organization, 2020)

With the complexities in defining and identifying 'trauma', few national surveys have estimated trauma prevalence in populations, particularly for children and young people. However, research about traumatic experiences indicates that rates of trauma and trauma-related disorders are likely to be high. For example, an estimated one-half of the world's children (approximately 1 billion children) are affected by physical, sexual, or psychological violence (World Health Organization, 2020). This includes abuse by parents/caregivers, peers, or community violence and sexual abuse (Hillis et al., 2016). A 2016 review found that at least 44% of children in developed countries and 59% in developing countries had been victims of physical, emotional, or sexual violence or had witnessed domestic or community violence in the preceding year (Hillis et al.).

The Australian Childhood Maltreatment Study (Mathews et al., 2023), incorporating a representative sample of over 8,000 people aged over 16 in Australia, identified that approximately 62% of survey respondents experienced abuse during childhood (including observed domestic violence). Specifically, 32.0% had experienced physical abuse, 28.5% sexual abuse, 30.9% emotional abuse, 8.9% neglect, and 39.6% exposed to domestic violence. Data, unfortunately now 20 years old, from the United Kingdom indicate that 21% of children experience some form of physical abuse perpetrated by parents or carers, with 7% experience 'serious' abuse, 6% of experienced serious absence of physical care (neglect), 6% emotional maltreatment, and 16% of sexual abuse (May-Chahal & Cawson, 2005). In New Zealand, 14% of adolescents reported being purposefully physically harmed by an adult in their home, with 20% of girls and 9% of boys experiencing sexual abuse (Clark et al., 2013).

Data from 2007 suggest that approximately 76% of men and 73.8% of women, respectively, have experienced at least one potentially traumatic event. As mentioned previously, First Nations peoples (United Nations, 2009), culturally and linguistically diverse people (O'Connor et al., 2020), and other specific populations experience higher adversity in many countries. In addition to intergenerational trauma, Indigenous peoples face further adversity; for instance, although their populations comprise only 5% of the global population, they are among 15% of the world's most impoverished people (United Nations, 2009). As mentioned previously, genocide, colonization, racism, displacement, and intergenerational trauma further increase risk of adversity and trauma for First Nations children and young people (Treloar & Jackson, 2015).

Impact

Immediate Impact

Stressors experienced by an individual may not create excessive stress, and indeed some amount of stress is considered appropriate, adaptive, and overall beneficial to an individual (Agorastos & Chrousos, 2022; Lu et al., 2021). However, distress occurs once stress intensity exceeds an individual's threshold (at which they become overwhelmed) (Lu et al., 2021). When an experience or circumstance is excessively stressful, the capacity and resources of an individual are exceeded which can cause harmful biological consequences (Agorastos & Chrousos, 2022). Distress threatening a person's 'physical integrity' can lead to uncontrollably intense emotions and behavioral responses (i.e., intense fear, helplessness, horror, dissociation, freezing), and pronounced hormonal output (Agorastos & Chrousos, 2022).

At the time of distress, the body responds by attempting to return itself to its normal state (homeostasis) (Marques et al., 2010). Following perception of threat/experiencing distress, a system in the body called the hypothalamic-pituitary-adrenal (HPA) axis is activated, stimulating organs within the body and the central nervous system (Lu et al., 2021) via the hypothalamus and brainstem (Chrousos, 2009). The hypothalamus's main role is to coordinate the endocrine system (which is involved in the control of hormones) and to regulate body temperature, the autonomic nervous system (ANS), and appetite (Shahid et al., 2018). The brainstem is involved in regulation of vital life functions including breathing, consciousness, blood pressure, heart rate, and sleep (Basinger & Hogg, 2019). Figure 2.1 (the acute stress response; reproduced with permission from Hackett (2016)) provides a summary of the body's physiological response to acute stress.

In response to acute stress (distress) (Hinds & Sanchez, 2022):

1. The outer layer of the brain (cerebral cortex) sends signals to stimulate the hypothalamus to release corticotropin-releasing hormone (CRH)
2. CRH stimulates the pituitary gland to produce and release the hormone known as adrenocorticotropic (ACTH) into the blood
3. ACTH activates pathways in the adrenal glands for the creation and release of the stress hormone called cortisol.

In addition, during a distressing experience, the ANS is activated (Marques et al., 2010). The HPA axis and ANS are highly interconnected (Rotenberg & McGrath, 2016). Together, they coordinate and impact the multiple physiological responses to stressors (Rotenberg & McGrath, 2016). The HPA axis is the neuroendocrine stress response and thus leads to the release of glucocorticoids (cortisol). The ANS is the neural route and results in the release of catecholamines (noradrenaline/adrenaline), and neuropeptides. Distress leads to secretion of pro-inflammatory cytokines, which coordinate immune

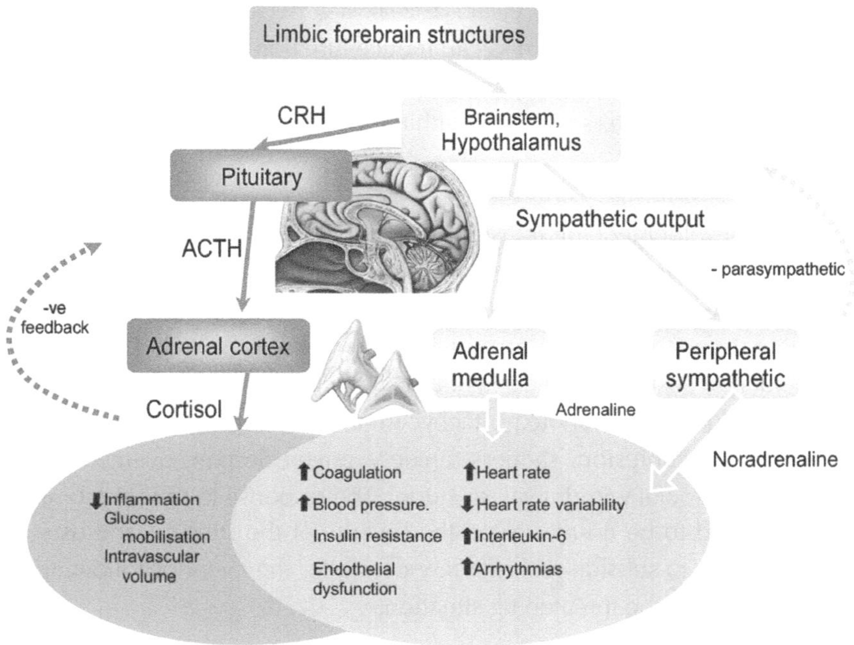

Figure 2.1 The acute stress response (reproduced with permission from Hackett (2016))

responses. See Hosseini-Kamkar et al. (2021) and Agorastos and Chrousos (2022) for more information about the acute stress response system.

The cascade of physiological stress responses throughout the body (Chrousos, 2009) impacts the:

- executive and/or cognitive system
- reward system
- fear system
- brain wake–sleep centers
- growth, reproductive, and thyroid hormone axes
- gastrointestinal system
- cardiorespiratory system
- metabolic system
- immune system.

For example, distress leads to immediate reduced functioning in the high-order part of the brain in which important learning processes occur (e.g., problem-solving (Woo et al., 2021)). If a person feels threatened or out of control, even mild distress can reduce functioning (Woo et al., 2021). Changes generated in these systems due to distress are evident in the definition of an 'acute stress reaction' within the ICD-11 (World Health Organisation, 2022b):

> ...the development of transient emotional, somatic, cognitive, or behavioral symptoms as a result of exposure to an event or situation (either short- or long-lasting) of an extremely threatening or horrific nature (e.g., natural or human-made disasters, combat, serious accidents, sexual violence, assault). Symptoms may include autonomic signs of anxiety (e.g., tachycardia, sweating, flushing), being in a daze, confusion, sadness, anxiety, anger, despair, overactivity, inactivity, social withdrawal, or stupor. The response to the stressor is considered to be normal given the severity of the stressor, and usually begins to subside within a few days after the event or following removal from the threatening situation.
>
> (no page)

Longer-Term Impact

Distressing events or life circumstances which are ongoing or repeated can lead to chronically altered physical and emotional states (Chrousos, 2009). While one single incident of distress may result in physiological consequences for the body, the chronic stress related to the ongoing impact of the event for an individual (and sometimes within the community) is likely to be the cause of disorders such as PTSD and other mental health disorders (McEwen, 2006; Hackett, 2016). The pathway to an individual experiencing long-term negative impacts from one or more traumatic or distressing events can be explored in relation to experiencing repeated episodes of or ongoing distress. Timing of the experience of trauma is also important. Trauma during critical periods of brain development can be particularly detrimental in relation to brain structure and function impact (Samson et al., 2024). There is significant evidence that very early traumatic experiences are especially important and may initiate a cascade of physiological and psychological processes that alter behavior as well as the structure and function of the brain (Bremner, 2003).

A wealth of prevalent research is available which describes elements protecting, exacerbating, or moderating the impact of trauma on children and young people. These factors can largely be categorized as: (1) developmental state when traumatic experience/s occurred, (2) individual physical characteristics (Ohashi et al., 2019), including epigenetics, (3) physiological impacts from trauma (De Bellis & Zisk, 2014), and (4) immediate, medial, and distal environments (such as family/community support, engagement in psychotherapy programs, and the physical environment).

Anatomy and Physiology

Although acute distress impacts physiological processes during and following one highly distressing event, the subsequent repeated stimulation of the stress system is likely to lead to the outcomes noted above for individuals who have experienced one traumatic event (McEwen, 2006). The knowledge about how stress impacts the body has been around for a long time; a commonly cited textbook from 1988 (Kaplan) noted physiological stress, which increases cortisol blood levels, can lead to high or low blood sugar (hyperglycemia or hypoglycemia), insulin resistance, decreased protein in bone and muscle, hyperlipemia, infection, decreased or increased ACTH, insulin sensitivity, weight loss, hypotension, and more.

More recent research provides more information about how trauma can impact the body. Overall, childhood maltreatment can impact brain neurological processes (Nemeroff, 2016) and structure (Carrion et al., 2007). Nerve pathways (neural circuits) within the brain's limbic system which regulate fear, executive function, learning, and memory are particularly sensitive to chronic stress (Roberts & Karatsoreos, 2021). Early-life adversity has consistently been shown to predict HPA dysregulation, and recent work has identified different cortisol reactivity for children who experience 'trauma' compared to children who experience adverse experiences (Hosseini-Kamkar et al., 2021).

Typically, the HPA axis produces a diurnal pattern, high levels of cortisol shortly after waking in the morning, followed by a steep decline in cortisol production throughout the day (Gunnar et al., 2015). Two main theoretical frameworks offer an explanation of the impact of chronic distress on HPA axis function (Hosseini-Kamkar et al., 2021). One is the 'toxic stress' model which purports the consequences of chronic stress as being harmful to the body (Nelson, 2018; Shonkoff & Garner, 2012). The other is the 'adaptationist' perspective which views the HPA axis calibration in response to changing stressors as evolutionarily adaptive (Del Giudice et al., 2011). Although the proposition herein is that trauma leads to chronic stress and thus impacts the body, this concept is not shared by all experts in this field. For instance, Thomason and Marusak (2017) promote the need in future research to disassociate trauma types from chronic stress in understanding brain development.

Table 2.2 presents examples of average physiological and anatomical differences detected for those exposed to trauma. Examples of potential challenges arising from these impacts which may be evident in the school setting are summarized. Clearly emerging from the research is the extensive impact that trauma can have on children and young people's bodies.

Examples of the impact of trauma on cardiovascular, muscular, reproductive, and skeletal systems are not included as examples in Table 2.2, however there is burgeoning research also highlighting the impact of chronic stress on these systems. For example, child abuse is associated with higher resting diastolic blood pressure and blunted blood pressure reactivity in adolescence (Gooding et al., 2015, 2016). Elevations in pro-inflammatory cytokines lead to vascular inflammation and elevations in blood pressure (Slopen et al., 2013). Physiological impacts from chronic stress such as disruption to the HPA axis and higher catecholamines have been theorized to be associated with muscle breakdown (Romero et al., 2009). Stress is proposed to impact reproductive physiology (Fietta et al., 2009) and more recent research has noted child abuse as a potential contributor to endometriosis (Liebermann et al., 2018). In addition, after controlling for confounders, childhood abuse has been found to be significantly associated with height deficits in young adults (Abajobir et al., 2017).

Mental Health Disorders

A wide range of stress-related mental, behavioral, and neurodevelopmental disorders can impact children and young people experiencing trauma. Such disorders were recently categorized by the World Health Organization (2022b) as a distinct group of diseases: 'Disorders Specifically Associated with Stress'. These are directly related to exposure to a stressful or traumatic event or a series of such events or adverse experiences (World Health Organisation, 2022a).

Table 2.2 Average difference/risk for those exposed to trauma and potential impact/implications by body systems

Evidenced differences between those experiencing trauma/adversity and those not	Average impact for those experiencing trauma/adversity
Brain and nervous system	
1. Reduced connectivity between brain regions (Thomason & Marusak, 2017)	• Reduced perception of emotional cues (Thomason & Marusak, 2017)
2. Peer abuse associated with depression symptoms and elevated cortisol (Vaillancourt et al., 2011)	• Challenges with memory (Vaillancourt et al., 2011)
3. Abuse in childhood and adolescence associated with whole-brain functional connectome; physiologic differences in intrinsic connectivity (independent of psychopathology) (Korgaonkar et al., 2023).	• Difficulties with perceptual processing and attention (Korgaonkar et al., 2023) • Heightened threat detection and response (Samson et al., 2024)
4. Early childhood abuse associated with brain development, specifically brain regions and circuits involved in stress response, emotional regulation, and autobiographical memory (Samson et al., 2024).	• Heightened stress response (Samson et al., 2024) • Challenges with emotional regulation (Samson et al., 2024) • Autobiographical memory differences (Samson et al., 2024)
5. Trauma experienced by young people associated with lower gray matter volume in the pre-front cortex (Thomason & Marusak, 2017) 6. Childhood maltreatment associated with gray matter disturbance in the brain frontal lobe (Begemann et al., 2023)	• Challenges in processes related to reinforcement-based decision-making, emotion regulation, and autobiographical memory (Begemann et al., 2023)
7. Parental verbal abuse to children associated with white matter tract abnormalities and altered brain region related to production and understanding of language (left arcuate fasciculus) (Choi et al., 2009)	• Challenges with production and understanding of language (Choi et al., 2009) • Challenges with verbal intelligence and verbal comprehension, depression, dissociation, limbic irritability, somatization, and anxiety (Choi et al., 2009)

(*Continued*)

Table 2.2 (Continued)

8. Early childhood stress (i.e., physical abuse, neglect, low socioeconomic status) associated with hippocampal reduction (Hanson & Nacewicz, 2021)	• Challenges with emotional processing and regulation (Hanson & Nacewicz, 2021)
9. Childhood maltreatment associated with differences in insular cortex (Fani et al., 2024)	• Difficulty recognizing internal bodily sensations (interception) (Löffler et al., 2018) • Reduced emotional awareness and heightened emotion dysregulation (Löffler et al., 2018)
10. Enhanced amygdala response to emotional stimuli in maltreated individuals compared with non-maltreated individuals (Teicher & Khan, 2019) 11. Child abuse maltreatment related PTSD associated with later abnormal amygdala volume (Woon & Hedges, 2008)	• Heightened emotional reactions, anxiety, and stress (Woon & Hedges, 2008) • May contribute to anxiety disorders or affect emotional regulation (Woon & Hedges, 2008)
12. Repeated activation of hormonal and inflammatory systems due to child abuse from heightened attention to and perception of threat over time (Pollak et al., 2005)	• Chronic hypervigilance (Pollak et al., 2005)
13. Generalized ANS hypo-arousal (Raine, 1996)	• Increased risks of aggressive, oppositional-defiant, or antisocial behaviors (Raine, 1996)
14. Adolescents experiencing neglect had reduced brain volumes in regions associated with social cognition and emotional processing (Trujillo-Llano et al., 2024)	• Lower performance in contextual emotional (recognition ability of systems to recognize emotions while considering the surrounding context) (Trujillo-Llano et al., 2024) • Challenges with ability to understand the thoughts, beliefs, desires, and emotions of other people (theory of mind), higher levels of envy, and Schadenfreude (pleasure felt at someone else's misfortune), and reduced empathy (Trujillo-Llano et al., 2024)

Table 2.2 (Continued)

Endocrine and immune systems	
15. Early-life adversity associated with hyper- and hypo activity of the HPA axis (Kirlic et al., 2020) 16. Peer-victimized children experience higher risk of dysregulation of HPA axis (Vaillancourt et al., 2008) 17. Individuals exposed to extreme and chronic stress that threaten a person's sense of safety associated with dysregulation of HPA axis (Miller et al., 2007)	• Challenges with executive function and subsequent self-regulation
18. Posttraumatic stress symptoms associated with higher levels of cortisol in youth (Carrion & Wong, 2012)	• Re-experiencing the traumatic event(s); avoidance of thoughts, memories, and activities that serve as reminders of the event; and persistent perceptions of heightened current threat (World Health Organ-isation, 2022a) • PTSD symptoms for adolescents may also include reluctance to pursue developmental oppor-tunities (e.g., to gain autonomy from caregivers), psychosocial impairment, self-injurious, or risky behaviors (World Health Organisa-tion, 2022a)
19. Moderate-to-severe childhood maltreatment associated with blunted cortisol reactivity (Tyrka et al., 2016) 20. Psychological and physical abuse associated with blunted cortisol reactivity slopes (Ouellet-Morin et al., 2011). 21. Childhood adversity is associated with blunted cortisol reactivity (Bunea et al., 2017)	• Blunted cortisol reactivity may prevent children from adaptively responding to stressors (Bunea et al., 2017)

(*Continued*)

Table 2.2 (Continued)

22. Childhood trauma is associated with elevations in pro-inflammatory cytokines (Slopen et al., 2013) 23. Elevated cytokines further impair glucocorticoid receptor functioning, thereby promoting further inflammation (Raison & Miller, 2003)	• Specific raised cytokines associated with socioemotional/behavioral problems in children including emotional symptoms, conduct problems, hyperactivity/inattention, and abnormal prosocial behavior (Barbosa et al., 2020) • Increased disease risk, such as a variety of cardiovascular risk factors for youth (Cook et al., 2000)
24. Strong inverse relationship between exposure to maltreatment in childhood and oxytocin concentrations (Heim et al., 2009)	• Impaired social signal reading and responding (Heim et al., 2009) • Interference with choosing an optimal partner (Heim et al., 2009)
25. Early maturation of the immune system for children and young people experiencing maltreatment (Marques-Feixa et al., 2022)	• Accelerated biological aging (Marques-Feixa et al., 2022)
26. Chronic stress exposure related to elevated inflammation and glucocorticoid-associated oxidative stress damage leads to the shorter telomeres (Kirlic et al., 2020)	• Increased cellular aging including biological aging and poorer physical health outcomes (Kirlic et al., 2020)
Digestion and excretory systems	
27. Distress associated with intestinal microbiota disturbance, impaired intestinal barrier function, immune dysfunction, and neuroendocrine system alterations (Konturek et al., 2011; Sun et al., 2019) 28. Distress associated with alterations in gastrointestinal motility, increase in visceral perception, changes in gastrointestinal secretion, increase in intestinal permeability, negative effects on regenerative capacity of gastrointestinal mucosa and mucosal blood flow, and negative effects on intestinal microbiota (Konturek et al., 2011)	• Various gastrointestinal diseases, including functional bowel disorders, inflammatory bowel disease, peptic ulcer disease, and gastroesophageal reflux disease (Konturek et al., 2011) • May experience poor growth and delayed puberty (Rosen et al., 2015)
29. Maltreated youth have increased risk for unexplained gastrointestinal symptoms partially mediated by psychological distress (van Tilburg et al., 2010)	• Unexplained gastrointestinal symptoms (van Tilburg et al., 2010)

Excessive stress can lead to disorders other than trauma which significantly impact an individual (Maercker & Eberle, 2022). For example, prolonged grief disorder and adjustment disorder are forms of stress-related disorders (World Health Organisation, 2022b). The ICD-11 signifies a specific stressor for the two trauma disorders (PTSD and CPTSD), specifying that potentially traumatic events are caused by *a stressor of an extremely threatening or horrific nature* (World Health Organisation, 2022a). The following definitions are taken from the ICD-11 (World Health Organisation, 2022b).

PTSD may develop following exposure to an extremely threatening or horrific event or series of events. It is characterized by all of the following: (1) re-experiencing the traumatic event or events in the present in the form of vivid intrusive memories, flashbacks, or nightmares. Re-experiencing may occur via one or multiple sensory modalities and is typically accompanied by strong or overwhelming emotions, particularly fear or horror, and strong physical sensations; (2) avoidance of thoughts and memories of the event or events or avoidance of activities, situations, or people reminiscent of the event(s); and (3) persistent perceptions of heightened current threat, for example, as indicated by hypervigilance or an enhanced startle reaction to stimuli such as unexpected noises. The symptoms persist for at least several weeks and cause significant impairment in personal, family, social, educational, occupational, or other important areas of functioning (World Health Organisation, 2022b).

Complex PTSD is defined as a disorder that may develop following exposure to an event or series of events of an extremely threatening or horrific nature, most commonly prolonged or repetitive events from which escape is difficult or impossible (e.g., torture, slavery, genocide campaigns, prolonged domestic violence, repeated childhood sexual, or physical abuse). All diagnostic requirements for PTSD are met. In addition, CPTSD is characterized by severe and persistent (1) problems in affect regulation; (2) beliefs about oneself as diminished, defeated, or worthless, accompanied by feelings of shame, guilt, or failure related to the traumatic event; and (3) difficulties in sustaining relationships and in feeling close to others. These symptoms cause significant impairment in 'personal, family, social, educational, occupational, or other important areas of functioning' (World Health Organization, 2022b).

Figure 2.2 is a proposed model (in line with the World Health Organization's International Classification of Diseases 11th Revision (2022b)) to demonstrate how 'Acute Stress Reaction/s' to one or more potentially

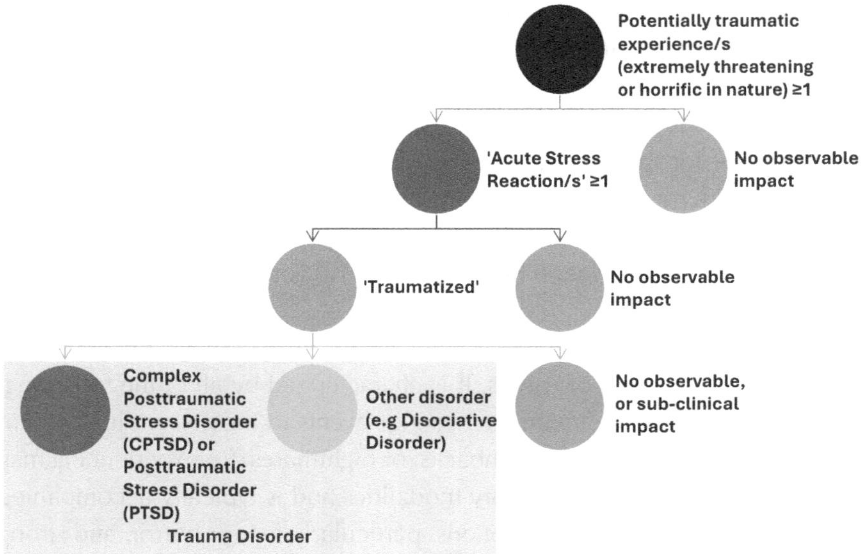

Figure 2.2 Proposed model demonstrating potential pathway from Acute Stress Reaction (from one or more potentially traumatic events) to 'traumatized', and then potential trauma disorder for an individual

traumatic events may lead to trauma. This model shows the development of 'trauma disorders' (e.g., PTSD, CPTSD, or other) which may emerge following trauma. This model also proposes different pathways which may be experienced by those who do not experience trauma or a trauma disorder after the event/s.

Emotions, Behavior, Learning, and Lifelong Wellbeing

In addition to trauma disorders, trauma is considered a risk factor for many other diseases and other health and wellbeing outcomes. Children and young people who experience trauma or adversity are more likely to experience mental health disorders including depression, non-suicidal self-injury (Ougrin et al., 2012), suicidality, and suicide (Dube et al., 2001; Lawrence et al., 2023; Perfect et al., 2016).

Childhood neglect and physical abuse are predictors of adult anxious attachment styles, avoidant attachment, and problems with depression, anxiety, and poor self-esteem (Widom et al., 2018). Poorer early-life socioeconomic status has been identified as the strongest lifelong driver of metabolic syndrome (Turner, 2018) incorporating impaired glucose metabolism, obesity, and hypertension, and hence increased risk of type 2 diabetes (Grundy et al., 2004). Trauma in childhood increases the risk of psychological distress, social exclusion, and development of chronic health conditions, such as heart disease, cancers, depression, and PTSD later in life (Hughes et al., 2017). Significant educational, social, and emotional well-being disadvantages are evident for children and young people who have experienced trauma (Houtepen et al., 2020; Kerker et al., 2015; Romano et al., 2014). Physiological impacts can lead to ongoing challenging behaviors (De Bellis & Zisk, 2014).

On average, significant learning, social, emotional, and behavioral disadvantages are experienced by children exposed to trauma compared with those who are not (Houtepen et al., 2020; Kerker et al., 2015; Romano et al., 2014). Domestic violence trauma is associated with negative outcomes in adulthood including psychosocial, economic, and educational achievement (Currie & Spatz-Widom, 2010; Zielinski, 2009). A child who experiences abuse is more likely to experience difficulties with focusing attention and completing learning tasks (van Harmelen et al., 2014). Experiencing domestic violence has been noted to be associated with cognition outcomes for students including poorer explicit memory (Jouriles et al., 2008) and decreased intelligence (Delaney-Black et al., 2002; Koenen et al., 2003). Experiencing two or more adverse childhood experiences for a child is associated with being disengaged from school (Bethell et al., 2014) and increases a child's risk of repeating a grade in school (Bethell et al., 2014) when compared with children with no adverse experiences.

Further, the higher number of adverse experiences encountered during childhood the higher the risk of negative mental health in adolescent and adult years (Lawrence et al., 2023). Children experiencing trauma or excessive stress are more likely to have problems with emotional self-regulation (Bettencourt et al., 2018; Hemphill et al., 2017; Wiley et al., 2020). Violent home or community environments and a lack of healthy role models can lead to maladaptive stress responses (such as violence) and self-regulation challenges (Kim & Cicchetti, 2010), increased avoidance, and emotional suppression (Gruhn & Compas, 2020). Children exposed to trauma may display challenging behaviors which are associated with lower levels of perceived safety (Crooks et al., 2011). Children and young people experiencing CPTSD may fear separation from loved ones, particularly when periods of separation from loved ones were experienced during the traumatic event (American Psychiatric Association, 2013).

Finding ways to reduce stress in the home and school environment could improve children's wellbeing and allow them to be more successful academically. Benefits from this will flow further afield to whole communities.

Recommendations

- Education about the impact of trauma on the body and associated challenges for students is implemented in initial teacher education along with changes to teaching curriculum
- Education about impact of trauma on the body and associated challenges for students is provided to students, families/caregivers, school staff including leaders, and education sector staff including policymakers
- Curriculum changes within primary and secondary education via the addition of education about the impact of trauma on the body and associated challenges
- Education to leaders at the system level creates and revises policies, processes, and environments to reduce stress within school environments for students and their caregivers, school leaders and staff, and caregivers
- School leaders create and revise school policies, processes, and environments to reduce stress for students, their caregivers, and school staff
- Teachers create and revise classroom-level policies, processes, and environments to reduce stress for students and their caregivers
- Government policies are amended to ensure they are trauma-informed.

Conclusion

The achievements of children and young people who are experiencing trauma are often profound. For some students, the challenges faced within their environment combined with their often compromised physical, emotional, and social states means that their very arrival at school each day is a significant achievement. This can inform the way in which schools change to encourage more supportive environments. Focusing on the strengths, achievements, and needs of children and young people experiencing trauma rather than perceived deficits in their emotions, learning, and behavior is a necessary shift in trauma-informed approaches.

This chapter emphasizes the range of challenges which children and young people who experience trauma are more likely to face. The research highlights that differences in physiology and anatomy are evident for many different stressful events and experiences. With such a range of challenges caused by trauma, it is clear why conforming to societal norms and expectations would be such a challenge for some children and young people. The school environment is challenging. Not only is attending school enforced for the majority of children and young people, but there are also many stressors and triggers in the environment likely to place them under increased strain. In addition, the impact of this on school staff and community members including parents/carers is clear. Education is imperative, but this must include cohesive, comprehensive, and consistent education for students, staff, leaders, families/carers, and the wider community.

References

Abajobir, A. A., Kisely, S., Williams, G., Strathearn, L., & Najman, J. M. (2017). Height deficit in early adulthood following substantiated childhood maltreatment: A birth cohort study. *Child Abuse & Neglect, 64*, 71–78.

Agorastos, A., & Chrousos, G. P. (2022). The neuroendocrinology of stress: The stress-related continuum of chronic disease development. *Molecular Psychiatry, 27*(1), 502–513. https://doi.org/10.1038/s41380-021-01224-9

Agorastos, A., Pervanidou, P., Chrousos, G. P., & Kolaitis, G. (2018). Early life stress and trauma: Developmental neuroendocrine aspects of prolonged stress system dysregulation. *Hormones, 17*, 507–520.

American Psychiatric Association. (2013). *Diagnostic and statistical manual of mental disorders: DSM-5* (Vol. 5). American Psychiatric Association.

Baes, N., Vylomova, E., Zyphur, M., & Haslam, N. (2023). The semantic inflation of "trauma" in psychology. *Psychology of Language and Communication, 27*(1), 23–45.

Barbosa, S., Khalfallah, O., Forhan, A., Galera, C., Heude, B., Glaichenhaus, N., & Davidovic, L. (2020). Serum cytokines associated with behavior: A cross-sectional study in 5-year-old children. *Brain, Behavior, and Immunity, 87*, 377–387.

Basinger, H., & Hogg, J. P. (2019). *Neuroanatomy, brainstem*. https://www.ncbi.nlm.nih.gov/books/NBK430685/

Begemann, M. J., Schutte, M. J., Van Dellen, E., Abramovic, L., Boks, M. P., Van Haren, N. E., Mandl, R. C., Vinkers, C. H., Bohlken, M. M., & Sommer, I. E. (2023). Childhood trauma is associated with reduced frontal gray matter volume: A large transdiagnostic structural MRI study. *Psychological Medicine, 53*(3), 741–749.

Bethell, C. D., Newacheck, P., Hawes, E., & Halfon, N. (2014). Adverse childhood experiences: Assessing the impact on health and school engagement and the mitigating role of resilience. *Health Affairs, 33*(12), 2106–2115.

Bettencourt, A. F., Gross, D., Ho, G., & Perrin, N. (2018). The costly consequences of not being socially and behaviorally ready to learn by kindergarten in Baltimore City. *Journal of Urban Health, 95*(1), 36–50. https://doi.org/10.1007/s11524-017-0214-6

Bremner, J. D. (2003). Long-term effects of childhood abuse on brain and neurobiology. *Child and Adolescent Psychiatric Clinics, 12*(2), 271–292.

Bunea, I. M., Szentágotai-Tătar, A., & Miu, A. C. (2017). Early-life adversity and cortisol response to social stress: A meta-analysis. *Translational Psychiatry, 7*(12), 1274.

Carrion, V. G., Weems, C. F., & Reiss, A. L. (2007). Stress predicts brain changes in children: A pilot longitudinal study on Youth Stress, Posttraumatic Stress Disorder, and the Hippocampus. *Pediatrics, 119*(3), 509–516. https://doi.org/10.1542/peds.2006-2028

Carrion, V. G., & Wong, S. S. (2012). Can traumatic stress alter the brain? Understanding the implications of early trauma on brain development and learning. *Journal of Adolescent Health, 51*(2), S23–S28.

Choi, J., Jeong, B., Rohan, M. L., Polcari, A. M., & Teicher, M. H. (2009). Preliminary evidence for white matter tract abnormalities in young adults exposed to parental verbal abuse. *Biological Psychiatry, 65*(3), 227–234. https://doi.org/10.1016/j.biopsych.2008.06.022

Chrousos, G. P. (2009). Stress and disorders of the stress system. *Nature Reviews Endocrinology, 5*(7), 374–381.

Clark, T. C., Fleming, T., Bullen, P., Denny, S., Crengle, S., Dyson, B., Fortune, S., Lucassen, M., Peiris-John, R., Robinson, E., Rossen, F., Sheridan, J., Teevale, T., & Utter, J. (2013). *Youth'12 overview: The health and wellbeing of New Zealand secondary school students in 2012.* University of Auckland, Faculty of Medical and Health Sciences.

Cook, D. G., Mendall, M. A., Whincup, P. H., Carey, I. M., Ballam, L., Morris, J. E., Miller, G. J., & Strachan, D. P. (2000). C-reactive protein concentration in children: Relationship to adiposity and other cardiovascular risk factors. *Atherosclerosis, 149*(1), 139–150.

Craig, S. L., Austin, A., Levenson, J., Leung, V. W., Eaton, A. D., & D'Souza, S. A. (2020). Frequencies and patterns of adverse childhood events in LGBTQ+ youth. *Child Abuse & Neglect, 107*, 104623.

Crooks, C. V., Scott, K., Ellis, W., & Wolfe, D. A. (2011). Impact of a universal school-based violence prevention program on violent delinquency: Distinctive benefits for youth with maltreatment histories. *Child Abuse & Neglect, 35*(6), 393–400.

Cross, D., Fani, N., Powers, A., & Bradley, B. (2017). Neurobiological development in the context of childhood trauma. *Clinical Psychology: Science and Practice, 24*(2), 111.

Currie, J., & Spatz-Widom, C. (2010). Long-term consequences of child abuse and neglect on adult economic well-being. *Child maltreatment, 15*(2), 111–120.

Dalenberg, C. J., Straus, E., & Carlson, E. B. (2017). Defining trauma. In S. N. Gold (Ed.), *APA handbook of trauma psychology: Foundations in knowledge* (pp. 15–33). American Psychological Association. https://doi.org/10.1037/0000019-002

Dallam, S. J. (2010). *A model of the retraumatization process: A meta-synthesis of childhood sexual abuse survivors' experiences in healthcare*. University of Kansas.

Davies, B. R., & Allen, N. B. (2017). Trauma and homelessness in youth: Psychopathology and intervention. *Clinical Psychology Review, 54*, 17–28.

De Bellis, M. D., & Zisk, A. (2014). The biological effects of childhood trauma. *Child and Adolescent Psychiatric Clinics of North America, 23*(2), 185–222.

Del Giudice, M., Ellis, B. J., & Shirtcliff, E. A. (2011). The adaptive calibration model of stress responsivity. *Neuroscience & Biobehavioral Reviews, 35*(7), 1562–1592.

Delaney-Black, V., Covington, C., Ondersma, S. J., Nordstrom-Klee, B., Templin, T., Ager, J., Janisse, J., & Sokol, R. J. (2002). Violence exposure, trauma, and IQ and/or reading deficits among urban children. *Archives of Pediatrics & Adolescent Medicine, 156*(3), 280–285.

Dube, S. R., Anda, R. F., Felitti, V. J., Chapman, D. P., Williamson, D. F., & Giles, W. H. (2001). Childhood abuse, household dysfunction, and the risk of attempted suicide throughout the life span: Findings from the adverse childhood experiences study. *JAMA, 286*(24), 3089–3096. https://doi.org/10.1001/jama.286.24.3089

Elhai, J. D., Gray, M. J., Kashdan, T. B., & Franklin, C. L. (2005). Which instruments are most commonly used to assess traumatic event exposure and posttraumatic effects?: A survey of traumatic stress professionals. *Journal of Traumatic Stress: Official Publication of the International Society for Traumatic Stress Studies, 18*(5), 541–545.

Fani, N., Fulton, T., & Botzanowski, B. (2024). *The neurophysiology of interoceptive disruptions in trauma-exposed populations*. Springer.

Felitti, V. J. (2002). The relation between adverse childhood experiences and adult health: Turning gold into lead. *The Permanente Journal, 6*(1), 44. https://doi.org/10.7812/tpp/02.994

Felitti, V. J., Anda, R. F., Nordenberg, D., Williamson, D. F., Spitz, A. M., Edwards, V., & Marks, J. S. (1998). Relationship of childhood abuse and household dysfunction to many of the leading causes of death in adults: The Adverse Childhood Experiences (ACE) Study. *American Journal of Preventive Medicine, 14*(4), 245–258. https://doi.org/10.1016/S0749-3797(98)00017-8

Fietta, P., Fietta, P., & Delsante, G. (2009). Central nervous system effects of natural and synthetic glucocorticoids. *Psychiatry and Clinical Neurosciences, 63*(5), 613–622.

Fowler, P. J., Tompsett, C. J., Braciszewski, J. M., Jacques-Tiura, A. J., & Baltes, B. B. (2009). Community violence: A meta-analysis on the effect of exposure and mental health outcomes of children and adolescents. *Development and Psychopathology, 21*(1), 227–259.

Gandham, S., Gunasekera, H., Isaacs, D., Maycock, A., & Britton, P. N. (2023). High prevalence of symptoms of post-traumatic stress in children of refugee and asylum seeker background. *International Journal of Mental Health and Addiction, 21*(1), 71–80.

Gooding, H. C., Milliren, C. E., Austin, S. B., Sheridan, M. A., & McLaughlin, K. A. (2015). Child abuse, resting blood pressure, and blood pressure reactivity to psychosocial stress. *Journal of Pediatric Psychology, 41*(1), 5–14. https://doi.org/10.1093/jpepsy/jsv040

Gooding, H. C., Milliren, C. E., Austin, S. B., Sheridan, M. A., & McLaughlin, K. A. (2016). Child abuse, resting blood pressure, and blood pressure reactivity to psychosocial stress. *Journal of Pediatric Psychology, 41*(1), 5–14.

Gradus, J. L., & Galea, S. (2022). Reconsidering the definition of trauma. *The Lancet Psychiatry, 9*(8), 608–609.

Gradus, J. L., & Galea, S. (2023). Moving from traumatic events to traumatic experiences in the study of traumatic psychopathology. *American Journal of Epidemiology, 192*(10), 1609–1612.

Gruhn, M. A., & Compas, B. E. (2020). Effects of maltreatment on coping and emotion regulation in childhood and adolescence: A meta-analytic review. *Child Abuse & Neglect, 103*, 104446.

Grundy, S. M., Brewer Jr, H. B., Cleeman, J. I., Smith Jr, S. C., & Lenfant, C. (2004). Definition of metabolic syndrome: Report of the National Heart, Lung, and Blood Institute/American Heart Association conference on scientific issues related to definition. *Circulation, 109*(3), 433–438.

Grych, J. H., Jouriles, E. N., Swank, P. R., McDonald, R., & Norwood, W. D. (2000). Patterns of adjustment among children of battered women. *Journal of Consulting and Clinical Psychology, 68*(1), 84.

Gunnar, M. R., Doom, J. R., & Esposito, E. A. (2015). *Psychoneuroendocrinology of stress: Normative development and individual differences. Handbook of Child Psychology and Developmental Science*, 1–46.

Hackett, R. (2016). *The role of psychosocial wellbeing and biological stress processes in linking type II diabetes and cardiovascular disease*. UCL (University College London).

Hanson, J. L., & Nacewicz, B. M. (2021). Amygdala allostasis and early life adversity: Considering excitotoxicity and inescapability in the sequelae of stress. *Frontiers in Human Neuroscience, 15*, 624705.

Heim, C., Young, L. J., Newport, D. J., Mletzko, T., Miller, A. H., & Nemeroff, C. B. (2009). Lower CSF oxytocin concentrations in women with a history of childhood abuse. *Molecular Psychiatry, 14*(10), 954–958.

Hemphill, S. A., Broderick, D. J., & Heerde, J. A. (2017). Positive associations between school suspension and student problem behaviour: Recent Australian findings. *Trends and Issues in Crime and Criminal Justice, 531*, 1–13.

Herman, J. L. (2015). *Trauma and recovery: The aftermath of violence--from domestic abuse to political terror*. Hachette.

Hillis, S., Mercy, J., Amobi, A., & Kress, H. (2016). Global prevalence of past-year violence against children: A systematic review and minimum estimates. *Pediatrics, 137*(3).

Hinds, J. A., & Sanchez, E. R. (2022). The role of the hypothalamus–pituitary–adrenal (HPA) axis in test-induced anxiety: Assessments, physiological responses, and molecular details. *Stresses, 2*(1), 146–155.

Hoover, D. W. (2020). Trauma in children with neurodevelopmental disorders: Autism, intellectual disability, and attention-deficit/hyperactivity disorder. *Childhood Trauma in Mental Disorders: A Comprehensive Approach* (pp. 367–383). Springer.

Hosseini-Kamkar, N., Lowe, C., & Morton, J. B. (2021). The differential calibration of the HPA axis as a function of trauma versus adversity: A systematic review and p-curve meta-analyses. *Neuroscience & Biobehavioral Reviews, 127*, 54–135.

Houtepen, L. C., Heron, J., Suderman, M. J., Fraser, A., Chittleborough, C. R., & Howe, L. D. (2020). Associations of adverse childhood experiences with educational attainment and adolescent health and the role of family and socioeconomic factors: A prospective cohort study in the UK. *PLoS Medicine, 17*(3), e1003031. https://doi.org/10.1371/journal.pmed.1003031

Hughes, K., Bellis, M. A., Hardcastle, K. A., Sethi, D., Butchart, A., Mikton, C., Jones, L., & Dunne, M. P. (2017). The effect of multiple adverse childhood experiences on health: a systematic review and meta-analysis. *The Lancet Public Health, 2*(8), e356–e366.

Johnson, S. B., Riley, A. W., Granger, D. A., & Riis, J. (2013). The science of early life toxic stress for pediatric practice and advocacy. *Pediatrics, 131*(2), 319–327.

Jouriles, E. N., Brown, A. S., McDonald, R., Rosenfield, D., Leahy, M. M., & Silver, C. (2008). Intimate partner violence and preschoolers' explicit memory functioning. *Journal of Family Psychology, 22*(3), 420.

Kaplan, E. (1988). The process approach to neuropsychological assessment. *Aphasiology, 2*(3–4), 309–311.

Kerker, B. D., Zhang, J., Nadeem, E., Stein, R. E. K., Hurlburt, M. S., Heneghan, A., Landsverk, J., & Horwitz, S. M. (2015). Adverse childhood experiences and mental health, chronic medical conditions, and development in young children. *Academic Pediatrics, 15*(5), 510–517. https://doi.org/10.1016/j.acap.2015.05.005

Kim, J., & Cicchetti, D. (2010). Longitudinal pathways linking child maltreatment, emotion regulation, peer relations, and psychopathology. *Journal of Child Psychology and Psychiatry, 51*(6), 706–716.

Kirlic, N., Cohen, Z. P., & Singh, M. K. (2020). Is there an ace up our sleeve? A review of interventions and strategies for addressing behavioral and neurobiological effects of adverse childhood experiences in youth. *Adversity and Resilience Science, 1*(1), 5–28.

Koenen, K. C., Moffitt, T. E., Caspi, A., Taylor, A., & Purcell, S. (2003). Domestic violence is associated with environmental suppression of IQ in young children. *Development and Psychopathology, 15*(2), 297–311.

Konturek, P. C., Brzozowski, T., & Konturek, S. J. (2011). Stress and the gut: Pathophysiology, clinical consequences, diagnostic approach and treatment options. *Journal of Physiology and Pharmacology, 62*(6), 591–599.

Korgaonkar, M. S., Breukelaar, I. A., Felmingham, K., Williams, L. M., & Bryant, R. A. (2023). Association of neural connectome with early experiences of abuse in adults. *JAMA Network Open*, *6*(1), e2253082.

Lawrence, D. M., Hunt, A., Mathews, B., Haslam, D. M., Malacova, E., Dunne, M. P., Erskine, H. E., Higgins, D. J., Finkelhor, D., & Pacella, R. (2023). The association between child maltreatment and health risk behaviours and conditions throughout life in the Australian Child Maltreatment Study. *Medical Journal of Australia*, *218*, S34–S39.

Liebermann, C., Kohl Schwartz, A., Charpidou, T., Geraedts, K., Rauchfuss, M., Wölfler, M., Von Orelli, S., Häberlin, F., Eberhard, M., & Imesch, P. (2018). Maltreatment during childhood: A risk factor for the development of endometriosis? *Human Reproduction*, *33*(8), 1449–1458.

Löffler, A., Foell, J., & Bekrater-Bodmann, R. (2018). Interoception and its interaction with self, other, and emotion processing: Implications for the understanding of psychosocial deficits in borderline personality disorder. *Current Psychiatry Reports*, *20*, 1–9.

Lu, S., Wei, F., & Li, G. (2021). The evolution of the concept of stress and the framework of the stress system. *Cell Stress*, *5*(6), 76.

Maercker, A., & Eberle, D. J. (2022). Disorders specifically associated with stress in ICD-11. *Clinical Psychology in Europe*, *4*(Spec Issue), e9711. https://doi.org/10.32872/cpe.9711

Marques, A. H., Silverman, M. N., & Sternberg, E. M. (2010). Evaluation of stress systems by applying noninvasive methodologies: Measurements of neuroimmune biomarkers in the sweat, heart rate variability and salivary cortisol. *Neuroimmunomodulation*, *17*(3), 205–208.

Marques-Feixa, L., Castro-Quintas, Á., Palma-Gudiel, H., Romero, S., Morer, A., Rapado-Castro, M., Martín, M., Zorrilla, I., Blasco-Fontecilla, H., & Ramírez, M. (2022). Secretory immunoglobulin A (s-IgA) reactivity to acute psychosocial stress in children and adolescents: The influence of pubertal development and history of maltreatment. *Brain, Behavior, and Immunity*, *103*, 122–129.

Mathews, B., Pacella, R., Scott, J. G., Finkelhor, D., Meinck, F., Higgins, D. J., Erskine, H. E., Thomas, H. J., Lawrence, D. M., & Haslam, D. M. (2023). The prevalence of child maltreatment in Australia: Findings from a national survey. *Medical Journal of Australia*, *218*, S13–S18.

May-Chahal, C., & Cawson, P. (2005). Measuring child maltreatment in the United Kingdom: A study of the prevalence of child abuse and neglect. *Child Abuse & Neglect*, *29*(9), 969–984.

McEwen, B. S. (2006). Protective and damaging effects of stress mediators: Central role of the brain. *Dialogues in Clinical Neuroscience*, *8*(4), 367–381.

Miller, G. E., Chen, E., & Zhou, E. S. (2007). If it goes up, must it come down? Chronic stress and the hypothalamic-pituitary-adrenocortical axis in humans. *Psychological Bulletin*, *133*(1), 25.

Nelson, C. (2018). 19. Hazards to early development: The biological embedding of early life adversity. *Biological Psychiatry*, *83*(9), S7–S8.

Nemeroff, C. B. (2016). Paradise lost: The neurobiological and clinical consequences of child abuse and neglect. *Neuron, 89*(5), 892–909.

Nie, Y., Wen, L., Song, J., Wang, N., Huang, L., Gao, L., & Qu, M. (2022). Emerging trends in epigenetic and childhood trauma: Bibliometrics and visual analysis. *Frontiers in Psychiatry, 13*, 925273.

Nielsen, M. B., Tangen, T., Idsoe, T., Matthiesen, S. B., & Magerøy, N. (2015). Post-traumatic stress disorder as a consequence of bullying at work and at school. A literature review and meta-analysis. *Aggression and Violent Behavior, 21*, 17–24.

Oberlander, T. F., Weinberg, J., Papsdorf, M., Grunau, R., Misri, S., & Devlin, A. M. (2008). Prenatal exposure to maternal depression, neonatal methylation of human glucocorticoid receptor gene (NR3C1) and infant cortisol stress responses. *Epigenetics, 3*(2), 97–106.

O'Connor, M., Slopen, N., Becares, L., Burgner, D., Williams, D., & Priest, N. (2020). Inequalities in the distribution of childhood adversity from birth to 11 years [Internet]. *Academic Pediatrics, 20*(5), 609–618. https://doi.org/10.1016/j.acap.2019.12.004

Ohashi, K., Anderson, C. M., Bolger, E. A., Khan, A., McGreenery, C. E., & Teicher, M. H. (2019). Susceptibility or resilience to maltreatment can be explained by specific differences in brain network architecture. *Biological Psychiatry, 85*(8), 690–702.

Ouellet-Morin, I., Odgers, C. L., Danese, A., Bowes, L., Shakoor, S., Papadopoulos, A. S., Caspi, A., Moffitt, T. E., & Arseneault, L. (2011). Blunted cortisol responses to stress signal social and behavioral problems among maltreated/bullied 12-year-old children. *Biological Psychiatry, 70*(11), 1016–1023.

Ougrin, D., Tranah, T., Leigh, E., Taylor, L., & Asarnow, J. R. (2012). Practitioner review: Self-harm in adolescents. *Journal of Child Psychology and Psychiatry, 53*(4), 337–350. https://doi.org/10.1111/j.1469-7610.2012.02525.x

Perfect, M. M., Turley, M. R., Carlson, J. S., Yohanna, J., & Gilles, M. P. S. (2016). School-related outcomes of traumatic event exposure and traumatic stress symptoms in students: A systematic review of research from 1990 to 2015 [journal article]. *School Mental Health, 8*(1), 7–43. https://doi.org/10.1007/s12310-016-9175-2

Pollak, S. D., Vardi, S., Putzer Bechner, A. M., & Curtin, J. J. (2005). Physically abused children's regulation of attention in response to hostility. *Child Development, 76*(5), 968–977.

Raine, A. (1996). Autonomic nervous system factors underlying disinhibited, antisocial, and violent behavior. Biosocial perspectives and treatment implications. *Annals of the New York Academy of Sciences, 794*, 46–59.

Raison, C. L., & Miller, A. H. (2003). When not enough is too much: The role of insufficient glucocorticoid signaling in the pathophysiology of stress-related disorders. *American Journal of Psychiatry, 160*(9), 1554–1565.

Rieder, H., & Elbert, T. (2013). Rwanda–lasting imprints of a genocide: Trauma, mental health and psychosocial conditions in survivors, former prisoners and their children. *Conflict and Health, 7*, 1–13.

Roberts, B. L., & Karatsoreos, I. N. (2021). Brain–body responses to chronic stress: A brief review. *Faculty Reviews, 10,* 83.

Romano, E., Babchishin, L., Marquis, R., & Fréchette, S. (2014). Childhood maltreatment and educational outcomes. *Trauma, Violence & Abuse, 16*(4), 418–437. https://doi.org/10.1177/1524838014537908

Romero, L. M., Dickens, M. J., & Cyr, N. E. (2009). The reactive scope model—a new model integrating homeostasis, allostasis, and stress. *Hormones and Behavior, 55*(3), 375–389.

Rosen, M. J., Dhawan, A., & Saeed, S. A. (2015). Inflammatory bowel disease in children and adolescents. *JAMA Pediatrics, 169*(11), 1053–1060.

Rotenberg, S., & McGrath, J. J. (2016). Inter-relation between autonomic and HPA axis activity in children and adolescents. *Biological Psychology, 117,* 16–25.

Samson, J. A., Newkirk, T. R., & Teicher, M. H. (2024). Practitioner review: Neurobiological consequences of childhood maltreatment–clinical and therapeutic implications for practitioners. *Journal of Child Psychology and Psychiatry, 65*(3), 369–380.

Sasaki, N., Watanabe, K., Kanamori, Y., Tabuchi, T., Fujiwara, T., & Nishi, D. (2024). Effects of expanded adverse childhood experiences including school bullying, childhood poverty, and natural disasters on mental health in adulthood. *Scientific Reports, 14*(1), 12015.

Shahid, Z., Asuka, E., & Singh, G. (2018). *Physiology, hypothalamus.* https://www.ncbi.nlm.nih.gov/books/NBK535380/

Shonkoff, J. P., & Garner, A. S. (2012). The lifelong effects of early childhood adversity and toxic stress. *Pediatrics, 129*(1), e232–e246. https://doi.org/10.1542/peds.2011-2663

Slopen, N., Kubzansky, L. D., McLaughlin, K. A., & Koenen, K. C. (2013). Childhood adversity and inflammatory processes in youth: A prospective study. *Psychoneuroendocrinology, 38*(2), 188–200.

Substance Abuse and Mental Health Services Administration (SAMHSA). (2014). *SAMHSA's concept of trauma and guidance for a trauma-informed approach* (HHS Publication No. (SMA) 14-4884). https://store.samhsa.gov/shin/content/SMA14-4884/SMA14-4884.pdf

Sun, Y., Li, L., Xie, R., Wang, B., Jiang, K., & Cao, H. (2019). Stress triggers flare of inflammatory bowel disease in children and adults. *Frontiers in Pediatrics, 7,* 432.

Teicher, M. H., & Khan, A. (2019). Childhood maltreatment, cortical and amygdala morphometry, functional connectivity, laterality, and psychopathology. *Child Maltreatment, 24*(4), 458–465.

Thomason, M. E., & Marusak, H. A. (2017). Toward understanding the impact of trauma on the early developing human brain. *Neuroscience, 342,* 55–67.

Treloar, C., & Jackson, L. C. (2015). Commentary on historical trauma, substance use, and indigenous people: Seven generations from a "big event". *Substance Use & Misuse, 50*(7), 891–893.

Troutt, D. D. (2017). Trapped in tragedies: Childhood trauma, spatial inequality, and law. *Marquette Law Review, 101,* 601.

Trujillo-Llano, C., Sainz-Ballesteros, A., Suarez-Ardila, F., Gonzalez-Gadea, M. L., Ibáñez, A., Herrera, E., & Baez, S. (2024). Neuroanatomical markers of social cognition in neglected adolescents. *Neurobiol Stress, 31*, 100642. https://doi.org/10.1016/j.ynstr.2024.100642

Turner, J. D. (2018). Childhood adversity from conception onwards: Are our tools unnecessarily hindering us? *Journal of Behavioral Medicine, 41*(4), 568–570.

Tyrka, A. R., Ridout, K. K., & Parade, S. H. (2016). Childhood adversity and epigenetic regulation of glucocorticoid signaling genes: Associations in children and adults. *Development and Psychopathology, 28*(4pt2), 1319–1331.

United Nations. (2009). *State of the world's indigenous peoples*. United Nations, Department of Economic and Social Affairs Division for Social Policy and Development.

Vaillancourt, T., Duku, E., Becker, S., Schmidt, L. A., Nicol, J., Muir, C., & MacMillan, H. (2011). Peer victimization, depressive symptoms, and high salivary cortisol predict poorer memory in children. *Brain and Cognition, 77*(2), 191–199.

Vaillancourt, T., Duku, E., Decatanzaro, D., Macmillan, H., Muir, C., & Schmidt, L. A. (2008). Variation in hypothalamic–pituitary–adrenal axis activity among bullied and non-bullied children. *Aggressive Behavior: Official Journal of the International Society for Research on Aggression, 34*(3), 294–305.

van Harmelen, A.-L., van Tol, M.-J., Dalgleish, T., van der Wee, N. J., Veltman, D. J., Aleman, A., Spinhoven, P., Penninx, B. W., & Elzinga, B. M. (2014). Hypoactive medial prefrontal cortex functioning in adults reporting childhood emotional maltreatment. *Social Cognitive and Affective Neuroscience, 9*(12), 2026–2033.

van Tilburg, M. A., Runyan, D. K., Zolotor, A. J., Graham, J. C., Dubowitz, H., Litrownik, A. J., Flaherty, E., Chitkara, D. K., & Whitehead, W. E. (2010). Unexplained gastrointestinal symptoms after abuse in a prospective study of children at risk for abuse and neglect. *The Annals of Family Medicine, 8*(2), 134–140.

Venet, A. S. (2023). *Equity-centered trauma-informed education*. Routledge.

Widom, C. S., Czaja, S. J., Kozakowski, S. S., & Chauhan, P. (2018). Does adult attachment style mediate the relationship between childhood maltreatment and mental and physical health outcomes? *Child Abuse & Neglect, 76*, 533–545.

Wiley, S. A., Slocum, L. A., O'Neill, J., & Esbensen, F.-A. (2020). Beyond the breakfast club: Variability in the effects of suspensions by school context. *Youth & Society, 52*(7), 1259–1284. https://doi.org/10.1177/0044118x19896716

Woo, E., Sansing, L. H., Arnsten, A. F., & Datta, D. (2021). Chronic stress weakens connectivity in the prefrontal cortex: Architectural and molecular changes. *Chronic Stress, 5*, 24705470211029254.

Woon, F. L., & Hedges, D. W. (2008). Hippocampal and amygdala volumes in children and adults with childhood maltreatment-related posttraumatic stress disorder: A meta-analysis. *Hippocampus, 18*(8), 729–736. https://doi.org/10.1002/hipo.20437

World Health Organisation. (2022a). *Disorders specifically related to stress in ICD-11 for mortality and morbidity statistics (V01/2023)*. Accessed 10/07/2025. https://icd.who.int/browse/2025-01/mms/en#991786158

World Health Organisation. (2022b). *ICD-11 International Classification of Diseases 11th revision*. Accessed 10/07/2025. https://icd.who.int/browse/2025-01/mms/en

World Health Organization. (2020). *Global status report on preventing violence against children 2020*. Geneva, World Health Organisation.

Zielinski, D. S. (2009). Child maltreatment and adult socioeconomic well-being. *Child Abuse & Neglect, 33*(10), 666–678.

Zhou, A., & Ryan, J. (2023). Biological embedding of early-life adversity and a scoping review of the evidence for intergenerational epigenetic transmission of stress and trauma in humans. *Genes, 14*(8), 1639.

3

Understanding Behavior through a Trauma-Informed Lens

A Framework for Educators

Govind Krishnamoorthy, Jessica Koslouski, Vicki C. Dallinger, Emma Gawthorne, and Sandra Chafouleas

Introduction

As summarized in prior chapters, trauma can create significant challenges for children and young people's learning and behavior at school (Cross et al., 2017; Koslouski et al., 2023a; Perfect et al., 2016). This chapter discusses the impact that trauma may have on behavior and how current school behavior management approaches risk re-traumatizing students. The concept that trauma-informed practice provides a more effective approach in responding to challenges related to student behavior in schools is introduced. Systemic, classroom, and student and/or teacher-led changes that can be made to improve the academic, social, emotional, and behavioral success of students experiencing trauma are then explored. Particular attention will be paid to building staff understanding of the impact of trauma on students and staff reflective practices for interpreting student behavior.

This chapter further provides practical, evidence-based trauma-informed strategies schools can apply to avoid triggers, responses, and patterns of behavior that may increase a child's risk of school exclusion and disengagement. The case study referred to throughout this chapter emphasizes key points, offers readers tangible examples, and highlights the potential of trauma-informed practices to support students. The case study[1] is a collection of experiences based on one author's years of teaching experience

DOI: 10.4324/9781003436034-3

with children exposed to trauma (pseudonyms have been used to protect the privacy and confidentiality of students and staff).

The 3 Es and 5 Cs of Trauma-Informed Practice in Schools

Trauma-informed schools not only recognize the prevalence of potentially traumatic events in students' lives, but also the varying impacts these events may have. Estimates of potentially traumatic events vary, in part, because proposed lists of potentially traumatic events may be narrower or more comprehensive (e.g., Felitti et al., 1998; World Health Organization, 2018). A key piece though, is that the events are *potentially* traumatic. What is traumatic to one student may not be to another. As described by the United States Substance Abuse and Mental Health Services Administration (SAMHSA, 2014), there are 3 Es of trauma: the *event, experience,* and *effect.* First, the *event* occurs. Potentially traumatic events might include child abuse or neglect, loss of a primary caregiver, or witnessing violence. Then, everyone will have an *experience*, or individual perception, of the event which contributes to whether the event will have traumatic effects. Individuals' experiences of the event can vary widely based on many factors, including developmental stage, prior mental health challenges, or trauma experiences, the duration of the event, and available social support (Chafouleas et al., 2019; Harvey, 1996). Events that threaten feelings of safety, agency, dignity, and belonging are more likely to be experienced as traumatic (McGlynn-Wright & Briner, 2021). Lastly, depending on the experience of the event, the *effects* will become clear. Traumatic effects include sustained negative effects on an individual's functioning and physical, mental, social, emotional, or spiritual wellbeing (SAMHSA, 2014).

SAMHSA has identified six principles of trauma-informed care. These six principles were designed to be applicable across multiple service settings (e.g., education, child welfare, primary health care, military). To maximize relevance to school settings, we have adapted SAMHSA's definitions to focus on school educators, students, and school environments. First, trauma-informed organizations promote physical and psychological *safety* for students and staff. Second, they promote *trustworthiness and transparency*, making transparent decisions and building and maintaining trust amongst students, families, and school staff. Third, SAMHSA recommends that trauma-informed organizations allow for *peer support*. In the case of working with children, this is often partnering with key caregivers in the child's recovery. Fourth, trauma-informed organizations establish *collaboration and mutuality*, sharing power and decision-making with students and amongst staff. Trauma-informed organizations also promote *empowerment, voice, and choice*, leveraging student strengths, creating shared goals with students, and providing frequent opportunities for choice. Lastly, trauma-informed organizations attend to *cultural, historical, and gender issues*. Trauma-informed schools address bias, provide culturally responsive instruction and care, and recognize and address the impacts of historical trauma.

SAMHSA (2014) also identifies four actions of trauma-informed organizations, which Chafouleas et al. (2016) tailored to school settings. First, school educators and leaders *realize* trauma and its effects and implement the six principles of a trauma-informed approach (see above) to create a positive learning environment for all students. By realizing trauma and its effects, school staff are then able to *recognize* the signs of trauma and *respond* with appropriate support. Finally, schools use their understandings of trauma to make short- and long-term decisions that *resist re-traumatization*. For example, exclusionary discipline practices prevent students from accessing learning, isolate them from their peers, and have not been shown to reduce future problem behavior (Michail, 2011; Valdebenito et al., 2019). A trauma-informed school might consider this evidence and engage positive behavioral interventions and supports or restorative justice practices to *resist re-traumatizing* students.

A Framework for Understanding: The 5Cs

The adaptation of trauma-informed care principles to the educational context and operationalizing of trauma-informed principles to tangible practices for school educators are emerging. Ayre and Krishnamoorthy (2020) propose a '5C' framework of understanding and practice that links key foundational theories of trauma-informed practice with best practice guidelines (e.g., Howard et al., 2022). The 5Cs refer to the five key considerations for educators to understand and respond to student behaviors through a trauma-informed practice lens. The 5Cs are: Care, Calm, Connect, Coach, and Collaborate. The following sections of this chapter will further discuss each of these components, provide a list of key questions for educators to consider when thinking about student behaviors, and offer a case study illustrating a teacher's use of the 5Cs in his classroom.

Care: Care before Curriculum

Trauma-informed schools consider the whole child, and how experiences of stress and trauma may get in the way of students' learning. As discussed in previous chapters, trauma-informed schools understand that addressing students' basic needs allows them to access the curriculum more successfully. Thus, trauma-informed schools consider *care before curriculum*. The 5C framework identifies four types of student needs: basic needs, safety needs, health needs, and developmental needs. This chapter defines each type of need and describes the care that can be provided by schools to address these needs.

First, all students have basic needs of food, water, clothing, shelter, sleep, and hygiene. Maslow's hierarchy of needs (Maslow, 1943, 1954) has proposed that if these basic physiological needs are not met, students are less prepared to engage in critical thinking or prosocial interactions. For example, dehydration impedes cognition (Edmonds & Burford, 2009). It is estimated that more than one half of school-age youth and adolescents are inadequately hydrated (Kenney et al., 2015). Simple strategies such as ensuring access to water throughout the school day can help students stay hydrated. In addition, research suggests that students experiencing food insecurity are at greater risk for lower academic achievement and increased emotional and behavioral concerns (Shankar et al., 2017). Many schools now serve breakfast, and examples of universal free meals are emerging (e.g., Langlois, 2024; Meisner, 2023). "Breakfast clubs" or opportunities to eat breakfast as the day begins allow students to approach learning without being distracted or dysregulated by hunger. Schools might also be able to provide support with clothing or hygiene needs by providing school uniforms, donated shoes and clothing, or hygiene products so that students are clean and ready to learn. Research indicates that increased access to resources to fulfill basic needs can improve students' mental and physical health (Gottlieb et al., 2016; Bellamy et al., 2022) and that schools are promising sites for connecting students to these resources (Koslouski et al., 2023).

Second, students need to experience physical and emotional safety. In many countries, educators are mandated reporters of abuse (Mathews,

2014). Such policies include that if educators are concerned that a student is in physical or emotional danger, they must follow legislative requirements and local procedures and report any suspected risk to a child to their school administration and/or child protective services (Mathews, 2014). In the United States, schools are required to provide training in these procedures – as part of a whole-of-school approach that aims to protect children from maltreatment (e.g., Abused and Neglected Child Reporting Act, 2019). In Australia, schools must adhere to the Federal Government's Child Safe Policy (2024), which also includes staff training to recognize abuse. The training in both the United States and Australia includes guidance for educators on warning signs of abuse. For example, this includes unexplained bruises or burns, especially where children do not frequently get hurt (e.g., torso, back, neck) or lacerations to any part of a child's face (Commonwealth of Massachusetts, 2023). Educators should also watch for signs of sexual exploitation, such as risky behavior, concerning relationships, and excessive money or material goods that seem incongruent with the student's life circumstances (Commonwealth of Massachusetts, 2023). As adults who work with children for extended periods of time each day, teachers are in an opportune position to notice and report these concerns.

Unaddressed physical health needs can also impact student behavior and impede school success. These might include untreated chronic illnesses, unaddressed mental health needs, or frequent somatic complaints (e.g., stomachaches, headaches, body aches; Bowyer et al., 2023). Educators might notice ongoing fatigue or withdrawal in students and partner with the school nurse or families/carers to address the concerns. Relationships with families/carers are crucial for addressing these needs (reference). Seeking supportive solutions with families using careful, considered discussions which avoid blame often assists. Unaddressed health needs are another component which is relevant to supporting students. In some cases, it may be a lack of health literacy, or knowledge, on the families' part. In other cases, barriers might include cost, transportation, insurance, or scheduling concerns which prevent access to adequate health care. Building relationships with families to identify applicable barriers allows for responsive and appropriate supports to be provided (e.g., Devoe et al., 2007; Sobo et al., 2006). Depending on identified needs, schools may support families by providing resources that promote health literacy (e.g., pamphlets, websites), transportation, referrals, or support in navigating insurance coverage or waitlists. School nurses, social workers, and school-based health center staff can all help to address these needs (e.g., Council on School Health, 2008; Kjolhede et al., 2021).

Lastly, school educators should watch for social-emotional or developmental needs of students. School educators can be supported to identify warning signs of delayed developmental capacities and milestones. Efforts to develop students' social and emotional skills can begin by consulting national and regional guidelines on evidence-based social-emotional instruction (e.g., Collaborative for Academic, Social, and Emotional Learning [CASEL], n.d.; Jones et al., 2021). This could include explicit instruction of routines, emotion regulation, and social skills that support students in successfully navigating the social, emotional, and academic demands of schools (e.g., Koslouski et al., revision under review; Jones et al., 2021). Transitions and unstructured times (e.g., recess, bus line) can be particularly difficult for some students (Jones et al., 2021). Thus, additional structure and support during these times can be very beneficial. Educators can also strengthen students' social and emotional development by communicating unconditional positive regard (i.e., care for the student regardless of behavior) and by modeling prosocial behaviors (Brunzell & Norrish, 2021).

Consider Sonia. Sonia has attended several schools due to being transitioned through several foster care placements. She is warm and friendly towards adults but has difficulty relating to her peers. Sonia currently resides in a residential care facility – with a rotating roster of youth workers who provide her care. There are frequent changes to the team of youth workers caring for Sonia, due to changes in funding mandates and staffing shortage. Reflecting on Sonia's basic needs, her teacher, Mr. Cruz recognizes that Sonia's basic needs of stable housing, clothing, food, and hygiene may be sources of challenge. Mr. Cruz connects with Sonia's team, including the school nurse and school adjustment counselor to discuss options for support. The team identifies available supports that the school adjustment counselor will share with Sonia's foster mom in their upcoming meeting.

Calm: De-escalate before You Educate

The influence of emotion and the stress response on behavior is well documented, and emotion regulation is essential for promoting learning amongst children. Humans must regulate their arousal levels as a prerequisite for engaging in higher-order cognitive processes, including reasoning and complex problem-solving (Perry, 2002). This phenomenon is underpinned by the inherent structural organization of the human brain, which dictates a hierarchical progression from fundamental physiological functions to progressively sophisticated cognitive functions (Perry, 2006). For example, when children experience heightened stress – in the form of fear or anger – neurological mechanisms prioritize short-term control and safety-seeking behaviors over tasks such as contemplating the longer-term consequences of one's actions. Children impacted by traumatic experiences often have a prolonged stress response (sometimes referred to as 'toxic stress reactions') resulting in frequent heightened emotional responses. The cumulative disadvantage of such prolonged stress responses and exposure to adverse experiences can result in challenges related to self-regulatory skills, social communication, cognition, and responsiveness to routine strategies for supporting emotion regulation (National Scientific Council on the Developing Child, 2012).

A trauma-informed approach to emotion regulation and de-escalation involves the use of four key skills (Ayre & Krishnamoorthy, 2020): (1) recruiting the use of external resources (external management), (2) communication and collaborative use of self-regulation skills (co-regulation), (3) support and coaching for the student in the use of the skills (supported regulation), and (4) reinforcement for autonomous use of self-regulatory skills (self-regulation; Ayre & Krishnamoorthy, 2020). The following section describes each of these skills in further detail.

It can be difficult to support students who are visibly upset or when their behavior becomes severely challenging or unsafe. Educators may not always understand the immediate cause of such reactions. Amongst children exposed to adversity or maltreatment, quick escalations of distress may reflect their heightened vulnerability to stress reactions (Grasso et al., 2013). Challenging behaviors, in this context, often represent flight, fight, or freeze reactions to perceptions of physical or social threat for the students within the school environment (National Child Traumatic Stress Network (NCTSN), n.d.). For students who may be at risk of being hurt, or hurting others, educators require skills in managing the student's environment to minimize the risk of harm and increase a sense of perceived safety for the student by removing them from the environment in the short term (Horowitz et al., 2015). A consistent, well-rehearsed process of managing such crisis situations in a least-restrictive manner represents skills in 'external regulation'.

Here, as a last option, students are provided with time away from a situation that may be triggering them – with a clear plan for reintegration into the classroom following these circumstances (Ayre & Krishnamoorthy, 2020). Equally, a process of debriefing and reflection for educators is important in understanding the use of other emotion regulation strategies for the students (Koslouski, 2022).

As students begin to develop a sense of safety and belonging in the school environment, their educators are often developing trust and becoming more attuned to early warning signs and cues of distress in the students (Wall, 2021). In such circumstances, students can become open to suggestions and feedback from trusted staff, and not excessively preoccupied with being shamed, manipulated, or excluded. These students can be more willing to discuss concerns with school staff and receptive to practicing social-emotional skills in collaboration with the educators. These experiences of regulating a student's distress through student-teacher communication are referred to as 'coregulation' (You and I do together; Ayre & Krishnamoorthy, 2020). Educators who co-regulate often model the use of self-regulation skills, while using communication and social-emotional skills rehearsal to calm the student and communicates genuine concern (Moos & Ringdal, 2012).

Students who are supported with co-regulation may begin to develop greater self-efficacy in using self-regulatory skills to manage their own physiological arousal and emotional reactions. However, given the effects that chronic stress may have on memory and higher-level problem-solving skills (Perry, 2006), students may require prompts from staff to utilize these social-emotional skills (Gan et al., 2020). Referred to as 'supported regulation', students who have emerging self-awareness and self-regulatory abilities may continue to require prompting and cueing from educators to use these skills in situations that are potentially upsetting or triggering to the student (Ayre & Krishnamoorthy, 2020). Educators often act as a 'skills coach,' supporting the student in the implementation of the social-emotional strategies – without necessarily engaging in the strategy with them (You do, I'll watch).

Supported regulation strategies represent the precursor for the final stage of students' regulatory capacities – self-regulation – where the child identifies emerging distress or discomfort, can remember suitable self-regulatory skills for the situation, and has the skills to effectively use the skills to optimize their levels of arousal. Self-regulation enables students to identify situations that require them to increase their physiological arousal (e.g., when bored in class) and decrease their heightened arousal (e.g., when frustrated or excessively excited; Moos & Ringdal, 2012). In this stage, the educator faces a unique challenge of identifying times when the student appears to have demonstrated the use of self-regulatory skills and provides encouragement and positive reinforcement for such efforts. A student's capacity to be autonomous in their self-regulatory capacities is dynamic – with certain situations at school and at home requiring educators to utilize skills in the previous phases (i.e., external regulation, co-regulation, and supported regulation; Johnson et al., 2023). Equally, an educator's capacity to provide such support may vary – depending on the competing demands of the classroom and school (Johnson et al., 2023). A thoughtful consideration of the needs of the student, the educator, and key people in the broader context of the child (e.g., other students, leadership, family members) is imperative in planning and implementing supports.

Sonia freezes when she is called on in the classroom. Color drains from her face and she begins to stammer as she tries to respond. Peers look at her and chuckle under their breath. Mr. Cruz recognizes that this is likely a freeze response. He decides to only call on Sonia in front of the class if she has raised her hand, and to work with her individually and in small groups to assess her learning and build her regulatory capacities for coping with academic challenges. Mr. Cruz works with the school adjustment counselor to identify strategies Sonia can use and creates a non-verbal signal to prompt Sonia to use the strategies before she becomes too dysregulated. Over time, Mr. Cruz fades his support, only co-regulating when needed, and instead coaching or praising Sonia's use of strategies.

Connect: Reach before You Teach

Student's level of trust in their educators is likely to influence their feeling of safety in school. Children exposed to harm and manipulation from adults at an early age are more likely to develop negative expectations of adults as not being trustworthy (Davey et al., 2020). Consequently, they can be less receptive to listening and learning from them (Jellesma et al., 2015). Such children are often sensitive to rejection, humiliation, and abandonment – often acting pre-emptively to avoid such experiences through disengagement and oppositionality in their relationships (Jellesma et al., 2015). Theories of attachment have proposed several mechanisms and patterns of influence from early childhood experiences of trauma. Attachment refers to the biobehavioral feedback system, where children express their needs, and caregivers in their environment respond to the child's expressions of need (Bowlby, 1969). This cycle of need expression and response forms the foundation for the emotional bond between the child and their parent/carer and shapes the child's expectations and behavior in and outside the family. There are several prominent proponents of attachment theory. A useful taxonomy of attachment styles was proposed by Mary Ainsworth, who outlined four primary childhood attachment styles: secure, anxious-avoidant, anxious-ambivalent, and disorganized (Ainsworth, 1979). While these styles do not constitute a formal diagnosis, they provide a useful description of relationship styles of children. The attachment theory (Ainsworth, 1979; Main & Solomon, 1990) proposes that securely attached children display trust in caregivers and explore their environment comfortably; anxious-ambivalent children exhibit clinginess and anxiety due to inconsistent caregiver responses; anxious-avoidant children avoid emotional connection with caregivers, stemming from caregiver unresponsiveness; disorganized attachment style often leads children to lack a consistent pattern of expressing their needs, moving between patterns of secure, anxious-ambivalent, and avoidant attachment (Ainsworth, 1979; Main & Solomon, 1990). Children exposed to traumatic experiences and cumulative harms are likely to be at higher risk of disorganized styles of attachment. While early experiences with caregivers have a significant impact on attachment styles, attachment styles are likely to change over time in response to relationships across contexts. Children often have greater success in the classroom when a teacher can recognize and respond appropriately to these attachment styles and patterns (Ayre & Krishnamoorthy, 2020).

Children exhibiting avoidant or disorganized relational styles can be challenging for educators to support. Their dynamic emotional states and reactivity can reflect their exposure to frightening situations in the past and their heightened vigilance for unsafe events and people in the future (Krishnamoorthy et al., 2023a; Perry & Szalavitz, 2017). The key challenge for such students is providing them with a sense of being 'seen and acknowledged'. The first step for educators is to work on "being present" – to be physically present in the child's environment, to communicate consistent availability and care and being mentally present, to attend and attune to the student's emotional state and behavior, and to actively reflect on the student's needs (Cozolino, 2013). Non-verbal cues aid in demonstrating that teachers are genuinely listening and also may serve as models for students to become better listeners themselves. It appears that a challenge for educators in this stage is to hone their observational capacities – in the face of competing demands and stimuli in a school. The thoughtful use of verbal and non-verbal cues to the student – moving from verbose instructions to small gestures and acknowledgment – are important skills in helping the student feel safe and supported (Cozolino, 2013).

Children with an anxious-avoidant attachment style may present as defensive, argumentative, and disagreeable. This frustration is often linked to the inconsistent presence and responsiveness of adults in their environment – requiring them to display distress, oppositional, or disruptive behavior to have their needs met (Ainsworth, 1979). In school, such behaviors may appear controlling or manipulative. Such learned behaviors are likely to be the child's bid at creating an environment in which their needs are attended. This difference in the intent and interpretation of their behaviors often leaves children feeling misunderstood (Columbia Embury et al., 2020). Understanding the child's perspective and their needs is likely to help students feel 'heard' and to 'reflect'. Skills in reflective listening need to be adapted to the speech and language capabilities of a child and used with an empathic spirit of accepting the child's perspective as valid – even if it does not concur with the views of those around them (Krishnamoorthy et al., 2023). Utilizing their own language as much as possible may assist the child in feeling truly heard and will teach them to construct a narrative to make sense of their experience. Non-judgmental listening of students does not require the educator to condone the actions of a student, and it does not preclude the enforcement of consequences for their behaviors. Often when students feel listened to and accepted, they are more likely to be responsive to learning, and accepting of consequences (Ayre & Krishnamoorthy, 2020).

As students begin to develop safety and trust in educators, they may tolerate longer conversations with educators and may be willing to be vulnerable and disclose worries and concerns. Such conversations can present a challenge for educators to operate within the scope of their training and expertise. When managed tactfully, however, such a conversation can be a unique opportunity for learning – prompting an emerging self-awareness of the student's own thoughts, feelings, and actions. Skills in 'validation' may include teachers saying, 'I wonder if you acted / thought / felt like this because...' (Bombèr et al., 2020). Such communication potentially invites the students to become curious about the context (or 'why') behind their actions, thoughts, and emotions. This language may be perceived as less threatening and shame-inducing for students compared to asking students 'why' they behaved or reacted in a certain way. These conversations also provide the educator with a deeper understanding of the student, and their needs. A broader contextual understanding of a student's challenges in and outside of school helps them transition from beliefs about themselves as 'I am bad', to more adaptive beliefs and self-compassionate beliefs such as 'that action was not good'. Such beliefs move the student to have a more hopeful view of themselves and their future and reduce experiences of stigma when engaging in counseling and mental health supports (Bombèr et al., 2020).

In this way, an increased sensitivity to a student's attachment style may help educators to formulate approaches to building trust with students and appropriately responding to their expressions of needs in the school context. The use of such relational pedagogy, however, requires educators to be skillful in their use of communication skills and reflective in ways to refine its implementation (Wilson-Ching & Berger, 2024). Every misattuned interaction with a student, or relational rupture, may represent another opportunity for forgiveness, restoration, repair, and learning in the student-teacher relationship. In this way, teachers and students may need help to go through repeated breaks and repairs in relationships and to strengthen students' sense of belonging.

Sonia demonstrates a disorganized attachment style, sometimes appearing content and cheerful in the classroom, and other times argumentative, sneaky, or disengaged. Sonia has lived in several foster homes, and her biological mother continues to seek reunification while struggling with addiction. It is not surprising that Sonia is unsure of who to trust, how long she will be at this school, or how to cope with the revolving door of caretakers in her life. Aware of the effects of trauma on attachment, Mr. Cruz works to observe Sonia's moods and interactions to guide his coaching and responses to her throughout the school day. Mr. Cruz enlists Sonia in taking care of classroom plants, feeling this will provide her with a specific caretaking role in the classroom and a task through which they can collaborate. Learning from previous conversations with Sonia in which she grew pale and silent while being asked about missing assignments or concerning behaviors, Mr. Cruz. Now tries to talk with Sonia about these topics away from the earshot of other students. He has made this choice transparent to Sonia, hoping to earn her trust and increase her self-awareness.

Coach: Inform before You Instruct

There is increasing recognition and discourse in Australia about the benefits students receive from effective and explicit instruction of the curriculum. This involves instruction and feedback to students which is consistent, specific, and tailored to suit students' individual needs and strongly aligned to learning objectives. Students exposed to adversity may require a differentiated approach to feedback that accommodates barriers in their capacity to engage with the curriculum. Challenges students may experience in receiving feedback may include cognitive, social-emotional, or developmental differences – that may hinder their understanding of instructions. Such difficulties may not always be apparent for students – as some children may 'camouflage' such difficulties by limiting their help-seeking behaviors to avoid judgment or shame and avoid feelings of embarrassment. For other children, such challenges may manifest in oppositional or challenging behaviors (Hobson & Lee, 2023).

Camouflaging involves deliberate or instinctive tactics sometimes employed by neurodiverse individuals to conceal their neurodivergent traits through masking and compensatory actions (Hull et al., 2017). Hobson and Lee (2023) have identified several forms of camouflaging behaviors amongst children that include relying excessively on the help of others, avoidance of challenging tasks, oppositional or disruptive behaviors, copying from or imitating peers, using phrases or scripts in conversations to avoid others from realizing they do not understood something, and using prosocial behaviors to be likable and minimize scrutiny or criticism of their work. For example, in the classroom, students who are aware of their difficulties with schoolwork are often preoccupied with the risk of a loss of social status amongst their peers. Students who have repeatedly experienced perceived or real 'failures' or difficulties at school are likely to be hypervigilant about the consequences of completing the task correctly. Their anxieties about making a mistake are at times so overwhelming that they have difficulties engaging their receptive language and high-order thinking capacities to understand instructions and complete tasks (Hobson & Lee, 2023). Such anxieties and heightened emotional states may reduce the capacity of students to complete tasks that they may otherwise have the capacity to complete when feeling calm and supported (Angelidis et al., 2019).

Research shows that specific teaching styles and techniques are effective in the diffusion of anxiety in students (LaBillois & Lagacé-Séguin, 2009). Students with low academic self-efficacy, for example, have been found to respond poorly to educators who have a controlling or authoritarian style of instruction (LaBillois & Lagacé-Séguin, 2009). Authoritarian educators are characterized by a "power over" dynamic with their students, in which they use their authority as an educator to be "highly demanding and inflexible" in their expectations of students (Ayre et al., 2022; Clark et al., 2023). For students who camouflage challenges, are reluctant to seek assistance, and are concerned about making mistakes, authoritarian educators may be perceived as uncaring, unfair, and punitive. Unintended consequences of such authoritarian teaching styles may include students disengaging from the curriculum, discrediting outcomes of grading and positive reinforcement contingencies, and lowering their expectations of their own performance on academic tasks (Angelidis et al., 2019). In contrast, authoritative educators adopt a style of instruction that is more collaborative with students – akin to a coach. A coaching or authoritative teaching style creates an environment that is encouraging of students to communicate their thoughts and desires, while still allowing the teacher to oversee the class (Burden, 2020). This style of teaching supports students thus is likely to support self-regulation skills by having developmentally appropriate expectations of behavior and engagement, and logical consequences. Involving students in developing classroom rules, with lots of opportunities to practice prosocial behaviors, is likely to be beneficial. There is an emphasis on building trust between teachers and students, and invitations for students to learn from mistakes and successes (Burden, 2020).

Trauma-informed educators are often mindful of the changing capacities for students to engage in tasks – particularly those with a history of academic difficulties – and the increased risk that they may be perceived negatively by these students when delivering the curriculum (Perry & Daniels, 2016). In addition to information about the student's learning needs, attending to the student's appearance, mood, demeanor, and behavior provides educators with valuable information to guide their differentiation of instruction (Downey & Greco, 2023). Students who appear agitated and not receptive to learning may require a modification of tasks provided, options, and choices for how to complete the task, and assistance with tasks provided in a way to minimize feelings of embarrassment and shame.

Individualized support plans that align with students' strengths, interests, and preferences may also support engagement, and a reduction in anxiety amongst students. The rationale and relevance of the lessons being taught may need to be revisited with students – especially in service to those who lack motivation and struggle to see the relevance of school-based tasks to their lives and future (Herrenkohl et al., 2019). Some guiding questions for educators in introducing and framing academic tasks can include: Who is doing the activity? What are we doing the activity about? When are we going to do the activity? Where are we going to complete the activity? Why are we doing the activity? And how is it going to be done? (Ayre & Krishnamoorthy, 2020). Drawing on principles of universal design for learning, using multiple media to convey instructions, such as simple language, pictures, and videos, will help provide different avenues for the child to understand what is required of them (Hall et al., 2012). Keeping within the boundaries of the classroom, choices for the student may involve having a menu of options for students to choose from, ordering activities but providing students with choices within the activity (e.g., choosing what material they would like to use to complete the activity, where they would like to sit when completing the activity, who they work with to complete the activity) (Downey & Greco, 2023). Explicit teaching and behavior rehearsal of school-wide expectations may aid students who lack sufficient positive role models and exposure to prosocial behaviors (Cavanaugh, 2016). Overall, differentiating instructions in a trauma-informed manner requires consideration of the psychosocial influences on a student's perception of school and academic work. Finding the balance between sufficiently engaging and challenging tasks, and modifications that accommodate their difficulties can be a complex task – requiring reflection and collaboration with colleagues and relevant partners.

> *Sonia's exposure to trauma and inconsistent schooling history contribute to her challenges with the curriculum. Witnessing these challenges firsthand, Mr. Cruz has rearranged students' desks to place Sonia with supportive peers and near where he teaches so he can provide her with non-verbal prompts and check-ins. Mr. Cruz has begun by showing Sonia her learning growth over time and celebrating small wins in her learning.*

Collaborate: Consult before You Commit

Supporting students with complex needs often require a 'wrap-around' approach – a collaboration between all support providers at all levels of experience. This includes external professionals and caregivers of children exposed to trauma. Coming together is integral to supporting children with trauma, and supporting all those involved in what can often be difficult or stressful circumstances (Morton & Berardi, 2018). Collaboration is not only important with adults but also with the children themselves, and this can be undertaken in many ways. Establishing the learning characteristics of students appears to be an important step – what do they like learning about (interests), why do they like it (goals), and how do they enjoy learning about it (strengths). This can be done individually with the student or as a group activity, depending on the child's needs. This information can then be applied to curriculum design, making learning more interesting and engaging for students (Arbour et al., 2024). It is also necessary to consider children's use of multisensory items that support self-regulation and, subsequently, learning. Having the flexibility to use various items available for students to access in times of need will support behavior management and help them engage in the learning process (Schimke et al., 2022).

The saying, 'It takes a village', underlines the importance of using a team approach to supporting children with complex needs. For teachers, adjusting perspectives to view the child not just as 'their student' but as part of the school community can help ease the sense for educators that they are solely responsible for the student's wellbeing. School staff can be encouraged to imagine themselves as being in a helicopter looking down at their school. Accessing this perspective enables them to take a broader view of the school culture and atmosphere (Krishnamoorthy & Ayre, 2022). It is still important for staff to engage with their team and students on the ground so staff can stay connected to the day-to-day workings and challenges of the system (Douglass et al., 2021). Issues are rarely linear with a definite cause, but are often reciprocal in nature – never solely a student problem or a teacher problem, and both require support to foster a culture of safety and trust. Engaging other teachers and establishing a team approach to support challenging students will help educators to share the load. Managing complex students and challenging behaviors can place a burden on everyone – practically and emotionally. Research supports the use of partnership and collaboration when offering practical supports, and sharing resources can have a significant impact on the wellbeing of all involved (Douglass et al., 2021).

A positive way to collaborate with caregivers and external stakeholders is to make time for regular contact, and to negotiate expectations and roles within the school community (Kataoka et al., 2018). Taking time to get to know each other by setting expectations for staff roles and how caregivers can influence their child's learning is a great place to start. This is also an excellent opportunity to demonstrate to the community that the school is trauma-informed – showcasing values, goals, pedagogical and wellbeing practices, and policies. It is worth noting here that not all parents will have positive associations with school, and some will also have varied levels of understanding and comprehension, including language and cultural differences (Garcia et al., 2023). How school leaders and educators interact with parents and external stakeholders should mirror the values and practices they use to interact with students (Bloom & Farragher, 2013). Sharing information with families on the progress of their child, and skills that they might find useful in supporting their children at home, may represent the start of a robust family-school partnership. Community building events such as 'book week' and 'festivals of learning' can bring the community together and engage both parents and students. In this way, collaborating with external providers and stakeholders through stakeholder meetings enables educators to understand each child's world more broadly (Collier et al., 2020; Kataoka et al., 2018). It offers the opportunity for educators to offer valuable insights and suggestions for holistic support.

Mr. Cruz completed a mid-year survey with his students to assess their connection to their classroom and peers, and their goals for the remainder of the school year. Sonia reported wanting a friend. After conferring with Sonia, Mr. Cruz reached out to the school adjustment counselor to collaborate on strategies for supporting Sonia is developing a meaningful friendship. Over time, the school adjustment counselor and Mr. Cruz supported Sonia in developing a friendship with a classmate, and eventually arranging a social outing together one weekend.

Recommendations for Schools in Understanding and Responding to Trauma

Promote physical and psychological safety for students: Develop and review school-wide policies and practices which prioritizes physical and psychological safety. Train school educators to recognize and report signs of child maltreatment. Foster a sense of belonging and an inclusive school climate that helps students feel supported and ready to learn.

Address basic needs: Recognize and address students' basic needs like food, water, clothing, shelter, sleep, and hygiene. Implement programs such as free meals and provide resources for clothing and hygiene to enhance students' wellbeing and prepare them for learning effectively.

Use trauma-informed de-escalation techniques: Train school staff in de-escalation techniques that focus on calming students before problem-solving. Recognize signs of distress and implement co-regulation strategies to help students self-regulate their emotions and stress effectively.

Adopt an authoritative teaching style: Use a coaching or authoritative teaching style that encourages collaboration and communication. This approach supports self-regulation, builds trust, and fosters a positive classroom environment, helping students feel valued and understood.

Foster a team approach and collaboration: Establish a 'wrap-around' approach involving collaboration with professionals, caregivers, and students. Regular communication and partnerships enhance support for students exposed to trauma, ensuring a comprehensive support network.

Conclusion

The experience of adversity, maltreatment, and exposure to traumatic events can influence children's behavior in a way that can make learning and school functioning challenging. Educators may view children's behavior through the lens of training or the role they play in their lives. Research has offered new insights and reminded forgotten practices to understand and respond to the needs of students. A trauma-informed approach requires an understanding that the needs of students are influenced by historical, biological, psychological, and social factors. The 5C framework provides a guide for educators to begin to reflect, refine, and redefine their practice to ensure the inclusion and support of all students. It is crucial to be mindful of the role played by educators – as one of many sources of support that the child and their caregivers require to enable positive learning and wellbeing outcomes. In this way, the task of inclusive education with students with complex needs requires a team effort – one that draws on the efforts and expertise of the classroom teacher, leadership at the school, family members, and interdisciplinary professionals working outside of the school. While a characteristic impact of trauma can be one of disrupted sense of self and the world, the journey of healing, learning, recovery, and resilience is one that requires the coming together of the school community. The impact of simple strategies for inclusion, implemented in a thoughtful and skillful manner, can foster feelings of belonging, agency, and hope in students who have experienced trauma, and the communities around them.

Note

1 Pseudonyms have been used to protect the privacy and confidentiality of students and staff.

References

Ainsworth, M. S. (1979). Infant–mother attachment. *American Psychologist, 34*(10), 932.

Angelidis, A., Solis, E., Lautenbach, F., van der Does, W., & Putman, P. (2019). I'm going to fail! Acute cognitive performance anxiety increases threat-interference and impairs WM performance. *PLoS One, 14*(2), e0210824.

Arbour, M., Walker, K., & Houston, J. (2024). Trauma-informed pedagogy: Instructional strategies to support student success. *Journal of Midwifery & Women's Health, 69*(1), 25–32.

Australian Institute of Family Studies. (2024, October). *Child safe policy*. https://aifs.gov.au/sites/default/files/2024-10/AIFS-Child-Safe-Policy-2024.pdf

Ayre, K., & Krishnamoorthy, G. (2020). *Trauma informed behaviour support: A practical guide to developing resilient learners* (N. Andersen, Ed.). University of Southern Queensland. https://doi.org/10.26192/q5zy0

Ayre, K., Krishnamoorthy, G., Rees, B., & Berger, E. (2022). Balancing the needs of the school community: Implementing trauma-informed behaviour supports in an Australian regional primary school. *Australian Journal of Teacher Education (Online), 47*(9), 43–61.

Bellamy, T., Krishnamoorthy, G., Ayre, K., Berger, E., Machin, T., & Rees, B. E. (2022). Trauma-informed school programming: A partnership approach to culturally responsive behavior support. *Sustainability, 14*(7), 3997.

Bloom, S. L., & Farragher, B. (2013). *Restoring sanctuary: A new operating system for trauma-informed systems of care*. Oxford University Press.

Bombèr, L. M., Golding, K. S., & Phillips, S. (2020). *Working with relational trauma in schools: An educator's guide to using Dyadic developmental practice*. Jessica Kingsley Publishers.

Bowlby, J. (1969). *Attachment and loss* (No. 79). Random House.

Bowyer, M., Fein, E. C., & Krishnamoorthy, G. (2023). Teacher mental health literacy and child development in Australian Primary Schools: A program evaluation. *Education Sciences, 13*(4), 329.

Brunzell, T., & Norrish, J. (2021). *Creating trauma-informed, strengths-based classrooms.* Jessica Kingsley Publishers.

Burden, P. (2020). *Classroom management: Creating a successful K-12 learning community*. John Wiley & Sons.

Cavanaugh, B. (2016). Trauma-informed classrooms and schools. *Beyond Behavior, 25*(2), 41–46.

Chafouleas, S. M., Johnson, A. H., Overstreet, S., & Santos, N. M. (2016). Toward a blueprint for trauma-informed service delivery in schools. *School Mental Health, 8*(1), 144–162. https://doi.org/10.1007/s12310-015-9166-8

Chafouleas, S. M., Koriakin, T. A., Roundfield, K. D., & Overstreet, S. (2019). Addressing childhood trauma in school settings: A framework for evidence-based practice. *School Mental Health, 11*(1), 40–53. https://doi.org/10.1007/s12310-018-9256-5

Clark, K. N., Blocker, M. S., Gittens, O. S., & Long, A. C. (2023). Profiles of teachers' classroom management style: Differences in perceived school climate and professional characteristics. *Journal of School Psychology, 100*, 101239.

Collaborative for Academic, Social, and Emotional Learning. (n.d.). *What is the CASEL framework?* Accessed January 19, 2024 from https://casel.org/fundamentals-of-sel/what-is-the-casel-framework/

Collier, S., Trimmer, K., & Krishnamoorthy, G. (2020). Evaluating frameworks for practice in mainstream primary school classrooms catering for children with developmental trauma: An analysis of the literature. *Children Australia, 45*(4), 258–265.

Columbia Embury, D., Clarke, L. S., & Leaver, C. (2020). Reactive attachment disorder in the classroom. *Preventing School Failure: Alternative Education for Children and Youth, 64*(3), 240–248.

Commonwealth of Massachusetts. (2023). https://www.mass.gov/info-details/warning-signs-of-child-abuse-and-neglect

Council on School Health. (2008). Role of the school nurse in providing school health services. *Pediatrics, 121*(5), 1052–1056. https://doi.org/10.1542/peds.2008-0382

Cozolino, L. (2013). *The social neuroscience of education: Optimizing attachment and learning in the classroom (the Norton Series on the Social Neuroscience of Education)*. WW Norton & Company.

Cross, D., Fani, N., Powers, A., & Bradley, B. (2017). Neurobiological development in the context of childhood trauma. *Clinical Psychology, 24*(2), 111–124. https://doi.org/10.1111/cpsp.12198

Davey, C. G., Keshavan, M. S., Frangou, S., Lee, F., Luna, B., Meyer-Lindenberg, A., ... Woo, T. W. (2020). A framework for understanding emerging mental disorders and early intervention. *Youth Mental Health: A Paradigm for Prevention and Early Intervention, 28*, 135.

Devoe, J. E., Baez, A., Angier, H., Krois, L., Edlund, C., & Carney, P. A. (2007). Insurance + access not equal to health care: Typology of barriers to health care access for low-income families. *Annals of Family Medicine, 5*(6), 511–518. https://doi.org/10.1370/afm.748

Douglass, A., Chickerella, R., & Maroney, M. (2021). Becoming trauma-informed: A case study of early educator professional development and organizational change. *Journal of Early Childhood Teacher Education, 42*(2), 182–202.

Downey, J., & Greco, J. (2023). Trauma sensitive schools: A comprehensive guide for the assessment planning and implementation of trauma informed frameworks. *Children and Youth Services Review, 149*, 106930.

Edmonds, C. J., & Burford, D. (2009). Should children drink more water? The effects of drinking water on cognition in children. *Appetite, 52*(3), 776–779. https://doi.org/10.1016/j.appet.2009.02.010

Felitti, V. J., Anda, R. F., Nordenberg, D., Williamson, D. F., Spitz, A. M., Edwards, V., … Marks, J. S. (1998). Relationship of childhood abuse and household dysfunction to many of the leading causes of death in adults: The adverse childhood experiences (ACE) study. *American Journal of Preventive Medicine, 14*(4), 245–258. https://doi.org/10.1016/S0749-3797(98)00017-8

Gan, Z., Liu, F., & Yang, C. C. R. (2020). Student-teachers' self-efficacy for instructing self-regulated learning in the classroom. *Journal of Education for Teaching, 46*(1), 120–123.

Garcia, A., Sprang, G., & Clemans, T. (2023). The role of school leaders in cultivating a trauma-informed school climate. *Children and Youth Services Review, 146*, 106816.

Gottlieb, L. M., Hessler, D., Long, D., Laves, E., Burns, A. R., Amaya, A., Sweeney, P., Schudel, C., & Adler, N. E. (2016). Effects of social needs screening and in-person service navigation on child health: A randomized clinical trial. *JAMA Pediatrics, 170*(11), e162521–e162528. https://doi.org/10.1001/jamapediatrics.2016.2521

Grasso, D. J., Ford, J. D., & Briggs-Gowan, M. J. (2013). Early life trauma exposure and stress sensitivity in young children. *Journal of Pediatric Psychology, 38*(1), 94–103.

Hall, T. E., Meyer, A., & Rose, D. H. (Eds.). (2012). *Universal design for learning in the classroom: Practical applications*. Guilford Press.

Harvey, M. (1996). An ecological view of psychological trauma and trauma recovery. *Journal of Traumatic Stress, 9*(1), 3–23. https://doi.org/10.1002/jts.2490090103

Herrenkohl, T. I., Hong, S., & Verbrugge, B. (2019). Trauma-informed programs based in schools: Linking concepts to practices and assessing the evidence. *American Journal of Community Psychology, 64*(3–4), 373–388.

Hobson, H. M., & Lee, A. (2023). Camouflaging in developmental language disorder: The views of speech and language pathologists and parents. *Communication Disorders Quarterly, 44*(4), 247–256.

Horowitz, D., Guyer, M., & Sanders, K. (2015). Psychosocial approaches to violence and aggression: Contextually anchored and trauma-informed interventions. *CNS Spectrums, 20*(3), 190–199.

Hull, L., Mandy, W., & Petrides, K. V. (2017). Behavioural and cognitive sex/gender differences in autism spectrum condition and typically developing males and females. *Autism, 21*(6), 706–727.

Jellesma, F. C., Zee, M., & Koomen, H. M. (2015). Children's perceptions of the relationship with the teacher: Associations with appraisals and internalizing problems in middle childhood. *Journal of Applied Developmental Psychology, 36,* 30–38.

Johnson, S. L., Maria, A., Guevara, M., & Preves, A. (2023). Developing a measure of educator self-efficacy around emotion co-regulation. *Trauma-Informed Education, 116,* 1–9.

Jones, S. M., Brush, K. E., Ramirez, T., Mao, Z. X., Marenus, M., Wettje, S., Finney, K., Raisch, N., Podoloff, N., Kahn, J., Barnes, S., Stickle, L., Brion-Meisels, G., McIntyre, J., Cuartas, J., & Bailey, R. (2021). *Navigating SEL from the inside out: Looking inside and across 33 leading SEL programs – A practical resources for schools and OST providers*. The EASEL Lab, Harvard University. Retrieved August 15, 2023 from https://www.wallacefoundation.org/knowledge-center/Documents/navigating-social-and-emotional-learning-from-the-inside-out-2ed.pdf

Kataoka, S. H., Vona, P., Acuna, A., Jaycox, L., Escudero, P., Rojas, C., … Stein, B. D. (2018). Applying a trauma informed school systems approach: Examples from school community-academic partnerships. *Ethnicity & Disease, 28*(Suppl 2), 417.

Kenney, E. L., Long, M. W., Cradock, A. L., & Gortmaker, S. L. (2015). Prevalence of inadequate hydration among US children and disparities by gender and race/ethnicity: National Health and Nutrition Examination survey, 2009–2012. *American Journal of Public Health, 105*(8), e113–e118. https://doi.org/10.2105/AJPH.2015.302572

Kjolhede, C., Lee, A. C., & Council on School Health. (2021). School-based health centers and pediatric practice. *Pediatrics, 148*(4), e2021053758. https://doi.org/10.1542/peds.2021-053758

Koslouski, J. B. (2022). Developing empathy and support for students with the "most challenging behaviors:" Mixed-methods outcomes of professional development in trauma-informed teaching practices. *Frontiers in Education, 7,* 1005887. https://doi.org/10.3389/feduc.2022.1005887

Koslouski, J. B., Chafouleas, S. M., Briesch, A. M., Caemmerer, J. M., Perry, H., Oas, J., Xiong, S., & Charamut, N. R. (2023a, Online first). School-based screening of social determinants of health: A scoping review. *School Mental Health.* https://doi.org/10.1007/s12310-023-09622-w

Koslouski, J. B., Stark, K., & Chafouleas, S. M. (2023b). Understanding and responding to the effects of trauma in the classroom: A primer for educators. *Social and Emotional Learning: Research, Practice, and Policy, 1,* 100004. https://doi.org/10.1016/j.sel.2023.100004

Krishnamoorthy, G., & Ayre, K. (2022). Sustaining interdisciplinary work in trauma-informed education. *The Australian Educational Researcher, 49*(3), 529–546.

Krishnamoorthy, G., Ayre, K., & Schimke, D. (2023). *Trauma-informed education: Interdisciplinary insights*. University of Southern Queensland.

Krishnamoorthy, G., Bryce, I, Mullens, A., & Gilmour, J. (2023). Post-traumatic stress in children and adolescents. In N. Beel (Ed.), *Counselling issues*. University of Southern Queensland.

LaBillois, J. M., & Lagacé-Séguin, D. G. (2009). Does a good fit matter? Exploring teaching styles, emotion regulation, and child anxiety in the classroom. *Early Child Development and Care, 179*(3), 303–315.

Langlois, J. (2024, January 8). School lunches are Brazil's secret—and delicious—weapon in halting hunger. *National Public Radio*. https://www.npr.org/sections/goatsandsoda/2024/01/08/1222567378/the-pandemic-sent-hunger-soaring-in-brazil-theyre-fighting-back-with-school-lunc

Main, M., & Solomon, J. (1990). Procedures for identifying infants as disorganized/disoriented during the Ainsworth Strange Situation. In M. T. Greenberg, D. Cicchetti, & E. M. Cummings (Eds.), *Attachment in the preschool years: Theory, research, and intervention* (pp. 121–160). The University of Chicago Press.

Maslow, A. H. (1943). A theory of human motivation. *Psychological Review, 50*(4), 370–396. https://doi.org/10.1037/h0054346

Maslow, A. H. (1954). *Motivation and personality*. Harpers.

Mathews, B. (2014). Mandatory reporting laws and identification of child abuse and neglect: Consideration of differential maltreatment types, and a cross-jurisdictional analysis of child sexual abuse reports. *Social Sciences, 3*(3), 460–482. https://www.mdpi.com/2076-0760/3/3/460

McGlynn-Wright, T., & Briner, L. (2021). *Integrative trauma and healing framework*. https://intheworksllc.squarespace.com/inflections/2021/3/30/integrative-trauma-and-healing-framework

Meisner, C. (2023, August 16). Massachusetts joins short list of states providing free school meals to all. *Education Week*. https://www.edweek.org/policy-politics/massachusetts-joins-short-list-of-states-providing-free-school-meals-to-all/2023/08

Michail, S. (2011). Understanding school responses to students' challenging behaviour: A review of literature. *Improving Schools, 14*(2), 156–171. https://doi.org/10.1177/1365480211407764

Moos, D. C., & Ringdal, A. (2012). Self-regulated learning in the classroom: A literature review on the teacher's role. *Education Research International, 2012,* 1–15. https://doi.org/10.1155/2012/423284

Morton, B. M., & Berardi, A. A. (2018). Trauma-informed school programming: Application for mental health professionals and educator partnerships. *Journal of Childhood and Adolescent Trauma, 11*(4), 487–493. https://doi.org/10.1007/s40653-017-0160-1

National Child Traumatic Stress Network. (n.d.). About child trauma. Retrieved from https://www.nctsn.org/what-is-child-trauma/about-child-trauma

National Scientific Council on the Developing Child. (2012). *The science of neglect: The persistent absence of responsive care disrupts the developing brain* (Working Paper 12). Retrieved from https://developingchild.harvard.edu/index.php/resources/ reports_and_working_papers/working_papers/wp12/

Perfect, M. M., Turley, M. R., Carlson, J. S., Yohanna, J., & Saint Gilles, M. P. (2016). School-related outcomes of traumatic event exposure and traumatic stress symptoms in students: A systematic review of research from 1990 to 2015. *School Mental Health, 8*(1), 7–43. https://doi.org/10.1007/s12310-016-9175-2

Perry, B. D. (2002). Childhood experience and the expression of genetic potential: What childhood neglect tells us about nature and nurture. *Brain and Mind*, 3, 79–100.

Perry, B. D. (2006). Applying principles of neurodevelopment to clinical work with maltreated and traumatised children: The neurosequential model of therapeutics. In N. B. Webb (Ed.), *Working with traumatised youth in child welfare* (pp. 27–52). The Guilford Press.

Perry, D. L., & Daniels, M. L. (2016). Implementing trauma-informed practices in the school setting: A pilot study. *School Mental Health*, *8*, 177–188.

Perry, B. D., & Szalavitz, M. (2017). *The boy who was raised as a dog: And other stories from a child psychiatrist's notebook--What traumatized children can teach us about loss, love, and healing*. Hachette.

Schimke, D., Krishnamoorthy, G., Ayre, K., Berger, E., & Rees, B. (2022, June). Multi-tiered culturally responsive behavior support: A qualitative study of trauma-informed education in an Australian primary school. In *Frontiers in Education* (Vol. 7, p. 866266). Frontiers.

Shankar, P., Chung, R., & Frank, D. A. (2017). Association of food insecurity with children's behavioral, emotional, and academic outcomes: A systematic review. *Journal of Developmental and Behavioral Pediatrics: JDBP*, *38*(2), 135–150. https://doi.org/10.1097/DBP.0000000000000383

Sobo, E. J., Seid, M., & Reyes Gelhard, L. (2006). Parent-identified barriers to pediatric health care: A process-oriented model. *Health Services Research*, *41*(1), 148–172. https://doi.org/10.1111/j.1475-6773.2005.00455.x

Substance Abuse and Mental Health Services Administration (SAMHSA). (2014). *SAMHSA's concept of trauma and guidance for a trauma-informed approach* (HHS Publication No. (SMA) 14-4884). https://store.samhsa.gov/shin/content/SMA14-4884/SMA14-4884.pdf

The Abused and Neglected Child Reporting Act, Illinois Public Act § 101-0564. (2019). https://www.ilga.gov/legislation/publicacts/fulltext.asp?Name=101-0564

Valdebenito, S., Eisner, M., Farrington, D. P., Ttofi, M. M., & Sutherland, A. (2019). What can we do to reduce disciplinary school exclusion? A systematic review and meta-analysis. *Journal of Experimental Criminology*, *15*, 253–287. https://doi.org/10.1007/s11292-018-09351-0

Wall, C. (2021). Relationship over reproach: Fostering resilience by embracing a trauma-informed approach to elementary education. *Journal of Aggression, Maltreatment & Trauma*, *30*(1), 118–137.

Wilson-Ching, M., & Berger, E. (2024). Relationship building strategies within trauma informed frameworks in educational settings: A systematic literature review. *Current Psychology*, *43*(4), 3464–3485.

World Health Organization. (2018). *Adverse Childhood Experiences International Questionnaire (ACE-IQ)*. https://www.who.int/publications/m/item/adverse-childhood-experiences-international-questionnaire-(ace-iq)

4

Healing Connections

Addressing Interpersonal Trauma through Belonging and Trauma-Informed Practice

Michelle Wilson-Ching, Kelly-Ann Allen, and Michelle Munyun

Introduction

Research suggests that traumatic events experienced during childhood are highly prevalent across Australia and worldwide World Health Organization, 2020). Given that childhood interpersonal trauma is commonly experienced within family systems, and perpetrated by a caregiver (Spinazzola et al., 2018), the home environment can become a place of stress for the child rather than a place where a healthy child-caregiver bond is established. This in turn can affect the child's ability to form relationships with others outside of the home environment and across their lifespan (Brown et al., 2017). Given that childhood trauma is also related to difficulties in mental health, socioemotional development, and learning (Tzouvara et al., 2023) and that teachers often report feeling ill-equipped to deal with students with trauma histories (Alisic, 2012), a greater understanding and awareness of trauma and its potential impacts is critical to best support all students within the school environment. The aim of this chapter is to discuss the prevalence and effects of interpersonal family trauma on children specifically within the school context. Schools have an important role in the life of a child who has experienced trauma (Thomas et al., 2019), and important connections can be established within schools to prevent children from experiencing adverse long-term outcomes from these experiences (Brunzell et al., 2015). This chapter will discuss the importance of fostering educational environments that are able to promote a sense of belonging for students through

DOI: 10.4324/9781003436034-4

the implementation of trauma-informed practices. Healthy connections among teachers and peers through such practices can ultimately contribute to building the wellbeing and academic success of all students (Chafouleas et al., 2019).

Interpersonal Trauma in Children

Various terms are employed in the trauma literature, including "potentially-traumatic event" and "posttraumatic stress", for example. For the purposes of this chapter, the term "trauma" will be used interchangeably to refer to both the types of experiences that may elicit a trauma response, as well as the response and outcomes that these adverse events cause. Also, given its high prevalence and the ongoing nature, the focus of this chapter will be on interpersonal trauma within the family home and specifically the impact that disrupted relational development has on self-regulation and emotional processes that can affect learning and school life.

Interpersonal or relational trauma[1] relates to experiences of emotional or physical violence, sexual abuse, neglect, or exposure to adverse circumstances, such as poor mental health or the use of drugs by caregivers or other individuals close to the child (Cook et al., 2005; van der Kolk, 2005). Interpersonal trauma is often chronic, that is, it occurs repeatedly over a prolonged period, and cumulative, that is, where multiple traumatic events are present (Cook et al., 2005; Gregorowski & Seedat, 2013). In such situations, the child commonly lacks the stability and predictability that is necessary to develop and thrive and, as will be discussed in more detail in subsequent sections, the child often operates from a heightened state where their body is in a constant and defensive fight-flight-freeze mode (van der Kolk, 2005).

Interpersonal trauma within the family home can result in disrupted attachment styles in children (Breidenstine et al., 2011; Moretti & Peled, 2004; Prather & Golden, 2009). Attachment styles, established early in life, reflect the quality of child-caregiver relationships (Ainsworth, 1978). Secure attachments form when caregivers are responsive and attuned to a child's needs, providing a foundation for socioemotional development and the formation of future relationships (Ainsworth, 1978; Sroufe, 2005). Therefore, insecure attachment styles often arise from interpersonal trauma within the home environment, which may hinder emotional bonding and disrupt caregiver responsiveness (Atkinson et al., 2000; Flowers et al., 2018;

Newman et al., 2015) and can have significant negative impacts on development across an individual's lifespan (Lünnemann et al., 2019; van Ijzendoorn & Bakermans-Kranenburg, 2019).

Impact of Interpersonal Family Trauma

Children with a history of interpersonal trauma can experience disrupted social and emotional development that can manifest as problems regulating emotional responses and an inability to establish emotional connectedness with others (Marusak et al., 2015). Research shows that childhood interpersonal trauma is commonly experienced within family systems and perpetrated by a caregiver (Dugal et al., 2016; Folger et al., 2017; Spinazzola et al., 2018). Therefore, the home environment becomes a place of stress for the child rather than a place where healthy child-caregiver attachment is established. That is, a child's ability to bond to significant caregivers is severely impacted (Gregorowski & Seedat, 2013). This in turn affects the child's ability to form bonds with others outside of the home environment. Students with a history of interpersonal trauma may be labeled as problematic, and teachers may interpret behavioral displays of dysregulation as defiance rather than an adaptive response and coping mechanism in response to trauma. Research also shows that insecure attachment can affect brain development, behavior, and learning outcomes of children at school and have long-term detrimental effects on a young person's life (O'Neill et al., 2010; Putnam, 2006).

Brain Mechanisms Related to Social-Emotional Development

Optimal brain development relies on supportive and healthy environmental conditions and quality of attachment in child-caregiver relationships (Anderson et al., 2019; Newman et al., 2015). Interpersonal trauma during childhood can disrupt brain development, causing prolonged activation of stress-response systems, such as the hypothalamic–pituitary–adrenal (HPA) axis (Newman et al., 2015; Ryan et al., 2017). Sometimes referred to as toxic stress, overactivation of the HPA system, alongside poor attachment, can lead to changes in brain connectivity, structure, and function, particularly in the prefrontal cortex, hippocampus, and amygdala (Hart & Rubia, 2012; van Bodegom et al., 2017). Early childhood trauma is associated with negative impacts on the development of brain structures related to social development, which may result in difficulties processing socioemotional information, emotional dysregulation, and challenges forming stable relationships (Putnam, 2006). Children who have experienced trauma are at higher risk for enduring developmental, mental health, and adaptive functioning issues, often exhibiting internalizing and externalizing behaviors, and are more likely to develop psychopathology later in life (McLaughlin & Lambert, 2017). Children and adolescents with a history of interpersonal trauma, when compared with those with no history, are more likely to exhibit internalizing behaviors, such as depression, anxiety, and withdrawal, as well as externalizing behaviors such as conduct problems, an increased number of high-risk-taking behaviors, and aggression (Dvir et al., 2014). Moreover, there is an association between Attention Deficit Hyperactivity Disorder (ADHD) diagnoses and insecure attachment (Storebø et al., 2016).

Impact of Interpersonal Family Trauma on Learning and Behavior

Children with interpersonal trauma histories, who have difficulty regulating their emotions, can also face additional challenges in the classroom environment (Brunzell et al., 2015; O'Neill et al., 2010). For example, they may struggle with transitioning between activities, exhibit behaviors at school which may appear abrupt and inappropriate, and may become easily triggered by the behavior of teachers and peers (Brunzell et al., 2015). Research suggests a relationship between the number of traumatic events experienced by a child and the challenges they face at school. For example, in a study evaluating the impact of trauma on social skills and problem behaviors in 500 students, a lower level of social skills and a higher level of problem behaviors were noted for students with a greater number of reported traumas (Creswell Báez et al., 2019). In addition, Blodgett and Lanigan (2018) found a relationship between school achievement and the number of Adverse Childhood experiences (ACEs).[2] The authors reported a relationship between the number of ACEs and poor school attendance, problems with behavior, and below-level performance for mathematics, reading, and writing. Similarly, Crouch et al. (2019) reported that primary and secondary school-aged children with four or more ACEs, including domestic abuse and family dysfunction, had less school engagement, poor school attendance, and were more likely to repeat a grade compared to children who had no ACEs history. A systematic review of academic difficulties in school-age populations with a history of trauma reported that students experiencing four or more ACEs have greater difficulties at school, evident by lower performance in various academic areas, such as English and Mathematics, greater likelihood of facing disciplinary measures or being suspended, lower school attendance, greater grade retention and access to learning support, as well as greater reports of behavioral difficulties reported by teachers (Perfect et al., 2016).

In summary, interpersonal trauma can significantly impact children's emotional and social development, brain development, learning, and behavior. Children who experience trauma are more likely to experience emotional dysregulation, relationship difficulties, and academic challenges, such as lower school performance and increased behavioral issues. Addressing these challenges using a strengths-based approach is essential for these students' academic and socioemotional success. The following sections will explore research and practices focused on fostering school belonging and implementing trauma-informed approaches to support these students.

School Belonging

Relationships that support children to feel safe and supported within schools are foundational to a healthy learning environment (Allen et al., 2021). School belonging, commonly referred to as school connectedness or school attachment, relates to a student's feelings of being accepted and valued by their school system (Allen et al., 2018; Goodenow & Grady, 1993). School belonging has been explored in multiple ways through educational research and has been found to predict a range of student outcomes related to wellbeing and academic success (Allen, 2023; Libbey, 2004; Slaten et al., 2016). The research evidence shows the critical importance of positive student-teacher relationships, peer interactions, and a safe school environment for fostering student belonging (Allen & Bowles, 2013; Roffey et al., 2019).

Underpinned in this concept of school belonging is the understanding that belonging is a fundamental psychological need (Allen, Gray et al., 2022). It has been well established over the decades that healthy attachments to others can have a significant impact on an individual's wellbeing and physical health (Baumeister & Leary, 1995). As such, it is essential that children have healthy attachment figures within the school environment in order for learning to take place (Allen, 2020). More specifically, having a stable network of teachers and peers provides a sense of security and value that enables the child to face academic and social challenges (Wong et al., 2022). In a review of the literature, McLaughlin and Clarke (2010) found that relationships with teachers and peers are key to positive academic outcomes, emotional wellbeing, and mental health in adolescence and concluded that encouraging these relationships is central to the goals of education. Research also suggests the importance of relationships and stability from the perspective of children (Allen, Berger, Grove et al., 2022; Wong et al., 2022). Several scholars evaluating the educational experiences of children in out-of-home care, who often experience poor attachment and trauma, have noted that these children considered schools to be a safe place and perceived good relationships with teachers and peers of great importance for their overall wellbeing (Allen, Berger, Campbell et al., 2022; Townsend et al., 2020).

Having a sense of belonging and stable relationships within the school community are therefore protective factors and become powerful influences for students with a history of interpersonal trauma within the family, as well as being key determinants of long-term outcomes for these children (Parker et al., 2022). With the support of the school community, students affected by interpersonal family trauma can develop better self-regulation strategies, as well as problem-solving and social skills, resulting in more favorable learning outcomes (Frydenberg et al., 2012; McLaughlin, 2016). Therefore, investing in developing school communities that encourage belonging is of benefit to the development of students impacted by trauma, as well as the school's primary goal of education. In addition, trauma-informed practices within schools can provide a framework that facilitates the development of healthy relationships, while also supporting school belonging. General principles of trauma-informed practice within the school system will be discussed particularly in relation to relationship building.

Trauma-Informed Practice and Interpersonal Trauma

Trauma-informed practices are implemented to promote healing and prevent re-traumatization (Keller-Dupree, 2013). The need to implement trauma-informed practices within the school system has been recognized given the large percentage of students who have experienced trauma (Thomas et al., 2019). Common aspects of trauma-informed practice in schools include the implementation of school policies across all staff levels, supportive classroom environments, professional development for teachers, collaboration between school and health professionals, self-care of school staff to protect against secondary trauma,[3] as well as the delivery of targeted interventions to trauma-exposed students (Thomas et al., 2019). Trauma-informed practices within schools are said to require a whole-school approach and culture change that is implemented across all staff and supported by policy (Berger & Martin, 2021).

Reviews and meta-analyses suggest that trauma-informed practices within educational environments are likely to reduce trauma-related symptoms in their students (Fondren et al., 2020). A recent systematic review evaluated the relationship-building strategies implemented as part of trauma-informed approaches in educational systems. While results suggested variability in the methods employed, improved teacher-student relationships as well as improved relationships between teachers and families were reported. A whole system of care, incorporating parental involvement and spaces for teachers to support each other, was found to be of key importance when supporting students affected by interpersonal trauma (Wilson-Ching & Berger, 2023).

Children affected by interpersonal family trauma benefit from establishing predictable and stable relationships that are promoted in many trauma-informed practice frameworks (Brown et al., 2017; Wall, 2020). Several models of trauma-informed practice implemented in schools have incorporated principles that encourage relationship building as a basis for the development of secure and safe school environments (e.g., Stokes et al., 2019). From a foundation of security and sense of safety, trauma-informed frameworks encourage teachers and schools to address the challenges common for students exposed to interpersonal family trauma, such as problems regulating emotions, impaired impulse control, and the development of student self-confidence and autonomy (Brunzell et al., 2016). Several examples of relationship-focused trauma-informed frameworks exist: The Attachment, Regulation, and Competency (ARC) framework (Blaustein & Kinniburgh, 2010), the Berry Street Educational Model (BSEM) (Stokes & Turnbull, 2016), and the Calmer Classrooms (Downey, 2008). These will be discussed.

Attachment, Regulation, and Competency Framework

The Attachment, Regulation, and Competency (ARC) framework provides guiding principles and interventions that address various critical areas in trauma-informed practice: attachment, self-regulation, and developmental competencies (Blaustein & Kinniburgh, 2010). The attachment domain is intended to strengthen bonds between the child and their caregiving system, including relationships with parents and the school community, by providing adequate resources, skills, and supports needed by the child. Caregivers are provided with guidelines to manage their own affect and respond to the child in a consistent manner, as well as providing strategies that encourage caregiver-child reciprocity. This provides the basis upon which other competencies are built. For example, the Healthy Environments and Response to Trauma in Schools (HEARTS) Program, based on the ARC framework, has been an approach to trauma-informed practice successfully implemented in schools (Dorado et al., 2016). The HEARTS program is a multi-tier approach where compassionate and dependable relationships are promoted across three tiers. At Tier 1, for instance, staff training includes education around the effect of trauma on relationships and strategies that should be implemented by all staff to address the adverse effects of trauma. An evaluation of the program suggests that, among other areas, students improved in their capacity to develop healthy relationships, and the principle of fostering positive relationships was seen as one of the integral principles required in creating the optimal environment for teaching and learning (Dorado et al., 2016).

Berry Street Educational Model

The Berry Street Educational Model (BSEM) (Stokes & Turnbull, 2016) is a strengths-based perspective on trauma-informed practice developed for educational settings. Similar to the ARC framework, it incorporates three tiers that focus on developing regulatory abilities (Tier 1), repairing disrupted attachments (Tier 2), and helping students to increase their psychological resources (Tier 3). In addition, the program comprises four domains (i.e., Body, Stamina, Engagement, and Character), all of which are anchored in a fifth domain named "relationship". The program recognizes that it is through relationships that students are able to learn and implement the skills learned. Safe and consistent classroom environments, where students feel a sense of belonging, trust, and worthiness, underpin all other strategies implemented in this model. Classrooms are also seen as the primary place for students to learn about relationships (Stokes & Turnbull, 2016). A review of this program across primary and secondary schools found positive outcomes, with teachers reporting that their focus has shifted to establishing positive relationships with students to enable learning (Stokes & Turnbull, 2016). Becoming more self-aware of the language being used in the classroom and showing the students' unconditional acceptance and support are other positive outcomes reported by teachers. Students also reported feeling more understood and accepted by teachers and classmates in comparison to previous years (Stokes & Turnbull, 2016).

Calmer Classrooms

The Calmer Classrooms (Downey, 2008) approach notes that schools are an essential part of the support system that promotes development and wellbeing of trauma-affected students, as well as improving their capacity to learn. This approach acknowledges that trauma-affected children have experienced disrupted attachments which may affect their ability to self-regulate and their ability to build healthy relationships. Hence, the principles in this approach focus on promoting the child's wellbeing by building strong attachments and connections within the school. Central to the practices promoted by this approach is the teacher's understanding of the effect childhood trauma has on the child's emotional, behavioral, and cognitive development. In addition, when the child exhibits difficult behavior, teachers are encouraged to focus on practices that will preserve the teacher-student relationship and promote trust rather than employing disciplinary action that solely focuses on managing the child's behavior. Importantly, given the challenging behaviors children impacted by trauma can exhibit, teachers are also encouraged to engage in self-care practices that prevent secondary traumatization, with the child's behavior and difficult circumstances also becoming an adverse experience for the teacher.

Summary of Trauma-Informed Models for Building Relationships

Although the above examples of trauma-informed frameworks consider relationship building strategies as central within educational settings to support students exposed to trauma, the way in which these strategies are implemented can vary. For example, the BSEM strategies are based on trauma-informed practice theory (e.g., enhancing emotional regulation) but also positive education theories (e.g., promoting a growth mindset), and, as such, the relationship-building strategies that are implemented in the curriculum differ. In addition, in the BSEM framework, these strategies are practiced in a sequential fashion. That is, the student's ability to self-regulate and build relationships is considered foundational in this model, therefore, multiple strategies to strengthen these areas are encouraged to be implemented first in the program. Subsequent strategies also support the building of connections with others, but are derived from positive education strategies and draw on a strengths-based perspective. This can include practices designed to enhance students' healthy relationships by increasing their emotional intelligence (i.e., stamina module) or encouraging students to identify character strengths in themselves and others (i.e., character module). By contrast, the focus of Calmer Classrooms (Downey, 2008) is to provide education to teachers to increase their awareness of the impact of traumatic events on children's learning and behavior. It is assumed that this awareness will enhance the educator's patience and compassion, resulting in more trauma-sensitive classrooms. Therefore, central to this model is enhancing teacher-student connections. For example, rather than encouraging "time-out" as a way of responding to challenging behavior (e.g., removing the student from the classroom), "time-in" is promoted (e.g., asking the student to move to a place in closer proximity to the teacher and/or having a one-on-one conversation with the student) as a way to preserve relationships and build trust. Although important in both models, relationship building strategies can vary across different trauma-informed frameworks, and the implementation can also vary across educational settings depending on the particular needs of the school (Chafouleas et al., 2019; Thomas et al., 2019). Given the importance of school belonging and the potential benefits of trauma-informed practice, integrating these two approaches can create a supportive and effective learning environment for students, especially for those with a history of trauma. By recognizing the impact of trauma on attachment and the need for healthy relationships in the school setting, educators can effectively promote school belonging and trauma-informed practices to build a safe school climate for all students.

Case Study: Navigating Trauma and Fostering Belonging in a Year Two Classroom

The following case study provided by an author of this chapter (MM), a teacher with over 20 years of experience, shows the transformative power of trauma-informed teaching and its role in fostering a sense of belonging in a Year Two classroom.

> As a teacher with over 20 years' classroom experience, I have always been aware of the diverse backgrounds and experiences that each student brings to the classroom. However, my encounter with Leon,[4] a student who had recently been showing increasing signs of challenging behavioral problems, highlighted like never before that I would need to understand how trauma-informed practice and a sense of belonging would make an impact in this child's educational journey.
>
> Leon's initial behavior in my classroom was characterized by disruptive actions, refusal to undertake learning tasks, and a noticeable difficulty in forming connections with his peers. Recognizing these as potential manifestations of his traumatic experiences, I felt a pressing need to adapt my teaching approach to better support him. I began by consciously cultivating a safe and welcoming environment in the classroom. This involved not only the physical arrangement of the space but also the emotional climate. I aimed to create an atmosphere where every student felt valued and accepted, where their voices were heard, and their individuality respected. This was particularly crucial for Leon, who needed reassurance that he was accepted as part of the group and on the same social level as his peers, a stark contrast to the turmoil he was experiencing at home.
>
> Building a strong, supportive relationship with Leon was another priority. I made an effort to show genuine interest in him and understand what worked (and what didn't) in terms

of boosting his self-esteem. This was not about prying into his personal life but about demonstrating that I cared about him as an individual. This was particularly difficult as he was extremely uncomfortable with positive curiosity from adults. I wanted him to know that he could trust me, that I was there to support him.

Fostering a sense of belonging within the classroom was another significant aspect of my approach. I made a conscious effort to highlight each student's unique strengths and contributions, so that each child could see the many and varied ways their peers thought and felt. For Leon, these strategies were instrumental in helping him feel part of the classroom community.

Over time, the impact of these trauma-informed practices became evident. Leon began to engage more positively with his peers, and his disruptive behaviors gradually gave way to a more engagement. His academic performance improved, which likely reflected his increasing comfort within the learning environment and increased feelings of being safe enough to make mistakes without fear of retribution.

This transformation was not immediate, but the gradual changes I observed in Leon were a testament to the power of trauma-informed practices and the cultivation of a sense of belonging. It was truly eye-opening to see the impact of trauma on a child's ability to learn and interact with others, and that my targeted intervention as his teacher was so critical.

My experience with Leon has profoundly shaped my approach to teaching. By responding with empathy and understanding, I was able to help Leon develop a sense of belonging and of safety in our school space, ultimately enhancing his learning experience. It has reinforced my belief I can make significant change as an educator, particularly for students who have experienced trauma, and what power and privilege there is in that.

Recommendations

1. Provide educators with tailored and individualized professional development on recognizing and responding to the impacts of interpersonal childhood trauma.
2. Integrate interpersonal trauma-informed practices into school policies and educational priorities.
3. Foster a sense of belonging by emphasizing the importance of positive relationships among students, peers, and teachers, while implementing strategies that promote social inclusion.
4. Choose trauma-informed frameworks that align with the school's unique context and needs, taking into consideration the student population, including developmental considerations.

Conclusion

Schools play a critical role in supporting children who have experienced interpersonal trauma since teachers and the school community exert significant influence on the lives of children. Trauma-informed practices and fostering healthy relationships within educational settings can greatly benefit students affected by trauma, especially by enhancing their sense of belonging within the school environment. Although several trauma-informed frameworks have been developed and implemented in schools, more research is needed to evaluate the effectiveness of these approaches, particularly those focused on cultivating belonging and relationship building. By examining various trauma-informed practices and their outcomes, we can better inform school practices, policymaking, and future research in this area.

Notes

1 The types of traumatic events experienced by people can be interpersonal (i.e., relational) or non-interpersonal in nature. Non-interpersonal trauma can result from adverse events caused by natural disasters, war, or poverty and it could be acute, that is, caused by one significant adverse event, or chronic.

2 ACEs largely relate to the exposure of traumatic experiences within the home environment associated with family dysfunction (e.g., child maltreatment, parental substance abuse, neglect) (Felitti et al., 1998), though additional adverse experiences have most recently been included in the research.

3 Secondary trauma refers to trauma-related symptoms (e.g., intrusion, avoidance, and hypervigilance) experienced by helping professionals (e.g., first responders, mental health providers, teachers) when supporting people exposed to trauma.

4 *Note.* All names and identifying information have been changed to preserve privacy and anonymity.

References

Ainsworth, M. D. S. (1978). *Patterns of attachment: A psychological study of the strange situation.* Lawrence Erlbaum Associates.

Alisic, E. (2012). Teachers' perspectives on providing support to children after trauma: A qualitative study. *School Psychology Quarterly, 27*(1), 51–59. https://doi.org/10.1037/a0028590

Allen, K. A. (2020). Do you feel like you belong? *Frontiers for Young Minds, 8,* Article 99. https://doi.org/10.3389/frym.2020.00099

Allen, K. A. (Discussant). (2023, April 13–16). Connecting research on belonging and motivation: Investigating the interplay between contextual, individual, and institutional factors. *2023 AERA annual meeting: Interrogating consequential education research in pursuit of truth,* Chicago, IL.

Allen, K. A. & Bowles, T. V. (2013). The importance of belonging for adolescents in secondary school settings. *The European Journal of Social & Behavioural Sciences, 5*(2), 976–984.

Allen, K. A., Berger, E., Campbell, T., U'Ren, M., & Andrews, M. L. (2022). Finding a sense of belonging in the absence of family. In M. Israelashvili & S. Mozes (Eds.), *Youth without family to lean on: Global challenges and local interventions* (pp. 41–58). Routledge.

Allen, K. A., Berger, E., Grove, C., Patlamazoglou, L., Gamble, N., May, F., Wurf, G., & Reupert, A. (2022). "Ask me how I am doing, be kind, and encourage me to get involved": Students' perspectives for improving belonging in secondary schools. OSF Preprints. https://doi.org/10.31219/osf.io/b4q6m

Allen, K. A., Gray, D. L., Baumeister, R. F., & Leary, M. R. (2022). The need to belong: A deep dive into the origins, implications, and future of a foundational construct. *Educational Psychology Review, 34*(2), 1133–1156. https://doi.org/10.1007/s10648-021-09633-6

Allen, K. A., Kern, M. L., Vella-Brodrick, D., Hattie, J., & Waters, L. (2018). What schools need to know about fostering school belonging: A meta-analysis. *Educational Psychology Review, 30*(1), 1–34. https://doi.org/10.1007/s10648-016-9389-8

Allen, K. A., Slaten, C. D., Arslan, G., Roffey, S., Craig, H., & Vella-Brodrick, D. A. (2021). School belonging: The importance of student and teacher relationships. In M. L. Kern & M. L. Wehmeyer (Eds.), *The Palgrave handbook of positive education* (pp. 525–550). Palgrave & Macmillan. https://www.palgrave.com/gp/book/9783030645366

Anderson, V., Northam, E., & Wrennall, J. (2019). *Developmental neuropsychology* (2nd ed.). Routledge.

Atkinson, L., Paglia, A., Coolbear, J., Niccols, A., Parker, K. C. H., & Guger, S. (2000). Attachment security: A meta-analysis of maternal mental health correlates. *Clinical Psychology Review, 20*(8), 1019–1040. https://doi.org/10.1016/S0272-7358(99)00023-9

Baumeister, R. F., & Leary, M. R. (1995). The need to belong: Desire for interpersonal attachments as a fundamental human motivation. *Psychological Bulletin, 117*(3), 497–529. https://doi.org/10.1037/0033-2909.117.3.497

Berger, E., & Martin, K. (2021). Embedding trauma-informed practice within the education sector. *Journal of Community & Applied Social Psychology, 31*(2), 223–227. https://doi.org/10.1002/casp.2494

Blaustein, M. E., & Kinniburgh, K. M. (2010). *Treating traumatic stress in children and adolescents: How to foster resilience through attachment, self-regulation, and competency*. Guilford Press.

Blodgett, C., & Lanigan, J. D. (2018). The association between adverse childhood experience (ACE) and school success in elementary school children. *School Psychology Quarterly, 33*(1), 137–146. https://doi.org/10.1037/spq0000256

Breidenstine, A. S., Bailey, L. O., Zeanah, C. H., & Larrieu, J. A. (2011). Attachment and trauma in early childhood: A review. *Journal of Child & Adolescent Trauma, 4*(4), 274. https://doi.org/10.1080/19361521.2011.609155

Brown, J. D., King, M. A., & Wissow, L. S. (2017). The central role of relationships with trauma-informed integrated care for children and youth. *Academic Pediatrics, 17*(7), S94–S101. https://doi.org/10.1016/j.acap.2017.01.013

Brunzell, T., Stokes, H., & Waters, L. (2016). Trauma-informed positive education: Using positive psychology to strengthen vulnerable students. *Contemporary School Psychology, 20*(1), 63–83. https://doi.org/10.1007/s40688-015-0070-x

Brunzell, T., Waters, L., & Stokes, H. (2015). Teaching with strengths in trauma-affected students: A new approach to healing and growth in the classroom. *American Journal of Orthopsychiatry, 85*(1), 3–9. https://doi.org/10.1037/ort0000048

Chafouleas, S. M., Koriakin, T. A., Roundfield, K. D., & Overstreet, S. (2019). Addressing childhood trauma in school settings: A framework for evidence-based practice. *School Mental Health, 11*(1), 40–53. https://doi.org/10.1007/s12310-018-9256-5

Cook, A., Spinazzola, J., Ford, J., Lanktree, C., Blaustein, M., Cloitre, M., DeRosa, R., Hubbard, R., Kagan, R., Liautaud, J., Mallah, K., Olafson, E., & van der Kolk, B. (2005). Complex trauma in children and adolescents. *Psychiatric Annals, 35*(5), 390–398. https://doi.org/10.3928/00485713-20050501-05

Creswell Báez, J., Renshaw, K. J., Bachman, L. E. M., Kim, D., Smith, V. D., & Stafford, R. E. (2019). Understanding the necessity of trauma-informed care in community schools: A mixed-methods program evaluation. *Children & Schools, 41*(2), 101–110. https://doi.org/10.1093/cs/cdz007

Crouch, E., Radcliff, E., Hung, P., & Bennett, K. (2019). Challenges to school success and the role of adverse childhood experiences. *Academic Pediatrics, 19*(8), 899–907. https://doi.org/10.1016/j.acap.2019.08.006

Dorado, J. S., Martinez, M., McArthur, L. E., & Leibovitz, T. (2016). Healthy Environments and Response to Trauma in Schools (HEARTS): A whole-school, multi-level, prevention and intervention program for creating trauma-informed, safe and supportive schools. *School Mental Health, 8*(1), 163–176. https://doi.org/10.1007/s12310-016-9177-0

Downey, L. (2008). Calmer classrooms: A guide to working with traumatised children. *Journal of the Home Economics Institute of Australia, 15*(1), 33–42. https://search.informit.org/doi/10.3316/aeipt.169828

Dugal, C., Bigras, N., Godbout, N., & Bélanger, C. (2016). *Childhood interpersonal trauma and its repercussions in adulthood: An analysis of psychological and interpersonal sequelae*. IntechOpen. https://doi.org/10.5772/64476

Dvir, Y., Ford, J. D., Hill, M., & Frazier, J. A. (2014). Childhood maltreatment, emotional dysregulation, and psychiatric comorbidities. *Harvard Review of Psychiatry, 22*(3), 149–161. https://doi.org/10.1097/HRP.0000000000000014

Felitti, V. J., Anda, R. F., Nordenberg, D., Williamson, D. F., Spitz, A. M., Edwards, V., Koss, M. P., & Marks, J. S. (1998). Relationship of childhood abuse and household dysfunction to many of the leading causes of death in adults: The Adverse Childhood Experiences (ACE) Study. *American Journal of Preventive Medicine, 14*(4), 245–258. https://doi.org/10.1016/s0749-3797(98)00017-8

Flowers, A. G. D., McGillivray, J. A., Galbally, M., & Lewis, A. J. (2018). Perinatal maternal mental health and disorganised attachment: A critical systematic review. *Clinical Psychologist, 22*(3), 300–316. https://doi.org/10.1111/cp.12145

Folger, A. T., Putnam, K. T., Putnam, F. W., Peugh, J. L., Eismann, E. A., Sa, T., Shapiro, R. A., Van Ginkel, J. B., & Ammerman, R. T. (2017). Maternal interpersonal trauma and child social-emotional development: An intergenerational effect. *Paediatric Perinatal Epidemiology, 31*(2), 99–107. https://doi.org/10.1111/ppe.12341

Fondren, K., Lawson, M., Speidel, R., McDonnell, C. G., & Valentino, K. (2020). Buffering the effects of childhood trauma within the school setting: A systematic review of trauma-informed and trauma-responsive interventions among trauma-affected youth. *Children and Youth Services Review, 109*, Article 104691. https://doi.org/10.1016/j.childyouth.2019.104691

Frydenberg, E., Deans, J., & O'Brien, K. A. (2012). *Developing everyday coping skills in the early years: Proactive strategies for supporting social and emotional development*. Bloomsbury.

Goodenow, C., & Grady, K. E. (1993). The relationship of school belonging and friends' values to academic motivation among urban adolescent students. *The Journal of Experimental Education, 62*(1), 60–71. https://doi.org/10.1080/00220973.1993.9943831

Gregorowski, C., & Seedat, S. (2013). Addressing childhood trauma in a developmental context. *Journal of Child and Adolescent Mental Health, 25*(2), 105–118. https://doi.org/10.2989/17280583.2013.795154

Hart, H., & Rubia, K. (2012). Neuroimaging of child abuse: A critical review. *Frontiers in Human Neuroscience, 6*(52). https://doi.org/10.3389/fnhum.2012.00052

Keller-Dupree, E. A. (2013). Understanding childhood trauma: Ten reminders for preventing retraumatization. *The Practitioner Scholar: Journal of Counseling and Professional Psychology, 2*(1), 1–11. https://www.thepractitionerscholar.com/article/view/10867

Libbey, H. P. (2004). Measuring student relationships to school: Attachment, bonding, connectedness, and engagement. *Journal of School Health, 74*(7), 274–283. https://link.gale.com/apps/doc/A122921723/AONE?u=monash&sid=AONE&xid=bf0cbf6c

Lünnemann, M. K. M., Horst, F. C. P. V. d., Prinzie, P., Luijk, M. P. C. M., & Steketee, M. (2019). The intergenerational impact of trauma and family violence on parents and their children. *Child Abuse & Neglect, 96*, Article 104134. https://doi.org/10.1016/j.chiabu.2019.104134

Marusak, H. A., Martin, K. R., Etkin, A., & Thomason, M. E. (2015). Childhood trauma exposure disrupts the automatic regulation of emotional processing. *Neuropsychopharmacology, 40*(5), 1250–1258. https://doi.org/10.1038/npp.2014.311

McLaughlin, C., & Clarke, B. (2010). Relational matters: A review of the impact of school experience on mental health in early adolescence. *Educational and Child Psychology, 27*(1), 91–103. https://psycnet.apa.org/record/2010-10870-008

McLaughlin, K. A. (2016). Future directions in childhood adversity and youth psychopathology. *Journal of Clinical and Child Adolescent Psychology, 45*(3), 361–382. https://doi.org/10.1080/15374416.2015.1110823

McLaughlin, K. A., & Lambert, H. K. (2017). Child trauma exposure and psychopathology: Mechanisms of risk and resilience. *Current Opinion in Psychology, 14*, 29–34. https://doi.org/10.1016/j.copsyc.2016.10.004

Moretti, M. M., & Peled, M. (2004). Adolescent-parent attachment: Bonds that support healthy development. *Paediatrics & Child Health, 9*(8), 551–555. https://doi.org/10.1093/pch/9.8.551

Newman, L., Sivaratnam, C., & Komiti, A. (2015). Attachment and early brain development – Neuroprotective interventions in infant–caregiver therapy. *Translational Developmental Psychiatry, 3*(1), 28647. https://doi.org/10.3402/tdp.v3.28647

O'Neill, L., Guenette, F., & Kitchenham, A. (2010). 'Am I safe here and do you like me?' Understanding complex trauma and attachment disruption in the classroom. *British Journal of Special Education, 37*(4), 190–197. https://doi.org/10.1111/j.1467-8578.2010.00477.x

Parker, P., Allen, K. A., Parker, R., Guo, J., Marsh, H. W., Basarkod, G., & Dicke, T. (2022). School belonging predicts whether an emerging adult will be not in education, employment, or training (NEET) after school. *Journal of Educational Psychology, 114*(8), 1881–1894. https://doi.org/10.1037/edu0000733

Perfect, M. M., Turley, M. R., Carlson, J. S., Yohanna, J., & Saint Gilles, M. P. (2016). School-related outcomes of traumatic event exposure and traumatic stress symptoms in students: A systematic review of research from 1990 to 2015. *School Mental Health, 8*(1), 7–43. https://doi.org/10.1007/s12310-016-9175-2

Prather, W., & Golden, J. A. (2009). A behavioral perspective of childhood trauma and attachment issues: Toward alternative treatment approaches for children with a history of abuse. *International Journal of Behavioral Consultation and Therapy, 5*(1), 56–74. https://doi.org/10.1037/h0100872

Putnam, F. W. (2006). The impact of trauma on child development. *Juvenile and Family Court Journal, 57*(1), 1–11. https://doi.org/10.1111/j.1755-6988.2006.tb00110.x

Roffey, S., Boyle, C., & Allen, K. A. (2019). School belonging – Why are our students longing to belong to school? *Educational and Child Psychology, 36*(2), 6–8.

Ryan, K., Lane, S. J., & Powers, D. (2017). A multidisciplinary model for treating complex trauma in early childhood. *International Journal of Play Therapy, 26*(2), 111–123. https://doi.org/ 10.1037/pla0000044

Slaten, C. D., Ferguson, J. K., Allen, K.-A., Brodrick, D.-V., & Waters, L. (2016). School belonging: A review of the history, current trends, and future directions. *The Educational and Developmental Psychologist, 33*(1), 1–15. https://doi.org/10.1017/edp.2016.6

Spinazzola, J., Van der Kolk, B., & Ford, J. D. (2018). When nowhere is safe: Interpersonal trauma and attachment adversity as antecedents of posttraumatic stress disorder and developmental trauma disorder. *Journal of Traumatic Stress, 31*(5), 631–642. https://doi.org/10.1002/jts.22320

Sroufe, L. A. (2005). Attachment and development: A prospective, longitudinal study from birth to adulthood. *Attachment & Human Development, 7*(4), 349–367. https://doi.org/10.1080/14616730500365928

Stokes, H., & Turnbull, M. (2016). *Evaluation of the Berry Street Education Model: Trauma informed positive education enacted in mainstream schools*. University of Melbourne Graduate School of Education, Youth Research Centre. http://education.unimelb.edu.au/__data/assets/pdf_file/0007/1962718/User_croftsj_Stokes_26_Turnbull_Final_Web_18-5-16.pdf

Stokes, H., Turnbull, M., Forster, R., & Farrelly, A. (2019). *Young people's voices, young people's lives: A Berry Street Education Model (BSEM) project*. University of Melbourne Graduate School of Education, Youth Research Centre.

Storebø, O. J., Rasmussen, P. D., & Simonsen, E. (2016). Association between insecure attachment and ADHD: Environmental mediating factors. *Journal of Attention Disorders, 20*(2), 187–196. https://doi.org/10.1177/1087054713501079

Thomas, M. S., Crosby, S., & Vanderhaar, J. (2019). Trauma-informed practices in schools across two decades: An interdisciplinary review of research. *Review of Research in Education, 43*(1), 422–452. https://doi.org/10.3102/0091732x18821123

Townsend, I. M., Berger, E. P., & Reupert, A. E. (2020). Systematic review of the educational experiences of children in care: Children's perspectives. *Children and Youth Services Review, 111*, Article 104835. https://doi.org/10.1016/j.childyouth.2020.104835

Tzouvara, V., Kupdere, P., Wilson, K., Matthews, L., Simpson, A., & Foye, U. (2023). Adverse childhood experiences, mental health, and social functioning: A scoping review of the literature. *Child Abuse & Neglect, 139,* 106092. https://doi.org/10.1016/j.chiabu.2023.106092

van Bodegom, M., Homberg, J. R., & Henckens, M. J. A. G. (2017). Modulation of the Hypothalamic-Pituitary-Adrenal axis by early life stress exposure. *Frontiers in Cellular Neuroscience, 11,* Article 87. https://doi.org/10.3389/fncel.2017.00087

van der Kolk, B. A. M. D. (2005). Developmental trauma disorder. *Psychiatric Annals, 35*(5), 401–408. https://www.ifemdr.fr/wp-content/uploads/2011/10/van-der-kolk-2005-Developmental-Trauma-Disorder-Psychiatric-annals.pdf

van Ijzendoorn, M. H., & Bakermans-Kranenburg, M. J. (2019). Bridges across the intergenerational transmission of attachment gap. *Current Opinion in Psychology, 25,* 31–36. https://doi.org/https://doi.org/10.1016/j.copsyc.2018.02.014

Wall, C. R. G. (2020). Relationship over reproach: Fostering resilience by embracing a trauma-informed approach to elementary education. *Journal of Aggression, Maltreatment & Trauma, 30,* 1–20. https://doi.org/10.1080/10926771.2020.1737292

Wilson-Ching, M., & Berger, E. (2023). Relationship building strategies within trauma informed frameworks in educational settings: A systematic literature review. *Current Psychology, 43,* 3464–3485. https://doi.org/10.1007/s12144-023-04590-5

Wong, D., Allen, K. A., & Cordoba, B. G. (2022). Examining the relationship between student attributional style, perceived teacher fairness, and sense of school belonging. *Contemporary Educational Psychology, 17,* Article 102113. https://doi.org/10.1016/j.cedpsych.2022.102113

5 Teachers, Burnout and Wellbeing

Emily Berger, India Bryce, and Liska Schramm

Introduction

Teaching is described as one of the most stressful and demanding professions, and rates of absenteeism and attrition in the profession are a significant concern (Liu & Onwuegbuzie, 2012; Reupert, 2020). Evidence suggests that teachers' wellbeing can influence the wellbeing and academic achievement of students (Arens & Morin, 2016; Harding et al., 2019). In addition, research shows that interactions with traumatized students can increase teachers' risk of experiencing burnout, secondary trauma, and compassion fatigue (Berger et al., 2021; Berger & Nott, 2023). The aim of this chapter is to outline evidence on the impact of exposure to traumatized students on teachers' mental health and professional fulfillment. Evidence-based programs and frameworks designed to improve outcomes for teachers exposed to traumatized students will also be discussed, as well as the role of school leaders and education departments in addressing the wellbeing of teachers. This chapter will conclude with discussion of important recommendations for whole-of-school policies and practices designed to promote teachers' wellbeing. The terms trauma, traumatic, and traumatization will be used interchangeably in this chapter to denote events that are experienced by students as physically, socially, emotionally, or spiritually harmful or threatening.

Definitions of Teacher Wellbeing

Over the past decade, researchers have attempted to define the construct and components of teacher wellbeing. Acton and Glasgow (2015) defined

DOI: 10.4324/9781003436034-5

teacher wellbeing as "an individual sense of personal professional fulfilment, satisfaction, purposefulness, and happiness, constructed in a collaborative process with colleagues and students" (p. 101). McCallum et al. (2017) conducted a review and analyzed 191 studies that used terms related to teacher wellbeing and concluded that: (1) teacher wellbeing is complex to define, (2) that teacher wellbeing should be prioritized in schools, and (3) to address teacher wellbeing, schools must improve personal, professional, leadership, and workplace standards. There is a growing consensus that teacher wellbeing encompasses both individual factors of professional fulfillment and personal happiness, as well as structural factors such as positive relationships with colleagues and healthy workplace conditions. McCallum and Price (2016) state that wellbeing is defined differently by different teachers and communities:

> Diverse and fluid respecting individual, family and community beliefs, values, experiences, culture, opportunities and contexts across time and change. It is something we all aim for, underpinned by positive notions, yet is unique to each of us and provides us with a sense of who we are which needs to be respected.
>
> (p. 17)

Cumming and Wong (2019) developed a definition of early childhood educator wellbeing, which resembles McCallum and Price's (2016) definition of teacher wellbeing. Cumming and Wong (2019) stated that early childhood educator wellbeing is determined by "individual, relational, work-environmental and socio-political aspects and contexts" (p. 276). Ecological frameworks have been used to illustrate the different components of teacher wellbeing, from individual factors that predict teachers' wellbeing, to workplace culture and policies designed to support teachers' wellbeing.

Frameworks to Understand and Promote Teacher Wellbeing

Ecological Framework of Teacher Wellbeing

To account for both individual and structural factors underpinning teacher wellbeing, several frameworks have been proposed, drawing from ecological models of wellbeing. Hine et al. (2022) conducted focus groups with

47 teachers, including early childhood educators, primary (elementary) and secondary teachers, and school principals and early childhood leaders, from a range of different personal and professional contexts. Hine et al. (2022) reported that teachers' wellbeing is impacted by several different factors including:

- Teacher's own personal coping and self-care strategies and possessing a positive and optimistic mindset
- Adequate access to mental health support and a positive workplace culture that encourages teachers to seek help from colleagues and education leaders
- Excessive workplace demands and workload, including long work hours, administrative tasks, working with families, and diverse responsibilities of teachers
- Experiences of discrimination and lack of culturally sensitive practices for Aboriginal and Torres Strait Islander, LGBTQIA+, and culturally and linguistically diverse educators
- Workplace relationships and support from colleagues, such as feeling a sense of belonging and inclusion in their school community
- Supportive and inclusive leadership in which leaders consult and collaborate with teachers and implement policies and initiatives designed to promote teachers' wellbeing.

Based on this study, Hine et al. (2022) developed a model of teacher and early childhood educator wellbeing, drawing on existing ecological models of wellbeing. The model starts with the individual educator and their own personal coping and self-care strategies, followed by the importance of positive workplace relationships and culture, supportive and inclusive leadership, and finally supportive community, governance, and policy that prioritizes the wellbeing of teachers (Hine et al., 2022).

From an ecological perspective, Hine et al. (2022) and others (e.g., Price & McCallum, 2015) have strongly advocated for teacher wellbeing to be addressed through explicit programs, such as teacher mindfulness and mental health literacy programs (Berger et al., 2022c), approaches to promote positive collegial relationships, inclusion, and sense of belonging among teachers, supportive leadership, resources, policies, and governance to address teacher wellbeing, and community recognition of the role and importance of teachers.

Positive Psychology Framework of Teacher Wellbeing

The paradigm shift which resulted in the positive psychology movement heralded a shift away from psychology as a field that focuses on psychopathology, to one that seeks to "understand and build the factors that allow individuals, communities, and societies to flourish" (Seligman & Csikszentmihalyi, 2000, p. 5). Positive psychology recognizes that people and their experiences are inseparable from social contexts and seeks to build positive systems and institutions for optimal wellbeing (Seligman & Csikszentmihalyi, 2000). The positive psychology movement has been adopted by schools in relation to promoting teacher wellbeing.

Job Demands-Resources (JD-R) theory adopts a positive psychology approach (Bakker & Demerouti, 2008) to explain employees' workplace experiences and holds that working conditions within all occupations can be broadly defined as either job demands or job resources (Demerouti et al., 2001). JD-R theory is considered valuable in understanding the occupational experiences of teachers and in shedding light on the nature of attrition and retention of teachers in the profession (Bakker & Demerouti, 2017; Demerouti et al., 2001). Skaalvik and Skaalvik (2017) noted that the concepts of job demands and job stressors can be viewed as interchangeable. According to Demerouti et al. (2001), job demands are:

> The physical, social, organizational, or psychological aspects of work that require the investment of physical and/or psychological effort, and are associated with energy depletion and psychological and/or physiological costs (e.g., workload, disciplinary issues, time pressure)
>
> (p. 2)

Conversely, job resources are:

> Those elements of work that enable employees to: achieve work goals; manage job demands, and the associated physical and psychological costs; and grow and develop in their position (e.g., perceived autonomy support, opportunities for professional learning, and relationships with colleagues)
>
> (Granziera et al., 2021, p. 231)

In recent years, researchers of JD-R theory have acknowledged the role of personal resources in influencing workplace environments, such as teachers' level of self-efficacy and adaptability. Personal resources are considered individual capabilities of teachers that can be nurtured or changed, and therefore provide a useful foundation from which interventions targeting teachers' wellbeing may be developed. The JD-R theory suggests that job demands and job/personal resources are two independent psychological processes, whereby job demands increase the likelihood of burnout, and job/personal resources lead to higher work engagement and wellbeing (Bakker & Demerouti, 2017). These two processes draw a thread between personal and occupational outcomes that can be influenced by teachers' interactions with students experiencing trauma. For example, when teachers feel under-resourced and overburdened, they may be more likely to experience burnout and poor wellbeing when supporting trauma-affected students. When teachers experience a sense of fulfillment when supporting students exposed to trauma, when working with trauma-exposed students aligns with their personal values, and when teachers have appropriate resources to support these students, greater job satisfaction and wellbeing can be achieved.

In addition to the associations between job demands and job resources, JD-R theory also highlights two equally important processes, the 'buffering' and the 'boosting' effects (Bakker et al., 2004). The 'buffering' effect refers to certain job resources that buffer or mitigate the effect of job demands on teachers' wellbeing (Bakker et al., 2004). Bakker et al. (2007) found that when Finnish school teachers reported high or positive ratings of support, the workplace environment, and access to appropriate resources, their perceptions of student misbehavior had a less negative impact on their work engagement. Thus, job resources provide teachers with strategies to better manage demanding situations. The 'boosting' effect refers to the job resources that 'boost' their engagement when job demands are high.

Teacher Wellbeing Frameworks in the Context of Student Trauma

Emotional Labor, Burnout, and Secondary Trauma

Emotional Labor, burnout, and secondary trauma are commonly described experiences of teachers and early childhood educators in response to their work with traumatized students and families. Emotional labor has been defined as "the management of feelings or create a publicly observable facial and body display" (Hochschild, 1983, p. 7), and "the act of displaying appropriate emotions, with the goal to engage in a form of impression management for the organization" (Ashforth & Humphrey, 1993, p. 90). A body of research conducted in response to the COVID-19 pandemic showed the high levels of emotional labor experienced by teachers and early childhood educators during the pandemic. This resulted from the pressure educators experienced around balancing their own health and wellbeing with the health and wellbeing of their own family and children, and the health and wellbeing of children and families attending their early learning setting or school. Educators also reported experiencing emotional labor due to the additional workload demands placed on them during the pandemic (Berger et al., 2022b; Quiñones et al., 2022). A review of the consequences of emotional labor found that emotional labor increases job-related stress and burnout and requires stress management support and organizational change to protect teachers against the negative effects of emotional labor (Jeung et al., 2018).

A growing body of research has shown that teachers are at risk of burnout and secondary trauma in response to exposure to students who have experienced trauma. According to the Professional Quality of Life (ProQOL) model, teachers and others in helping professionals can experience both positive and negative reactions to their work with people impacted by trauma, and how they respond can be influenced by the work environment (e.g., workplace policies, and leadership support), the nature of their work (e.g., degree of exposure to traumatized people), and personal circumstances of the worker (e.g., experience and training to support their response to trauma-affected people) (Stamm, 2002, 2010). The ProQOL model includes both compassion satisfaction and compassion fatigue as the most common consequences of working with traumatized people. The concept of compassion satisfaction was originally defined by Stamm (2002, 2010) as a sense of personal growth that professionals achieve when supporting trauma-impacted clients. In comparison, compassion fatigue refers to any negative physical, emotional, and psychological impacts helping professionals experience when exposed to traumatized people (Stamm, 2002, 2010). Compassion fatigue is further classified as experiences of burnout and secondary traumatic stress. Studies have provided support for this two-dimensional model of compassion fatigue, including the two constructs of burnout and secondary trauma among teaching populations (Berger & Nott, 2023; Yang, 2021).

Secondary trauma is defined in the literature as an acute stress reaction which can manifest as fear or avoidance, sleep problems, and/or intrusive thoughts from exposure to details of another person's trauma (Stamm, 2010). These impacts can impair the personal and professional functioning of helping professionals. The concept of burnout is defined as chronic, work-related stress, feelings of hopelessness, loss of productivity, and lethargy at work (Stamm, 2010). Burnout can manifest as low self-efficacy and job satisfaction, leading to high stress and anxiety, reduced empathy, and occupational performance, as well as negative physical and mental health outcomes. Research suggests that burnout is the consequence of chronic strain due to a lack of trauma-informed training, inadequate resources, and undue demands placed on workers (Hydon et al., 2015).

There is currently limited evidence examining burnout and secondary trauma of teachers and other school staff. The majority of research has been conducted with emergency service workers, hospital and medical staff, and social and other mental health care workers. Furthermore, few studies have investigated the combination of work, client, and personal circumstances that contribute to burnout and secondary trauma of teachers. One study conducted in Australia found that inexperience, inadequate training, greater exposure to traumatized students, and teachers with mental illness or a history of trauma experienced higher burnout and secondary trauma, and lower compassion satisfaction compared to other workers (Berger & Nott, 2023).

Similar to secondary trauma and stress, there is limited evidence on strategies to promote compassion satisfaction of teachers and other school staff. Research has found that compassion satisfaction is determined by individual (e.g., self-care) and systematic (e.g., role recognition and workplace policies) factors that increase levels of compassion satisfaction among staff (Harr, 2014). These concepts can be linked back to ecological and positive psychology frameworks of teacher wellbeing, which indicate that teachers' sense of wellbeing in response to trauma-exposed students is governed by both individual and school structure factors. Together, these frameworks provide strong support for the importance of a systematic, whole-school approach to address and maintain the wellbeing of teachers in the context of exposure to students who have experienced trauma. The whole-school approach includes policies and school leaders that prioritize teachers' wellbeing, professional development, and support for teachers to help them manage their own wellbeing, positive workplace culture, and reduced workload demands that can negatively impact teacher wellbeing.

Current Trends in Impacts on Teacher Wellbeing

Exposure to Students Impacted by Trauma

Alisic (2012) conducted one of the first studies on teacher perspectives of supporting traumatized students in the Netherlands. This research found that teachers experience difficulty carrying the "emotional burden of their work", wanted "better knowledge and skills", expressed "uncertainty and struggle" in providing optimum care to traumatized students, sought clearer understanding of their role and responsibilities, and desired "good balance" while juggling the conflicting demands of working with children exposed to trauma and other children in the classroom (Alisic, 2012, pp. 51–59). An Australian study of 182 school leaders and 169 teachers in Queensland found that 76% of those surveyed reported a need to develop their skills in dealing with traumatized students and 74% expressed a need for more knowledge (Howard, 2019). Additionally, on dealing with traumatized students, 46% reported feeling sadness, 49% reported feeling frustration, and 59% reported lingering negative feelings. Others reported feeling "unsafe, overwhelmed, underappreciated", "thrown off the deep-end", "powerless, and at times helpless", and "not equipped to work with these students" (Howard, 2019, p. 14).

These examples are consistent with research by Berger et al. (2021) and Berger and Nott (2023) showing teachers' experience burnout and secondary trauma in response to exposure to students impacted by trauma. Specifically, Berger et al. (2021) conducted interviews with 27 school teachers and found teachers expressed feeling of detachment and disengagement from students, feelings of inadequacy, feelings of being overwhelmed, anxious, and fatigued, become preoccupied with the experiences of students, experience increased cynicism and loss of hope, and reported greater absenteeism from teaching due to their exposure to trauma-affected students. Berger et al. (2021) likened these symptoms to teachers' experiences of burnout and secondary trauma when exposed to traumatized students. Berger and Nott (2023) completed a study with 302 teachers to explore levels and predictors of burnout and secondary trauma among Australian teachers when exposed to students who had experienced trauma. It was identified that over 80% of Australian teachers have been exposed to at least one traumatized student, and 45% of teachers had experienced their own trauma in their lifetime. Teachers exposed to traumatized students were found to be more likely to experience their own trauma symptoms and higher rates of burnout compared to teachers not exposed to students who had experienced trauma (Berger & Nott, 2023).

A body of research has identified several common challenges of teachers and other school staff when managing the needs and supporting students impacted by trauma (Barrett & Berger, 2021; Berger et al., 2021, 2022a; Berger & Samuel, 2020), including:

- The emotional impact of working with students impacted by trauma, including burnout and secondary trauma, experienced by teachers and educators
- Challenges associated with working with parents, especially parents who are the perpetrators of the student's trauma, respond with anger or aggression to offers of help from teachers, parents who deny or refuse to acknowledge trauma experienced by students, and parents who do not enact strategies recommended by teachers at home
- The challenge of balancing student confidentiality with teachers' responsibility to ensure that students are supported by their parents, caregivers, and mental health services
- Challenges balancing the social, emotional, behavioral, and learning needs of students exposed to trauma with the needs of other students and the other responsibilities of teachers
- Teachers need more professional development and ongoing training and support to respond to the needs of trauma-exposed students. This includes professional development and coaching for all members of school staff, including teachers, school leaders, and school mental health staff
- That schools require policies designed to address student trauma, trauma-informed practice, and teacher wellbeing, including alignment between existing mandatory reporting and other school policies and practices with trauma-informed policies and practices
- Challenges of working with external mental health and social service providers, including a lack of consultation between child protection workers and school staff, and between external mental health services and school teachers

- The importance of creating inclusive and culturally sensitive learning and school environments for students and families impacted by trauma, especially for families from Aboriginal and Torres Strait backgrounds, culturally and linguistically diverse families, and other marginalized and disadvantaged groups
- Challenges responding to students' trauma and implementing trauma-informed practices in instances when teachers are exposed to the same traumatic experience as students, such as the recent COVID-19 pandemic and environmental disasters.

Overall, evidence has illustrated the emotional burden teachers experience in response to students exposed to trauma, and that teachers require additional assistance and school policies and procedures for managing their own health wellbeing when working with students exposed to trauma.

Occupational Violence and Aggression Experienced by Teachers

Violence experienced by teachers during the course of their work, perpetrated either by students or parents, appears to be increasing (Stevenson et al., 2022). By definition, occupational violence is "any incident where an employee is abused, threatened or assaulted in circumstances arising out of or in the course of, their employment" (Shea et al., 2017, p. 237). Examples of occupational violence perpetrated toward teachers may include:

- physical or verbal intimidation and threatening behavior
- spitting, biting, hitting, kicking, and punching
- malicious damage to an individual's property
- gendered violence
- online/virtual harassment.

Occupational violence can have significant short- and long-term impacts on a teacher's psychological and physical health (Ribeiro et al., 2022; Stevenson et al., 2022). Small instances of exposure to occupational violence can also have a negative cumulative effect on teachers.

Occupational violence is a problem confronted by many educators, irrespective of age, gender, and years of experience. An Australian study found 80% of surveyed teachers had experienced some form of bullying and harassment in the preceding 12-month period and close to half

(44.6%) reported this behavior as coming from both students and parents (Billett et al., 2019). Riley (2018) revealed that of the 2,385 school leaders surveyed, over 84% reported being subjected to some form of offensive behavior by parents or students in the past 12-month period. Of the teachers who reported verbal or physical bullying and harassment, 25.3% reported experiencing threats of violence exclusively from students and 13.4% from parents (Riley, 2018). The proportion of school leaders who reported experiencing physical violence increased from 27.3% in 2011 to 42.2% in 2018 (Riley, 2018). Research shows that occupational violence is a global issue for educators, with teachers from the United States, Canada, the United Kingdom, and Israel sharing their experiences (Bare et al., 2021; Del Riccio, 2021; Holt & Birchall, 2022; Wilson et al., 2011). Studies conducted in South Africa reveal that schools, both primary and secondary, are considered unsafe for teachers as they experience various forms of occupational violence (Govender, 2015; Fakude, 2022). All these experiences of maltreatment and victimization are harmful to the health and psychophysical wellbeing of teachers.

From putting a strain on personal relationships to feeling unsafe in local communities, the impacts of school staff abuse reach far beyond the school environment. Concerningly, abuse from parents can have negative consequences for an educator's sense of self-efficacy and wellbeing (Billett et al., 2019). Moreover, experiencing abuse from students can undermine an educator's confidence, causing additional stress, unease, and uncertainty in the classroom. In turn, this can leave school staff feeling emotionally and mentally drained, requiring them to seek psychological support and time off work to seek respite from the abusive behavior (Billett et al., 2019). The burden of protecting school staff from abusive behavior from students, parents, and community members means school leaders may also become victims of abuse in schools (Riley, 2018). Abuse against school leaders can affect leaders' mental health and wellbeing, act as a deterrent to others who might otherwise seek leadership roles, and impact the ability of school leaders to effectively perform their leadership duties (Riley, 2018).

Interventions to Promote Teacher Wellbeing

To mitigate factors which foster negative workplace experiences and increase teacher burnout and mental ill-health, researchers have attempted to design and implement interventions to support teachers' wellbeing.

Berger et al. (2022c) completed a systematic review of programs designed to promote teacher and early childhood educators' wellbeing and identified 17 different programs shown to improve the wellbeing of teachers. The majority of interventions were mindfulness-based programs which were found to lower educators' stress, anxiety, and depression, and improve educators' positive emotions, distress tolerance, and teaching practices. Other programs incorporated elements of mental health literacy, such as improving teachers' knowledge and confidence to support their own and colleagues' mental health, programs incorporating school leadership and policy changes, and evidence-based positive psychology approaches to improve teachers' wellbeing. Based on the results of this review, Berger et al. (2022c) concluded that there is a lack of high-quality, evidence-based programs designed to promote teachers' and especially early childhood educators' wellbeing. The results of this review also align with previous research showing the lack of trauma-informed interventions to support teachers' wellbeing when exposed to traumatized students (Berger, 2019).

Trauma-Informed Interventions for Teachers

Unfortunately, there is currently a lack of trauma-informed programs specifically designed to address the mental health and wellbeing needs of teachers and other staff in schools (Berger et al., 2022c). The majority of trauma-informed research and programs in schools focus on teachers' capacity, knowledge, and skills to respond to students exposed to trauma (Berger, 2019) and the emotional toll that exposure to traumatized students can have on teachers and other school staff (Alisic, 2012).

The ERASE-Stress program was designed to provide psychoeducation, mindfulness approaches, and art-therapy to improve the emotional wellbeing of teachers in response to the Christchurch earthquake in New Zealand. Research evaluating the ERASE-Stress program revealed that the program decreased symptoms of posttraumatic stress and secondary trauma and improved levels of optimism and positive coping strategies among teachers (Berger et al., 2016). Davis et al. (2023) implemented a trauma-informed yoga program with teachers in the United States and found that the program reduced symptoms of depression, anxiety, burnout, and trauma among teachers and increased their resilience, self-efficacy, and quality of sleep. Finally, Kim et al. (2021) evaluated a trauma-informed mindfulness program with teachers in the United States, designed to increase teachers' social, emotional, and coping capacity, and found the program decreased levels of emotional exhaustion, and improved self-efficacy and personal sense of accomplishment among teachers. These are examples of the small number of programs that have focused on increasing teachers' capacity to cope with the emotional burdens of working with students exposed to trauma. There continues to be a notable lack of trauma-informed programs and policies in schools focused on enhancing the wellbeing and coping strategies of teachers in response to student trauma.

Case Study of Support for Teachers in Response to Student Trauma

The following case study illustrates an interaction between a secondary school teacher and students exposed to trauma in Australia, with the aim of highlighting the support provided to her at an individual, leadership, and whole-school level. Names have been redacted to protect the privacy and anonymity of individuals mentioned in the case study.

> A classroom teacher teaching a senior secondary school class was stood over, verbally abused, and sworn at on two separate occasions by two separate students as a result of her respectfully challenging behaviors exhibited by the students in the classroom. Both students had a history of significant trauma and had been continually exposed to several adverse events, including parental substance abuse, familial mental health problems, emotional, physical, mental, and verbal abuse, as well as neglect, and frequent family breakdown (at times resulting in having to leave the family home for a period). This classroom teacher was significantly impacted by these two interactions and became visibly distressed after she had experienced these events. She approached members of the leadership team for support and advice on how to proceed. The following actions were put into place to support the classroom teacher's wellbeing.

Individual Support

The classroom teacher identified that they needed to take a day of personal leave to take care of their own mental health. This was supported and encouraged by the leadership team.

The classroom teacher was encouraged to seek support from the Employee Assistance Program[1] created for education staff to access counseling and debriefing when needed.

School Response to Events

Leadership members spoke to both the classroom teacher and the students involved to obtain an accurate and objective account of the events that had occurred.

Leadership members reinforced to the classroom teacher that they had followed the appropriate school process when challenging the behavior of the students.

Conversations were held with both students separately by members of the leadership team. These conversations occurred with curiosity, empathy, and with the aim to understand what was possibly sitting behind the verbal outbursts so that appropriate supports could be identified and put in place for them. These conversations also created a learning opportunity for the students to reflect on how they could respond to similar interactions in the future.

Where appropriate, parent meetings were held so that parents and school staff could work together in setting up supports and expectations for the students moving forward.

Restorative conversations were held between the students and the classroom teacher when the teacher was ready, which was facilitated by a member of the Leadership Team.

The classroom teacher was checked on by members of the Leadership Team across a couple of days to ensure they felt supported in returning to work.

Whole-School Policies and Ongoing Supports for Staff Wellbeing

The Leadership Team has a common aim of ensuring a strong and positive presence within the school community with the aim of building up positive connections with students as well as maintaining high expectations across the school. Examples of this include members of the Leadership Team based at the school gates every morning ready to greet and interact with the students at the start of the school day, leadership members having a strong and consistent presence across the school day, and leadership members organizing school events for students to attend (i.e., dodgeball games, staff vs. student sporting games).

Pre-conditions for learning have been set up to ensure students are "Ready to Learn". These are clearly and frequently communicated out to the school community using positive and explicit language. The pre-conditions were created to set clear expectations for students and their parents/carers around what is required of them so that they are ready to learn. By having these in place, the responsibility of high expectations sits across multiple parties and not just on the classroom teacher. Explicit teaching of the pre-conditions has allowed for classroom teachers to have a greater sense of predictability and control in their day as well as being able to share the responsibility of preparing students for learning; resulting in less stress and mental load. Students have also provided positive feedback on the pre-conditions for learning as they feel more equipped in knowing what is expected of them and what actions will occur if they choose not to follow the policy.

Consequences for repetitive student behavioral concerns are not the responsibility of the classroom teacher. This responsibility sits with leadership to ensure that classroom teachers can focus on the teaching and learning, and general wellbeing of the student. This process has also assisted classroom teachers in building up positive relationships with students which has helped both students and teachers to feel connected.

Classroom Removals Process – this is an immediate response by the leadership team for those students who are presenting as dysregulated in the classroom and in-classroom responses are not proving to be successful. Upon removal, students have the opportunity for a reset where they get to walk and talk, have a check-in with the leadership staff,; and (if appropriate) a discussion is had around expected behaviors, resulting in time for the student to reflect and co-regulate before being reintroduced back into the classroom.

A well-resourced and skilled school team – this includes increased time provided for planning, creation of individual support plans, and student/parent meetings; and multiple and varied opportunities for professional learning so that teachers feel confident to respond to students using a trauma-informed approach. A recent example of professional development focused on how to put in place a clear, consistent, and thorough support plan that is both proactive and responsive for students who had engaged in disruptive or inappropriate behavior.

Frequent check-ins with identified students post-incident to ensure that appropriate support is provided for them based on their point of need (i.e., learning support, mental health support, employment/careers support, mentorship/connection). These supports are identified and enacted to reduce future dysregulation in the classroom, thereby protecting the wellbeing of the classroom teachers.

A well-resourced and multidisciplinary wellbeing team to support the more significant mental health concerns of students. A clear referral pathway exists for teachers which is easy to access.

Frequent professional development run by wellbeing-trained staff for classroom teachers on identifying and responding to initial student wellbeing concerns as well as what processes to follow to ensure appropriate wellbeing supports are put in place. These sessions always include a focus on reminding staff around what they can do to personally take care of their own wellbeing if needed.

Recommendations for Addressing Teacher Wellbeing

1. *Incorporate teacher wellbeing into school policies and practices*

   The first recommendation is for schools and education departments to better incorporate and prioritize teacher wellbeing within existing trauma-informed models and programs. Evidence shows that student wellbeing and learning are dependent on the wellbeing of teachers, and teachers' wellbeing can be severely impacted by their interactions with traumatized students (Berger & Nott, 2022). Thus, incorporating teacher wellbeing policies and practices into school trauma-informed frameworks and programs is of vital importance. This will also ensure there is an organizational culture which overtly acknowledges, supports, and resources trauma-informed practice.

2. *Incorporate different levels of support for teachers and other school staff*

   Evidence shows that all school staff, including teachers, school leaders, and school mental health staff require professional development and support when managing the needs of students exposed to trauma (Alisic, 2012; Berger et al., 2021). The professional development and support required by teachers may be dependent on the types of interactions and frequency of their interactions with students exposed to trauma. This will ensure that trauma-informed interventions are timely, flexible, and responsive. Therefore, school policy and practices should consider the different roles and responsibilities of staff when planning professional learning and support for teachers and other school staff in response to traumatized students. Evidence also shows that younger teachers, teachers with fewer years of experience, and teachers with higher exposure to student trauma, with their own exposure to trauma, and/or with their own history of mental illness, are at greater risk of negative mental health outcomes when exposed to students who have experienced trauma (Berger & Nott, 2023). Thus, professional development, support, and school policies which acknowledge that some teachers may be at a greater risk of poor mental health in response to traumatized students are required.

3. *Develop policies and interventions which acknowledge the multifaceted role of teachers in response to student trauma*

   Teachers hold varied roles and responsibilities when responding to students exposed to trauma. Teachers may be responsible for making classroom adjustments, managing the needs of families exposed to trauma, or responsible for referring students exposed to trauma to mental health professionals. These are some examples of the many different roles teachers play when supporting students exposed to trauma. It is essential that school policies and processes acknowledge and provide advice and services to support teachers when undertaking these varied roles in response to student trauma.

4. *Develop policies and interventions to support teachers from marginalized groups and exposed to their own traumatic events*

   Evidence shows that teachers from marginalized backgrounds, including Aboriginal and Torres Strait Islander teachers, teachers from culturally and linguistically diverse groups, teachers located in regional and rural areas, and LGBTQIA+ educators are at greater risk of discrimination in the workplace and mental ill-health compared to teachers not from these groups (Hine et al., 2022). Therefore, school trauma-informed policies and processes should prioritize and consider strategies to support these teachers' mental health and inclusive school environments. Teachers will also have their own experiences of trauma which may result in teachers experiencing mental ill-health or re-traumatization as a result of their exposure to details of a student's trauma (Berger & Nott, 2023). The study by Berger and Nott (2023) found that 45% of teachers reported their own experiences of trauma, and there is potential that these earlier experiences of trauma may place teachers at risk of re-traumatization and mental illness when exposed to student trauma.

5. *Ensure that policies and programs designed to address teacher wellbeing incorporate individual and systemic change*

   An important recommendation from this chapter is that teachers' wellbeing should be viewed as an individual, school, and community responsibility. Teachers' wellbeing is determined by several factors, including their own coping resources and mental health, their relationships and support provided by colleagues in schools, supportive school leadership that prioritizes the wellbeing of teachers, workload considerations that take into account the impact of excessive workloads on teacher wellbeing, school policies that center teacher wellbeing within wellbeing policies for students, and recognition and acknowledgment from the community about the essential role of teachers for the community (Hine et al., 2022; Berger et al., 2022b). Unfortunately, the evidence and approaches to address teacher wellbeing have focused on what teachers can do to support their own wellbeing, with limited programs focused on improving school and community support to ensure the wellbeing of teachers (Berger et al., 2022c). The evidence base concerning systematic school change to support teacher wellbeing in relation to student trauma and trauma-informed practice is limited and requires significant consideration.

Conclusion

There is growing consensus that teacher wellbeing is determined by a number of personal and professional factors, such as personal coping strategies, workload demands, and positive workplace culture. However, there is a recognized lack of school programs and policies designed to promote and maintain teachers' wellbeing, and prevent emotional labor, burnout, and secondary trauma. The evidence presented in this chapter can be used to advocate for change and prioritize teachers' wellbeing within existing school wellbeing and mental health initiatives. Recommendations from this chapter can also be used to improve school and early childhood policies and trauma-informed approaches designed to address and improve wellbeing of all teachers, school staff, and early childhood educators.

Note

1 The Employee Assistance Program (EAP) is a free, short-term, and strictly confidential counseling service available to all Department of Education staff. This service is available 24 hours, seven days a week for up to four sessions for Department employees to discuss any personal or work-related issues.

References

Acton, R., & Glasgow, P. (2015). Teacher wellbeing in neoliberal contexts: A review of the literature. *Australian Journal of Teacher Education, 40*(8), 99–114. https://doi.org/10.14221/ajte.2015v40n8.6

Alisic, E. (2012). Teachers' perspectives on providing support to children after trauma: A qualitative study. *School Psychology Quarterly, 27*(1), 51–59. https://doi.org/10.1037/a0028590

Arens, A. K., & Morin, A. J. (2016). Relations between teachers' emotional exhaustion and students' educational outcomes. *Journal of Educational Psychology, 108*(6), 800–813. https://doi.org/10.1037/edu0000105

Ashforth, B. E., & Humphrey, R. H. (1993). Emotional labor in service roles: The influence of identity. *Academic Management Review, 18*, 88–115.

Bakker, A. B., Demerouti, E., & Verbeke, W. (2004), Using the job demands-resources model to predict burnout and performance. *Human Resources Management, 43*, 83–104. https://doi.org/10.1002/hrm.20004

Bakker, A. B., & Demerouti, E. (2008). Towards a model of work engagement. *The Career Development International, 13*(3), 209–223. https://doi.org/10.1108/13620430810870476

Bakker, A. B., & Demerouti, E. (2017). Job demands–resources theory: Taking stock and looking forward. *Journal of Occupational Health Psychology, 22*(3), 273–285. https://doi.org/10.1037/ocp0000056

Bakker, A. B., Hakanen, J. J., Demerouti, E., & Xanthopoulou, D. (2007). Job resources boost work engagement, particularly when job demands are high. *Journal of Educational Psychology, 99*(2), 274–284. https://doi.org/10.1037/0022-0663.99.2.274

Bare, K., McMahon, S. D., Gonzalez Molina, E., Tergesen, C., & Zinter, K. E. (2021). Educator experiences as victims of school violence: Emerging perspectives and research. In R. Blasdell, L. Krieger-Sample, & M. Kilburn (Eds.), *Invisible victims and the pursuit of justice: Analyzing frequently victimized yet rarely discussed populations* (pp. 1–25). IGI Global. https://www.igi-global.com/gateway/chapter/281352

Barrett, N., & Berger, E. (2021). Teachers' experiences and recommendations to support refugee students exposed to trauma. *Social Psychology of Education, 24*, 1259–1280. https://doi.org/10.1007/s11218-021-09657-4

Berger, E. (2019). Multi-tiered approaches to trauma-informed care in schools: A systematic review. *School Mental Health, 11*, 650–664. https://doi.org/10.1007/s12310-019-09326-0

Berger, R., Abu-Raiya, H., & Benatov, J. (2016). Reducing primary and secondary traumatic stress symptoms among educators by training them to deliver a resiliency program (ERASE-Stress) following the Christchurch earthquake in New Zealand. *The American Journal of Orthopsychiatry, 86*(2), 236–251. https://doi.org/10.1037/ort0000153

Berger, E., Bearsley, A., & Lever, M. (2021). Qualitative evaluation of teacher trauma knowledge and response in schools. *Journal of Aggression, Maltreatment & Trauma, 30*(8), 1041–1057. https://doi.org/10.1080/10926771.2020.1806976

Berger, E., Martin, K., & Phal, A. (2022a). Dealing with student trauma: exploring school leadership experiences and impact. *Leadership and Policy in Schools, 21*(4), 780–790. https://doi.org/10.1080/15700763.2020.1836231

Berger, E., & Nott, D. (2023). Predictors of compassion fatigue and compassion satisfaction among Australian teachers. *Psychological Trauma: Theory, Research, Practice, and Policy*. Advance online publication. https://doi.org/10.1037/tra0001573

Berger, E., Quiñones, G., Barnes, M., & Reupert, A. E. (2022b). Early childhood educators' psychological distress and wellbeing during the COVID-19 pandemic.

Early Childhood Research Quarterly, 60, 298–306. https://doi.org/10.1016/j.ecresq.2022.03.005

Berger, E., Reupert, A., Campbell, T. C. H., Morris, Z., Hammer, M., Diamond, Z., Hine, R., Patrick, P., & Fathers, C. (2022c). A systematic review of evidence-based wellbeing initiatives for schoolteachers and early childhood educators. *Educational Psychology Review, 34*, 2919–2969. https://doi.org/10.1007/s10648-022-09690-5

Berger, E., & Samuel, S. (2020). A qualitative analysis of the experiences, training, and support needs of school mental health workers regarding student trauma. *Australian Psychologist, 55*(5), 498–507. https://doi.org/10.1111/ap.12452

Billett, P., Fogelgarn, R., & Burns, E. (2019). *Teacher targeted bullying and harassment by students and parents: Report from an Australian exploratory survey*. La Trobe University. https://doi.org/10.26181/12655880.v2

Cumming, T., & Wong, S. (2019). Towards a holistic conceptualisation of early childhood educators' work-related well-being. *Contemporary Issues in Early Childhood, 20*(3), 265–281. https://doi.org/10.1177/1463949118772573

Davis, L., Aylward, A., Scott, B. G., & Jacobs, J. (2023). "Following the Breath:" A trauma-informed intervention for educator wellness in rural montana. *Education Sciences, 13*(1), 23. https://doi.org/10.3390/educsci13010023

Del Riccio, J. (2021). Classrooms in crisis: Workplace violence and harassment experienced by educators in Ontario. *Education & Law Journal, 30*(2), 149–172. https://www.proquest.com/scholarly-journals/classrooms-crisis-workplace-violence-harassment/docview/2575543812/se-2

Demerouti, E., Bakker, A. B., Nachreiner, F., & Schaufeli, W. B. (2001). The job demands-resources model of burnout. *The Journal of Applied Psychology, 86*(3), 499–512.

Fakude, X. S. (2022). Teachers' experiences of teaching learners with violent behaviour: A case of contextually selected high schools in KwaZulu-Natal. Ph.D. Thesis, University of KwaZulu-Natal, Durban, South Africa. Retrieved from https://ukzn-dspace.ukzn.ac.za/bitstream/handle/10413/21064/Fakude_Xolani_Simangaye_2022.pdf?sequence=1&isAllowed=y

Govender, K. (2015). Primary school teachers' experiences of violence towards them perpetrated by learners. Master's Thesis, University of KwaZulu-Natal, Durban, South Africa. Retrieved from https://ukzn-dspace.ukzn.ac.za/bitstream/handle/10413/15383/Govender_Komashni_2015.pdf?sequence=1&isAllowed=y

Granziera, H., Collie, R., & Martin, A. (2021). Understanding teacher wellbeing through job demands-resources theory. In C. F. Mansfield (Ed.), *Cultivating teacher resilience*. Springer. https://doi.org/10.1007/978-981-15-5963-1_14

Harr, C., Brice, T., Riley, K., & Moore, B. (2014). The impact of compassion fatigue and compassion satisfaction on social work students during field internship: An exploratory study. *Journal of the Society for Social Work and Research, 5*, 233–251. https://doi.org/10.1086/676518

Holt, A., & Birchall, J. (2022). *Violence towards teaching/classroom assistants in mainstream UK schools: Research findings and recommendations*. University of

Roehampton. Retrieved from https://pure.roehampton.ac.uk/ws/files/8540822/Holt_Birchall_2022_ViolenceTowardsTAs_Summary_Report_FINAL.pdf

Hydon, S., Wong, M., Langley, A. K., Stein, B. D., & Kataoka, S. H. (2015). Preventing secondary traumatic stress in educators. *Child and Adolescent Psychiatric Clinic of North America, 24*, 319–333. https://doi.org/10.1016/j.chc.2014.11.003

Harding, S., Morris, R., Gunnell, D., Ford, T., Hollingworth, W., Tilling, K., Evans, R., Bell, S., Grey, J., Brockman, R., Campbell, R., Araya, R., Murphy, S., & Kidger, J. (2019). Is teachers' mental health and wellbeing associated with students' mental health and wellbeing? *Journal of Affective Disorders, 242*, 180–187. https://doi.org/10.1016/j.jad.2018.08.080

Hine, R., Patrick, P., Berger, E., Diamond, Z., Hammer, M., Morris, Z. A., Fathers, C., & Reupert, A. (2022). From struggling to flourishing and thriving: Optimizing educator wellbeing within the Australian education context. *Teaching and Teacher Education, 115*, 1–12. https://doi.org/10.1016/j.tate.2022.103727

Hochschild, A. R. (1983). *The managed heart: Commercialization of human feeling*. University of California Press.

Howard, J. A. (2019). A systemic framework for trauma-informed schooling: Complex but necessary! *Journal of Aggression, Maltreatment & Trauma, 28*(5), 545–565. https://doi.org/10.1080/10926771.2018.1479323

Jeung, D. Y., Kim, C., & Chang, S. J. (2018). Emotional labor and burnout: A review of the literature. *Yonsei Medical Journal, 59*(2), 187–193. https://doi.org/10.3349/ymj.2018.59.2.187

Kim, S., Crooks, C. V., Bax, K., & Shokoohi, M. (2021). Impact of trauma-informed training and mindfulness-based social–emotional learning program on teacher attitudes and burnout: A mixed-methods study. *School Mental Health, 13*(1), 55–68. https://doi.org/10.1007/s12310-020-09406-6

Liu, S., & Onwuegbuzie, A. J. (2012). Chinese teachers' work stress and their turnover intention. *International Journal of Educational Research, 53*, 160–170. https://doi.org/10.1016/j.ijer.2012.03.006

McCallum, F., & Price, D. (2016). *Nurturing wellbeing development in education*. Routledge.

McCallum, F., Price, D., Graham, A., & Morrison, A. (2017). *Teacher wellbeing: A review of the literature*. The Association of Independent Schools of New South Wales Limited.

Price, D., & McCallum, F. (2015). Ecological influences on teachers' well-being and "fitness." *Asia-Pacific Journal of Teacher Education, 43*(3), 195–209. https://doi.org/10.1080/1359866X.2014.932329

Quiñones, G., Barnes, M., & Berger, E. (2022). Australian early childhood educators' emotional support to families and children during COVID-19 pandemic. In O. N. Saracho (Ed.), *Contemporary perspectives on research on coronavirus disease 2019 (COVID-19) in early childhood education* (1st ed., pp. 87–103). Information Age Publishing.

Reupert, A. (2020). *Mental health and academic learning in schools: Approaches for facilitating the wellbeing of children and young people*. Routledge.

Ribeiro, B. M. D. S. S., Martins, J. T., Moreira, A. A. O., Galdino, M. J. Q., Lourenço, M. D. C. F. H., & Dalri, R. D. C. D. M. B. (2022). Association between burnout syndrome and workplace violence in teachers. *Acta Paulista de Enfermagem, 35*, eAPE01902.

Riley, P. (2018). *The Australian principal occupational health, safety and wellbeing survey 2018 data*. Australian Catholic University.

Stamm, B. H. (2002). Measuring compassion satisfaction as well as fatigue: Developmental history of the compassion satisfaction and fatigue test. In C. R. Figley (Ed.), *Treating compassion fatigue* (pp. 107–119). Routledge. https://doi.org/10.4324/9780203890318

Stamm, B. H. (2010). *The concise ProQOL manual*. Retrieved 1 December 2021 from https://proqol.org/proqol-manual

Seligman, M. E., & Csikszentmihalyi, M. (2000). *Positive psychology: An introduction* (Vol. 55, No. 1). American Psychological Association.

Shea, T., Sheehan, C., Donohue, R., Cooper, B., & De Cieri, H. (2017). Occupational violence and aggression experienced by nursing and caring professionals. *Journal of Nursing Scholarship: An Official Publication of Sigma Theta Tau International Honor Society of Nursing, 49*(2), 236–243. https://doi.org/10.1111/jnu.12272

Sigad, L. I. (2024). "I keep warning the new teachers, you'll have elephant skin": Teachers coping with physical violence perpetrated toward them by their pupils. *Journal of Family Trauma, Child Custody & Child Development, 21*(1), 76–95. https://doi.org/10.1080/26904586.2023.2202204

Skaalvik, E. M., & Skaalvik, S. (2017). Dimensions of teacher burnout: Relations with potential stressors at school. *Social Psychology of Education, 20*, 775–790. https://doi.org/10.1007/s11218-017-9391-0

Stevenson, D. J., Neill, J. T., Ball, K., Smith, R., & Shores, M. C. (2022). How do preschool to year 6 educators prevent and cope with occupational violence from students? *Australian Journal of Education, 66*(2), 154–170.

Wilson, C. M., Douglas, K. S., & Lyon, D. R. (2011). Violence against teachers: Prevalence and consequences. *Journal of Interpersonal Violence, 26*(12), 2353–2371. https://doi.org/10.1177/0886260510383027

Yang, C. (2021). Online teaching self-efficacy, social–emotional learning (SEL) competencies, and compassion fatigue among educators during the COVID-19 pandemic. *School Psychology Review, 50*, 505–518. https://doi.org/10.1080/2372966X.2021.1903815

6 Designing School-Built Environments for Trauma-Informed Education

Sophie Lea and Emily Berger

Introduction

An overlooked aspect of trauma-informed practices in schools is the impact of the school-built environment. In this chapter, we discuss the impact and importance of the school setting and how these spaces support all students' learning, specifically those requiring a trauma-informed approach. We present three major foundations of design: the physical, ambient, and aesthetic elements that should be considered when designing school-built environments, with practical and achievable recommendations for implementing a suitable trauma-informed built environment in a school setting. In architecture and design, the definition of the 'built environment' pertains to the human-created surroundings that facilitate and underpin a wide range of human activities and social interactions (Gifford, 2002; Gifford et al., 2011), for example, classrooms. Surprisingly, there exists a need for greater awareness to address the significant impact of the built environment when implementing trauma-informed practices in order to safeguard students' wellbeing (Wang et al., 2023).

Research indicates that people's interactions with the built environment can directly influence their behavior and experience (Pardeck, 1996; Wang et al., 2023). A central theoretical objective within environmental psychology is the cultivation of a built environment that promotes greater humaneness and enhances interactions between individuals and their surroundings (Gifford, 2002; Gifford et al., 2011). Ecology theory proposes that the relationship between people and their environment can be straightforward, based on cause and effect, with one condition changing another, or this

DOI: 10.4324/9781003436034-6

relationship can be transactional, whereby both elements interconnect and influence each other (Germain, 1991). Transactionalism has emerged as a fundamental theoretical perspective when assessing the impact of the physical environment on children's behavior. This perspective underscores the dynamic interplay between the built environment and children, recognizing that meaningful exchanges continually occur between a child and their physical surroundings (Gifford, 2002; Stokols, 1995; Stokols & Shumaker, 1981). Elements within the built environment, such as windows and artworks, can shape and facilitate a child's transactional response to these stimuli, informed by the environmental context (Gifford, 2002; Ungar, 2002). Considering the profound influence that the built environment wields over our responses and behaviors, there is a compelling rationale for the deliberate and thoughtful design of schools for all students.

The Importance of the School 'Built Environment'

Humans take in information, assessing surroundings and taking on meaning from essential places, which can influence their thinking and behavioral responses in different environments (Augustin et al., 2009). Attachment can be formed toward certain environments and places, known as 'place attachment,' which is described as 'the cognitive-emotional bond that forms between individuals and their important settings' (Scannell & Gifford, 2017, p. 256). Depending on the quality of the place experience, this bond can be beneficial or disruptive to children and young people's wellbeing, including their sense of self (Ranieri, 2021) and sense of belonging (Eyles & Williams, 2008; Scannell & Gifford, 2017); however, youth trauma and its impacts on place attachment are currently an emerging research field.

Behavior Setting Theory (BST), originally proposed by Roger Barker in 1968, substantiates the core premise that the specific characteristics and context of an environment, termed the 'behavior setting', exerts a significant influence on individuals' conduct and interpersonal interactions within that setting (Görlitz, 1998). As we navigate our spaces, functional issues within spaces can negatively influence our behaviors and experiences of the space. Additionally, behaviorists acknowledge that our engagement with the physical space is pivotal in shaping our socialization behaviors (Pardeck, 1996).

For example, if a classroom is too hot, it compromises students' comfort and ability to concentrate, which might increase students' irritability, reducing their tolerance toward others, and contribute to disruptive behavior and compromise students' social relationships.

Symbolic Interactionism (SI) contributes to the sociological perspectives and theoretical frameworks explaining how individuals create and interpret meaning in their social interactions. Developed primarily by George Herbert Mead (Mead & Morris, 1934) and Herbert Blumer (1969), SI emphasizes the importance of symbols, gestures, and language in shaping human behavior and social reality. SI helps us understand how people construct their sense of self and navigate and make sense of the social world around them. When applying SI to the built environment, the emphasis is on how the physical spaces and structures we inhabit are imbued with symbolic meaning and how this contributes to our social interactions and behaviors. SI in the built environment suggests that our perception of spaces, such as homes, schools, or public places, is shaped by the symbolic significance we attach to them, impacting our behaviors, identity, and social relationships within those spaces.

Knowing people interpret and develop direct associations and responses to places, young people who experience trauma are often grappling with a disrupted sense of self and security, which can mean they are more likely to interpret the built environment through the lens of their trauma (Ranieri, 2021). For example, spaces that evoke feelings of confinement or danger can perpetuate a sense of vulnerability, while environments that promote safety, comfort, and personal agency can facilitate healing and recovery. Through meticulous attention to evidence-based design principles and a specific focus on school environments, schools can craft spaces that empower and cultivate a positive self-identity among all students, particularly those exposed to trauma (Geldard et al., 2019). In the context of trauma-informed school design, the physical layout and features of educational spaces can have a profound impact on how traumatized youth perceive their safety and sense of self (Knight et al., 2018; Westergaard, 2013). Understanding how the physical environment can impact students exposed to trauma can guide the planning and construction of new school facilities or the redesign of old school facilities, ensuring they offer a sense of refuge, inclusion, and flexibility, which is important for students with a history of trauma.

The School-Built Environment and Trauma

Beyond the pursuit of academic excellence, school leadership and teaching teams acknowledge the importance of establishing safe and nurturing environments tailored to the needs of students with a history of trauma (Nicholson et al., 2023). When approaching the design of school environments, there is a need for an informed sensitivity to youth mental health and trauma history. Research has shown that those grappling with mental health challenges tend to be particularly susceptible to the impact of poorly designed surroundings (Golembiewski, 2016). Ames and Loebach (2023) stated that the role of the built environment can become 'powerfully amplified' for children and young people experiencing trauma. When children or young people perceive the school environment as a potential threat or unsafe, they instinctively initiate protective behaviors and responses. For instance, the 'fight, flight, freeze or fawn' response can be triggered, prompting children to seek escape from the setting or engage in management strategies to insulate themselves from perceived threats (Freeman & Freeman, 2008; Nicholson et al., 2023).

Research by Northoff et al. (2004) states that individuals grappling with severe mental illness and trauma exhibit heightened sensitivity to their surroundings; the built environment can either exacerbate mental health symptoms or protect children's mental health. Environmental adjustments were instituted within a trauma-informed Juvenile Justice facility in the United States (Marrow et al., 2012). These adjustments included staff training, trauma-informed group therapy, and enhancements to the built infrastructure. In addition, noise reduction through the introduction of carpeting and sound paneling, the allocation of designated areas for youth to employ coping mechanisms, changing the wall color to evoke a sense of tranquility, and comfortable furniture to promote social engagement were employed. Marrow et al. (2012) reported that these changes resulted in reduced clinical depression, anxiety symptoms, and behavioral concerns, improved optimism and hope among the youth population, and reduced the need for staff to resort to seclusion or restraint measures due to the improved emotional self-regulation capabilities exhibited by the young people.

Montero and Zouhouri (2022) advocate that schools should be seen and valued as settings that support mental health promotion, alongside playing a role in students' healing and recovery from trauma. Purposefully designed trauma-informed school spaces can play a role in supporting all students' academic learning, social communication and cohesion, and behavioral and emotional regulation (Maxwell & Schechtman, 2012; Montero & Zouhouri, 2022; Nicholson et al., 2023). Research has found that young people function within ecological systems and develop connections with their essential places, particularly their home and school, due to the time spent in these settings. A study by Wang et al. (2023) identified the importance of a trauma-informed physical environment to remove triggers and facilitate a welcoming and secure space for people exposed to trauma. One participant stated:

> Trauma-informed practice means being aware and sensitive to the client's presentation and needs. It's about providing a safe (physically and emotionally) and culturally appropriate environment. It's providing choice to the client, and working collaboratively with them. And empowering them in their recovery journey.
>
> (Wang et al., 2023, p. 24)

The Physical, Ambient, and Aesthetic Environment

The physical, ambient, and aesthetic components of school-built environments have been found to influence young people's wellbeing and academic performance directly (Earthman et al., 1995; Maxwell & Schechtman, 2012; Whipple et al., 2010) and contribute to both children's positive and negative associations and experiences of a particular place (Maxwell & Schechtman, 2012; Northoff et al., 2004; Rossen et al., 2020). For example, Rossen et al.'s (2020) research on trauma-informed school design recommends that teachers address common trauma triggers for students by providing an open seating plan to reduce feelings of entrapment and the provision of 'reregulation' safe spaces where children can de-escalate. However, as illustrated throughout this chapter, the need for quiet physical spaces for students to de-escalate and regulate their emotions is also essential when creating trauma-informed school settings. The remainder of this chapter will outline three components for creating trauma-informed built school environments. These three specific built environment components can provide us with a guiding framework to assess and facilitate school spaces purposeful design and function to address the needs of students who have experienced trauma.

Physical Spaces

A trauma-informed school needs to begin with the physical space, which aims to provide students with physical and psychological safety (Earthman et al., 1995; Maxwell & Schechtman, 2012; Whipple et al., 2010). When designing optimal built spaces, there needs to be a consideration of its users' mental health. Golembiewski (2016) suggests improving or removing built environments that may trigger negative emotional reactions and distress of people using the space. Students experiencing trauma may encounter a range of triggers that can significantly impact them psychologically and compromise their ability to function optimally in an educational setting. Trauma triggers among students can vary widely but often include situations or stimuli that remind them of the traumatic event (Brewer-Smyth, 2022). These triggers can include loud noises (e.g., school bell), crowded or cramped school settings (e.g., school assembly), or crowded, overstimulated classrooms (Evans et al., 1998). Some triggers can be subtler for students, such as their proximity to classroom entry and exit doors, including preferences of students to be seated near open or closed classroom doors, or their preference to face toward open or closed classroom doors (Rossen et al., 2020). Creating an emotionally and physically safe and supportive environment that acknowledges and accommodates students' trauma triggers has been shown to help them cope in different environments and improve academically (Earthman et al., 1995; Maxwell & Schechtman, 2012; Whipple et al., 2010).

In addition, specific classroom building features, including adjustable lighting, coverable windows, and easily movable comfortable seating have also been suggested to assist with achieving a soothing and conducive learning environment that can adapt to the needs of students and teachers (Kaplan, 2001; Pressly & Heesacker, 2001; Rossen et al., 2020). Primary and secondary schools have increasingly focused on accommodating students' emotional needs by creating allocated safe 'calming' spaces within the classroom or a designated room in the school setting that students can easily access (see Figures 6.1 and 6.2). These safe and 'calm corners' (Berger, 2018) provide a quieter, relaxing environment that facilitates opportunities for students to de-escalate behavioral and emotional responses, while also allowing students to remain in the classroom (Baroni et al., 2020) connected to the teacher and able to re-engage with their learning once soothed.

Figure 6.1 The 'calm corner' in an Australian primary school classroom

Implementing *hygge* in these calm corners and the wider school environment can help soothe students. Hygge originates from a Danish concept emphasizing coziness, comfort, and a sense of togetherness (Wiking, 2017), creating an atmosphere that promotes physical and emotional comfort. In a school setting, this can be achieved by incorporating warm and inviting elements such as soft lighting, comfortable seating, calm color palettes, cozy decorative items, and natural materials.

Weighted blankets, fidget toys, and noise-canceling headphones are popular items provided in varied calming spaces and rooms in school settings to support neurodivergent and trauma-experienced young people. Creating soothing spaces in the classroom or a nearby location monitored by staff, where students can implement their coping strategies and access items that help them relax, connect, and engage in meaningful activities, can reduce school stressors and improve self-regulation and feelings of safety and security at school.

Figure 6.2 The 'chill out' room in an Australian secondary school

Ambient Spaces

To support teachers in implementing classroom conditions that provide their students with optimal conditions to learn and engage with peers, the ambient attributes of sound, temperature, and lighting are fundamental elements to address (Wineman & Barnes, 2018). The ambient interplay between elements, including fluctuating temperature, lighting changes, and noise management, is relevant to trauma-informed schools, given that the impact of the ambient environment on students' behavior can directly affect their comfort, security, and psychological wellbeing (Xiong et al., 2018).

Temperature and thermal comfort are key ambient factors to manage for a functional school setting. Frontczak and Wargocki (2011) define optimum thermal comfort as a building in which the 'user will wish to feel neither warmer nor cooler if asked about thermal state and preference' (p. 4); they conclude that temperature is frequently viewed as the most crucial aspect of ambient comfort. Research suggests that uncomfortable temperatures can be a thermal stressor if a room is too hot or cold (Anderson et al., 2000; Patterson & Quadflieg, 2015). The repercussions of experiencing higher than preferred temperature include a reduction in concentration energy, increased feelings of hostility, and possible escalation of disruptive behavior (Anderson et al., 2000). Pressly and Heesacker (2001) determine that most people feel comfortable with a temperature range of 20.5–26.6 degrees Celsius, with 30–60% relative humidity.

Sounds and noise levels are also aspects of our ambient ecosystem that require attention (Iyendo et al., 2016). Research has found that one of the most significant environmental impacts on mental health is the negative impact of noise exposure (Evans, 2003). Intrusive external noise within school environments can range from annoying and exhausting to a trauma-triggering stressor (Blomkvist et al., 2005). Providing ambient background music of nature sounds can be psychologically soothing, reducing depression and anxiety symptoms (Biley, 1996; Caspari et al., 2010; Robertson, 2001). Providing structural soundproofing, carpeted flooring, and numerous indoor plants has also been shown to reduce noise and dull classroom acoustics (Biley, 1996; Han, 2009).

Ideally, schools should provide natural, non-fluorescent lighting and a pleasant classroom window views (Lawson, 2010). Windows have importance partly because their view can positively shift attention, providing respite from thinking and reducing stress (Kaplan & Kaplan, 1989; Kaplan, 2001; Ulrich, 1984). Kaplan and Kaplan's (1989) research concludes that when cognitive fatigue is experienced in a more relaxed setting, like a room with a nice window view, it can replenish and restore focus and attention. Benfield et al.'s (2015) research concluded that students reported higher ratings toward their learning experiences when in a classroom with a natural view, compared to learning in a classroom without one. Including windows improves mood and contributes to reduced stress and fatigue (Kaplan, 2001; La Torre, 2006; Lawson, 2010; Ulrich, 1984; Ulrich et al., 1993).

Aesthetic Spaces

When considering the aesthetics of the school-built environment from a trauma-informed viewpoint, it is helpful to be aware that the aesthetic environment can positively and negatively influence students' feelings, thoughts, and associations (Caspari et al., 2011; Golembiewski, 2016).

'Aesthetics' refers to a person's experienced sensory perception, including an appreciation and criticism of what is considered beautiful.

Unsuitable color palettes can increase children's arousal and stress when experiencing school spaces. Ou and Luo's (2006) research findings reported that blue was often selected as the most harmonious color, and red was the least. Blue and green hues have also been found to elicit reduced arousal and aggressive behaviors, and an improved sense of calm and relaxation for people in hospital settings (Mazuch & Rona, 2005). Liu et al. (2014) conducted a mixed-method study measuring optimal color design, finding that blue and green were preferred colors for males and females among all age groups. Children report associations of positive emotions with light colors and negative emotions with dark colors (Dalke et al., 2005; Pressly & Heesacker, 2001). Color harmony principles applied in school settings suggest preference for lighter blues and greens, with greys, purples, and reds less commonly used in school classroom design (Biley, 1996; Liu et al., 2014; Ou & Luo, 2006). Overall, it is reasonable to conclude that color preferences are somewhat subjective, but it is useful to be aware of the possible psychological effects of color choice in trauma-informed school design.

Exposure to the natural environment and its influence on mental health are relevant to schools. Outdoor spaces influence our mental health, with a lack of green spaces and poor walkability in nature being associated with depression (Gong et al., 2016). Neighborhood noise, artificial light exposure, and proximity to polluting traffic are associated with stress among young people; green spaces may buffer such effects (Dreger et al., 2015; Franklin et al., 2020). In addition, regular exposure to green space (e.g., parks, playgrounds) is associated with less psychological distress and anger (Bowler et al., 2010; Klompmaker et al., 2019), and specifically, exposure to green spaces in schools supports primary-aged children's cognitive development (Dadvand et al., 2015).

Nature interactions can provide a stress buffer and regulate mood (Beute & de Kort, 2014) and can be experienced in both outdoor and indoor settings wherever nature elements are provided. Potthoff (1995) evaluated adolescents' satisfaction with the interior design of drug and alcohol treatment facilities, concluding that adolescent patients responded favorably to rooms with plants and recognizable artworks. Studies have concluded that plants enhance the aesthetic look and attractiveness of indoor spaces and are a cost-effective way to improve their appeal (Park & Mattson, 2009).

Research conducted in Taiwanese high school classrooms found that adding plants in the classroom improved students' comfort and increased friendliness (Han, 2009).

Practical Recommendations

Implementing a trauma-informed school-built environment conducive to optimal learning, socialization, and psychological wellness for all students, specifically those who have experienced trauma, is beneficial. Golembiewski (2016) suggests removing any built environment attributes that may be triggering and focus on elevating built environment elements that promote a sense of safety, comfort, learning, and engagement for all students. Understandably, optimum results will occur when school infrastructure is architecturally designed from the ground up, but realistically, most schools do not have the luxury of being in this position. Making some achievable adjustments to classroom spaces with a trauma-informed design focus can improve the benefits and functionality of the spaces for both students and teachers.

Key Recommendations to Improve the School-Built Environment

1. *Safety and Privacy*

    - Provide a spatial flow between buildings, inside the classroom, and in playgrounds, which allows groups of students to move freely about safely.
    - All users of school buildings need to be able to view clear signage indicating exit, entry, and emergency gathering points.
    - In classrooms, a clear delineation between learning and regulation spaces is required; furniture, bookshelves, and flooring can create specific zones. Structuring the classroom space into specific zones gives students a choice between privacy and interaction, and allows teachers to monitor individual students' needs while supervising the whole class.
    - Expansive open-plan classrooms can be overwhelming to students experiencing trauma. Implementing a 'calm corner' provides a place

for students to be reflective, implement self-soothing strategies, and provides privacy, but it is still accessible by the teacher.

- Consider the type of noise and foot traffic that may occur throughout the school day. Include adjustable window blinds for required privacy and temperature control and implement soundproofing to reduce the impact of external noise and distractions.

2. *Ambient Comfort*

- The temperate climate in learning and play areas substantially impacts students' learning and psychological wellbeing. The temperature of indoor spaces needs to be comfortable, with adjustable sources of heating and cooling that can be easily controlled, and ideally, classrooms should have access to fresh air through open windows and doors.
- Playground areas need to facilitate shade and sheltered areas from the changing weather, which allow students to regulate temperature and manage their comfort when needed.
- Natural light sources are preferred in all indoor buildings through windows. Fluorescent lighting is the least conducive to learning, with dimmable LED downlights a suitable option for classroom spaces.

3. *Functional Comfort*

- Consideration of students' age and stage of development should inform what types of seating they may require.
- Classroom seating for desk or table learning must be comfortable and easily movable. Memory foam seating, beanbags, and chairs that rock gently can assist with relaxation and regulation.
- Along with the seating choice, the way the seating is arranged in learning and social spaces informs the preferred behaviors of its users. Sociopetal spaces are designed to bring people together (e.g., table groups), and sociofugal spaces are designed to reduce the contact between people (e.g., book nooks). Ideally, schools and classrooms need to provide both.
- In classrooms, numerous seating configurations exist, from individual seats in rows to double horseshoe patterns, in which rows of tables and chairs are arranged in a horseshoe pattern, nested within each other. Being flexible rather than fixed in classroom seating

arrangements can be suitable for students experiencing trauma, giving them the agency to adjust their seating position depending on the learning task. However, monitoring a class's dynamics and group needs is an ongoing process, and having allocated seating at particular times of the day may be warranted.

- Students experiencing trauma can be highly responsive to the way the seating is arranged in a classroom; feelings of entrapment or high exposure are common; the calm corner provides a place of retreat. Each classroom and school setting that a student interacts with (e.g., different classrooms for different school subjects, sports, and recreation facilities in schools) should be assessed for suitability and potential triggering elements for students who have experienced trauma.
- Playgrounds are often busy and noisy and can be intense and overwhelming; a balance of active and sedentary zones allows students to be selective in how they engage with the playground space.

4. *Inclusive Design*

- A trauma-informed school needs to support students' functional relationships and contribute to an inclusive environment for all, encouraging healthy socialization between students and staff. Students may require quite time and space away from peers and teachers to encourage healthy school relationships. Students may also benefit from collaboration with teachers during allocation of classroom seating plans and desk arrangements.
- Consideration for the naming of spaces (e.g., wellbeing hub) can help to clarify the built space's identity and eliminate associated stigmas that could prevent students from accessing spaces when required.
- Accessibility needs (e.g., wheelchair use) in the school setting and how a variety of students experience the school space, from a physical perspective, particularly bathrooms and outdoor areas, need attention.
- Bathroom spaces can be triggering and a stressor for many vulnerable students. Providing multiple locations and choices and permission to access the bathroom at differing points of the day can significantly reduce student anxiety and stress.

5. *Aesthetic Design*

    - The intention and tone of a trauma-informed school setting are partly created by the aesthetic design of the built environment. Welcoming signage and positive messaging in posters and artworks support students' feelings of belonging and inclusion. Trauma-informed cultural inclusion and safety can be promoted through displaying artwork, flags, and celebrating culturally significant days in schools (Miller & Berger, 2022).
    - Soothing, natural color palettes with pops of primary color to add energy and vibrancy in specific classroom learning areas are recommended. Acknowledge that color and decorative items can be subjective; however, accents of color and personality can be provided to the school space by including artworks, furnishings, and plants, which can be interchangeable.
    - A balance of soothing and productive learning spaces can be delineated using practical (e.g., chairs, desks) and soft furnishings (e.g., cushions, decorative items). Overall, schools should aim to find a balance between school settings which are educational, soothing, and personable, and setting that are not too sterile, but not too cluttered.

6. *Resources*

    - Investing in a variety of affordable resources in school spaces can effectively support students when they require tools to implement to manage their trauma triggers and assist with emotional regulation.
    - The inclusion of weighted blankets and lap pads for student use can be beneficial. These apply a deep, soothing pressure which can regulate breathing and reduce heart rate, helping manage feelings of being overwhelmed and supporting focus and concentration. Accurate weight-to-size ratios are important to consider, and not all students experience benefits from their use.
    - Easily accessible sensory and neurodivergent toys, such as stress balls, fidget spinners, glitter wands, and headphones, can support individual students' need to regulate and re-engage with learning and social interaction.
    - Calming soft music sets a tone of intention, which can help all students settle into the new school day or re-focus after an active lunchtime play.

7. *Nature Elements*

- Natural elements and exposure to nature to assist with improved feelings of wellbeing provide respite from stress and contribute to trauma healing or management. Given that nature is restorative, its inclusion in a trauma-informed school is paramount.
- Windows are particularly beneficial in facilitating natural light and fresh air to assist with temperature control, and an outlook for respite.
- The inclusion of indoor plants to purify the air, while fake plants can also provide aesthetic appeal. Both options bring the natural world into learning spaces.
- The value of outdoor green spaces for play, exercise, productive socialization, and tranquility and calmness for students cannot be underestimated. Berger et al. (2018) reported on the benefits of outdoor experiences for students exposed to trauma to regulate their emotions and re-engage in classroom activities.

Conclusion

By recognizing the prevalence of students with a history of trauma and the potential impact of the school's physical surroundings on their wellbeing and educational experiences, school leaders are presented with a significant opportunity to implement functional changes to the built environment. When schools are attentive to trauma-informed design, students find themselves in an environment that prioritizes their unique wellbeing needs, contributing to improved academic performance, classroom engagement, enhanced social interactions, suitable emotional response management, and an increased sense of belonging.

Prioritizing trauma-informed design principles benefits not only students with trauma histories but the entire school community. By creating an environment that is sensitive to the needs of those who have experienced trauma, educators can simultaneously cultivate a setting that promotes safety, comfort, improved learning, and achievement for all. The positive implications of this approach extend far beyond just accommodating a specific group of students; it transcends to enhance the educational experience and mental wellbeing of every individual within a school environment.

In essence, the significance of adopting a trauma-informed perspective in evaluating and shaping the school-built environment is a commitment to creating a space where the physical, emotional, and psychological wellbeing of all students (and staff) is considered paramount. It is an investment in the future, where new schools and school facilities can evolve into places of tranquility, optimum learning, and transformative and inclusive educational environments that benefit the wellbeing and success of every student.

References

Ames, R. L., & Loebach, J. E. (2023). Applying trauma-informed design principles to therapeutic residential care facilities to reduce retraumatization and promote resiliency among youth in care. *Journal of Child & Adolescent Trauma, 16*(4), 805–817. https://doi.org/10.1007/s40653-023-00528-y

Anderson, C. A., Anderson, K. B., Dorr, N., DeNeve, K. M., & Flanagan, M. (2000). Temperature and aggression. *Advances in Experimental Social Psychology, 32,* 63–133.

Augustin, S., Frankel, N., & Coleman, C. (2009). *Place advantage: Applied psychology for interior architecture*. John Wiley & Sons.

Barker, R. G. (1968). *Ecological psychology: Concepts and methods for studying the environment of human behavior*. Standford University Press.

Baroni, B., Day, A., Somers, C., Crosby, S., & Pennefather, M. (2020). Use of the monarch room as an alternative to suspension in addressing school discipline issues among court-involved youth. *Urban Education, 55*(1), 153–173. https://doi.org/10.1177/0042085916651321

Benfield, J. A., Rainbolt, G. N., Bell, P. A., & Donovan, G. H. (2015). Classrooms with nature views: Evidence of differing student perceptions and behaviors. *Environment and Behavior, 47*(2), 140–157. https://doi.org/10.1177/0013916513499583

Berger, E., Carroll, M., Maybery, D., & Harrison, D. (2018). Disaster impacts on students and staff from a specialist, trauma-informed Australian school. *Journal of Child and Adolescent Trauma, 11*(4), 521–530. https://doi.org/10.1007/s40653-018-0228-6

Berger, T. (2018, February 5). An inside look at trauma-informed practices. *Edutopia*. https://www.edutopia.org/article/inside-look-trauma-informed-practices

Beute, F., & de Kort, Y. A. W. (2014). Natural resistance: Exposure to nature and self-regulation, mood, and physiology after ego-depletion. *Journal of Environmental Psychology, 40,* 167–178. https://doi.org/10.1016/j.jenvp.2014.06.004

Biley, F. C. (1996). Hospitals: Healing environments? *Complementary Therapies in Nursing & Midwifery, 2*(4), 110–115. https://doi.org/10.1016/S1353-6117(96)80087-4

Blomkvist, V., Eriksen, C. A., Theorell, T., Ulrich, R., & Rasmanis, G. (2005). Acoustics and psychosocial environment in intensive coronary care. *Occupational and Environmental Medicine, 62*(3), e1. https://doi.org/10.1136/oem.2004.017632

Blumer, H. (1969). *Symbolic interactionism: Perspective and method*. https://edisciplinas.usp.br/pluginfile.php/2747599/mod_folder/content/0/COMPLEMENTAR%20-%201969%20-%20Blumer%20-%20Symbolic%20Interactionism.pdf

Bowler, D. E., Buyung-Ali, L. M., Knight, T. M., & Pullin, A. S. (2010). A systematic review of evidence for the added benefits to health of exposure to natural environments. *BMC Public Health, 10*, 456. https://doi.org/10.1186/1471-2458-10-456

Brewer-Smyth, K. (2022). Adverse childhood experiences and neurodevelopment. In *Adverse childhood experiences*. Springer. https://doi.org/10.1007/978-3-031-08801-8_2

Caspari, S., Eriksson, K., & Nåden, D. (2011). The importance of aesthetic surroundings: A study interviewing experts within different aesthetic fields. *Scandinavian Journal of Caring Sciences, 25*(1), 134–142. https://doi.org/10.1111/j.1471-6712.2010.00803.x

Dadvand, P., Nieuwenhuijsen, M. J., Esnaola, M., Forns, J., Basagaña, X., Alvarez-Pedrerol, M., Rivas, I., López-Vicente, M., De Castro Pascual, M., Su, J., Jerrett, M., Querol, X., & Sunyer, J. (2015). Green spaces and cognitive development in primary schoolchildren. *Proceedings of the National Academy of Sciences – PNAS, 112*(26), 7937–7942. https://doi.org/10.1073/pnas.1503402112

Dalke, H., Little, J., Niemann, E., Camgoz, N., Steadman, G., Hill, S., & Stott, L. (2005). Colour and lighting in hospital design. *Optics and Laser Technology, 38*(4–6), 343. https://doi.org/10.1016/j.optlastec.2005.06.040

Dreger, S., Meyer, N., Fromme, H., Bolte, G., & Study Group of the GME Cohort. (2015). Environmental noise and incident mental health problems: A prospective cohort study among school children in Germany. *Environmental Research, 143* (Pt A), 49–54. https://doi.org/10.1016/j.envres.2015.08.003

Earthman, G. I., Cash, C. S., & Van Berkurn, D. (1995). *A statewide study of student achievement and behavior and school building condition*. https://files.eric.ed.gov/fulltext/ED387878.pdf

Evans, G. (2003). The built environment and mental health. *Journal of Urban Health, 80*(4), 536–555. https://doi.org/10.1093/jurban/jtg063

Evans, G. W., Lepore, S. J., Shejwal, B. R., & Palsane, M. N. (1998). Chronic residential crowding and children's well-being: An ecological perspective. *Child Development, 69*(6), 1514–1523. https://doi.org/10.1111/j.1467-8624.1998.tb06174.x

Eyles, J., & Williams, A. (2008). *Sense of place, health and quality of life*. Ashgate.

Franklin, M., Yin, X., McConnell, R., & Fruin, S. (2020). Association of the built environment with childhood psychosocial stress. *JAMA Network Open, 3*(10), e2017634. https://doi.org/10.1001/jamanetworkopen.2020.17634

Freeman, D., & Freeman, J. (2008). *Paranoia the 21st century fear*. Oxford University Press. https://doi.org/10.1192/bjp.bp.108.061499

Frontczak, M., & Wargocki, P. (2011). Literature survey on how different factors influence human comfort in indoor environments. *Building and Environment, 46*(4), 922–937. https://doi.org/10.1016/j.buildenv.2010.10.021

Geldard, K., Geldard, D., & Foo, R. Y. (2019). *Counselling adolescents: The proactive approach for young people*. Sage.

Germain, C. B., & Columbia University Press. (1991). *Human behavior in the social environment: An ecological view*. Columbia University Press.

Gifford, R. (2002). *Environmental psychology: Principles and practice* (3rd ed.). Optimal Books.

Gifford, R., Steg, L., & Reser, J. P. (2011). Environmental psychology. In P. R. Martin, F. M. Cheung, M. C. Kyrios, L. Littlefield, M. Knowles, J. B. Overmier, & J. M. Prieto (Eds.), *The IAAP handbook of applied psychology* (pp. 440–471). Blackwell Publishing. https://doi.org/10.1002/9781444395150.ch18

Golembiewski, J. A. (2016). The designed environment and how it affects brain morphology and mental health. *HERD, 9*(2), 161–171. https://doi.org/10.1177/1937586715609562

Gong, Y., Palmer, S., Gallacher, J., Marsden, T., & Fone, D. (2016). A systematic review of the relationship between objective measurements of the urban environment and psychological distress. *Environment International, 96*, 48–57. https://doi.org/10.1016/j.envint.2016.08.019

Görlitz, D. (1998). Introduction. In D.Görlitz, H. J., Harloff, G. Mey, & J. Valsiner (Eds.), *Children, cities, and psychological theories: Developing relationships* (pp. 9–22). De Gruyter.

Han, K. (2009). Influence of limitedly visible leafy indoor plants on the psychology, behavior, and health of students at a junior high school in Taiwan. *Environment and Behavior, 41*(5), 658–692. https://doi.org/10.1177/0013916508314476

Iyendo, T. O., Uwajeh, P. C., & Ikenna, E. S. (2016). The therapeutic impacts of environmental design interventions on wellness in clinical settings: A narrative review. *Complementary Therapies in Clinical Practice, 24*, 174–188. https://doi.org/10.1016/j.ctcp.2016.06.008

Kaplan, R. (2001). The nature of the view from home: Psychological benefits. *Environment and Behavior, 33*(4), 507–542. https://doi.org/10.1177/00139160121973115

Kaplan, R., & Kaplan, S. (1989). *The experience of nature: A psychological perspective*. Ulrich's Bookstore. https://doi.org/10.1177/030913259201600333

Klompmaker, J. O., Hoek, G., Bloemsma, L. D., Wijga, A. H., van den Brink, C., Brunekreef, B., Lebret, E., Gehring, U., & Janssen, N. A. H. (2019). Associations of combined exposures to surrounding green, air pollution and traffic noise on mental health. *Environment International, 129*, 525–537. https://doi.org/10.1016/j.envint.2019.05.040

Knight, K., Gibson, K., & Cartwright, C. (2018). "It's like a refuge": Young people's relationships with school counsellors. *Counselling and Psychotherapy Research, 18*(4), 377–386. https://doi.org/10.1002/capr.12186

Kristiina Montero, M., & Al Zouhouri, A. (2022). Fear not the trauma story: A trauma-informed perspective to supporting war-affected refugees in Schools and Classrooms. In L. J. Pentón Herrera (Ed.), *English and students with limited or interrupted formal education. educational linguistics*, vol 54. Springer. https://doi.org/10.1007/978-3-030-86963-2_6

La Torre, M. (2006). Creating a healing environment. *Perspectives in Psychiatric Care, 42*(4), 262–264. https://doi.org/10.1111/j.1744-6163.2006.00086.x

Lawson, B. (2010). Healing architecture. *Arts & Health, 2*(2), 95–108. https://doi.org/10.1080/17533010903488517

Liu, W., Ji, J., Chen, H., & Ye, C. (2014). Optimal color design of psychological counseling room by design of experiments and response surface methodology. *PLoS One, 9*(3), E90646. https://doi.org/10.1371/journal.pone.0090646

Marrow, M. T., Knudsen, K. J., Olafson, E., & Bucher, S. E. (2012). The value of implementing target within a trauma-informed juvenile justice setting. *Journal of Child & Adolescent Trauma, 5*(3), 257–270. https://doi.org/10.1080/19361521.2012.697105

Maxwell, L. E., & Schechtman, S. L. (2012). The role of objective and perceived school building quality in student academic outcomes and self-perception. *Children, Youth and Environments, 22*(1), 23–51. https://doi.org/10.7721/chilyoutenvi.22.1.0023

Mazuch, R., & Rona, S. (2005). Creating healing environments: Humanistic architecture and therapeutic design. *Journal of Public Mental Health, 4*(4), 48–52. https://doi.org/10.1108/17465729200500031

Mead, G. H., & Morris, C. W. (1934). *Mind, self and society from the standpoint of a social behaviorist*. The University of Chicago press.

Miller, J., & Berger, E. (2022). Supporting First Nations students with a trauma background in schools. *School Mental Health, 14*, 485–497. https://doi.org/10.1007/s12310-021-09485-z

Nicholson, J., Perez, L., Kurtz, J., Bryant, S., & Giles, D. (2023). *Trauma-informed practices for early childhood educators: Relationship-based approaches that reduce stress, build resilience and support healing in young children* (2nd ed.). Taylor & Francis Group.

Northoff, G., Kötter, R., Baumgart, F., Danos, P., Boeker, H., Kaulisch, T., Schlagenhauf, F., Walter, H., Heinzel, A., Witzel, T., & Bogerts, B. (2004). Orbitofrontal cortical dysfunction in akinetic catatonia: A functional magnetic resonance imaging study during negative emotional stimulation. *Schizophrenia Bulletin, 30*(2), 405–427. https://doi.org/10.1093/oxfordjournals.schbul.a007088

Ou, L., & Luo, M. (2006). A colour harmony model for two colour combinations. *Color Research & Application, 31*(3), 191–204. https://doi.org/10.1002/col.20208

Pardeck, J. T. (1996). *Social work practice: An ecological approach*. Auburn House.

Park, S., & Mattson, R. (2009). Ornamental indoor plants in hospital rooms enhanced health outcomes of patients recovering from surgery. *Journal of Alternative and Complementary Medicine, 15*(9), 975–980. https://doi.org/10.1089/acm.2009.0075

Patterson, M., & Quadflieg, S. (2015). The physical environment and nonverbal communication. In D. Matsumoto, H. C. Hwang, & M. G. Frank (Eds.), *APA handbook of nonverbal communication* (pp. 189–220). APA Books.

Potthoff, J. K. (1995). Adolescent satisfaction with drug/alcohol treatment facilities: Design implications. *Journal of Alcohol and Drug Education, 41*(1), 62–73.

Pressly, P., & Heesacker, M. (2001). The physical environment and counseling: A review of theory and research. *Journal of Counseling & Development, 79*(2), 148–160. https://doi.org/10.1002/j.1556-6676.2001.tb01954.x

Ranieri, F. (2021). Trauma and place identity: The breaking and repairing of place attachment in the mind of an adolescent with developmental trauma. *Journal of Child Psychotherapy, 47*(3), 338–356. https://doi.org/10.1080/0075417X.2021.2012498

Robertson, P. (2001). Music and health. In A. Dilani (Ed.), *Design and health – The therapeutic benefits of design* (pp. 73–79). Elanders Svenskt Tryck AB.

Rossen, E., Kopec, D., & Harte, J. D. (2020). Design as the missing variable in trauma-informed schools. In E. Rossen (Ed.), *Supporting and educating traumatized students* (pp. 343–358). Oxford University Press. https://doi.org/10.1093/med-psych/9780190052737.003.0019

Scannell, L., & Gifford, R. (2017). The experienced psychological benefits of place attachment. *Journal of Environmental Psychology, 51*, 256–269. https://doi.org/10.1016/j.jenvp.2017.04.001

Stokols, D. (1995). The paradox of environmental psychology. *American Psychologist, 50*(10), 821–837. https://doi.org/10.1037/0003-066X.50.10.821

Stokols, D., & Shumaker, S. A. (1981). *People in places: A transactional view of settings* (pp. 441–488). Lawrence Erlbaum Associates.

Ulrich, R. S. (1984). View through a window may influence recovery from surgery. *Science (New York, N.Y.), 224*(4647), 420–421. https://doi.org/10.1126/science.6143402

Ulrich, R. S., Lundén, O., & Eltinge, J. L. (1993). Effects of exposure to nature and abstract pictures on patients recovering from heart surgery. In *Thirty-third meeting of the Society of Psychophysiological Research*, Rottach-Egern, Germany (Vol. 30, No. 7).

Ungar, M. (2002). A deeper, more social ecological social work practice. *The Social Service Review, 76*(3), 480–497. https://doi.org/10.1086/341185

Wang, S., Schramm, L., & Berger, E. (2023). Psychologists' perceptions of assessing and treating trauma-exposed clients. *Australian Psychologist, 58*(1), 18–30. https://doi.org/10.1080/00050067.2022.2120381

Westergaard, J. (2013). Counselling young people: Counsellors' perspectives on "what works" – An exploratory study. *Counselling and Psychotherapy Research, 13*(2), 98–105. https://doi.org/10.1080/14733145.2012.730541

Whipple, S. S., Evans, G. W., Barry, R. L., & Maxwell, L. E. (2010). An ecological perspective on cumulative school and neighborhood risk factors related to achievement. *Journal of Applied Developmental Psychology, 31*(6), 422–427. https://doi.org/10.1016/j.appdev.2010.07.002

Wiking, M. (2017). *The little book of Hygge: The Danish way to live well.* Penguin Life.

Wineman, J. D., & Barnes, J. (2018). Workplace settings. In *Environmental psychology and human well-being: Effects of built and natural settings* (pp. 167–192). Academic Press. Elsevier Academic Press. https://doi.org/10.1016/B978-0-12-811481-0.00007-X

Xiong, L., Huang, X., Li, J., Mao, P., Wang, X., Wang, R., & Tang, M. (2018). Impact of indoor physical environment on learning efficiency in different types of tasks: A 3 × 4 × 3 full factorial design analysis. *International Journal of Environmental Research and Public Health, 15*(6), 1256. https://doi.org/10.3390/ijerph15061256

7

Systemic Harms Call for Systemic Healing

Trauma-Informed Systems of Care for Black Students

Allisyn L. Swift and Theodore McGlynn-Wright

Introduction

One of the critiques leveled against trauma-informed schools (TIS) – specifically for populations of Black students in urban American schools – is that it can seem to operate within a historical vacuum that does not consider the root cause of anti-blackness that is axiomatic within the system itself. Further, there is little consideration of the specific ways that schools have been weaponized and complicit in the maintenance of these structural systems. This makes whole-school implementation of these strategies particularly fraught. In this chapter, we promote the idea of schools as a site of healing specifically because they have been a site of trauma. We argue that because group-based oppression is collective, not individual, analyses and interventions need to take place at the collective level, rather than the individual level of a socioecological model. In this chapter, we begin with a review of the literature on schools as a locale of harm and then discuss how they can be a site of healing. We provide recommendations illustrated by exploring several instances where schools have worked toward a trauma-informed framework that considers the historic and contemporary circumstances of their Black student population. We posit that whole-school implementation of trauma-informed strategies that are historically located/contextualized are most effective, especially for marginalized populations. Although we focus on the specific needs and factors that affect urban, predominantly Black schools in the United States, given the effects of colonialism on a global level, we believe that the discussion is relevant for most educational contexts for systemically marginalized youth.

DOI: 10.4324/9781003436034-7

The benefits of TIS are illustrated, in abundance, elsewhere so we have taken this as fact in preparation of this chapter (National Education Alliance, 2024; National Education Association. 2024; National Traumatic Stress Network, 2017). Thomas et al.'s (2019) interdisciplinary review of the literature on TIS in the past two decades (i.e., 1998–2018) revealed that in the 33 studies that were reviewed, 30 different interventions were named. Most cater to individual students or small groups, not the school or systems level, indicating an absence in the literature of models that address trauma-informed care at the systems level. At the Coalition for Compassionate Schools (CforCS), located in New Orleans, Louisiana, we advocate and consistently adapt our approach to and for systemic change in our schools and our city toward the goal of safe and compassionate schools. After an intensive search, we have not found any current models of trauma-informed, mainstream schools that successfully incorporate trauma-informed care on the systems level, from leadership development and school policies, to guidance on individual interactions that meet the bar of evidence-based practice in mainstream school although some discussed here are emerging (Avery et al., 2020; Maynard et al., 2019). Therefore, an actual comprehensive case study illustration of whole-school, evidence-based, trauma-informed practice does not exist, to our knowledge. Consequently, this chapter will present examples of best practices that encourage a comprehensive systems change model of TIS, and lessons learned from attempts at encouraging a systems change model.

Schools as a Site of Black Suffering

We must begin with the ways that schools in the United States, specifically post-segregation schools, have been weaponized through cultural and political practices to be the sites of harm, which has been insidiously normalized in our society. Given the plethora of initiatives for equitable education, specifically aimed at Black schools in America (see Same et al., 2018 for a comprehensive discussion), the reality of suffering in Black schools is not in question. The starting point for many Black schools is an assumption, building on the premise of inequitable opportunities and disparate outcomes. We normalize and even expect that predominantly Black urban schools will not achieve as highly as white ones, that Black students will not be accepted into predominantly white higher education institutions at the same rate as their white or Asian counterparts. We take Black low achievement as if it is almost inevitable, not realizing how this normalizing of Black suffering has "systemic, deleterious effects, every day, on specific social groups" (Dumas, 2014, p. 7). I There are clear differences in the expectations for the achievement of Black children vs. white children which has negatively impacted Black student achievement (Carter Andrews & Gutwein, 2017; Malone et al., 2023). Further, schooling in America has not held up to its promise of achieving greater proximity to social advancement and humanity for its Black citizens, who then are subject to a form of cultural gaslighting as our plight is not seen as an act of or outcome of suffering, but rather as an individual or collective failure to fully engage in schooling as a result of laziness at best, or lack of innate ability at worst (Dumas, 2014).

Stark racial differences in access to adequate education, low expectations for Black child academic achievement, and resulting disparities in academic achievement are well documented and well known. Comprehensive documentation of limited access to adequate education, when compared to their white peers, includes Black students having limited access to high-level math and science courses, less access to experienced teachers, and disparate and harsher discipline practices (National Center for Education Statistics, 2017; Annie E. Casey Foundation, 2017; United States Government Accountability Offices, 2016). Dumas, in his seminal 2014 article discussion of schools as a site of Black suffering, notes that there is a 'psychic link' between the historical memory of antebellum slavery and the post-civil rights era of black suffering in schools. Our current predicament of politicians using schools as sites of white supremacist tactics of erasing history, banning books, and anti-critical race theory rhetoric indeed reinforces the uncertainty of the state of education as "Black educators, children, and families are never quite sure when they will be taken (back) to the place of trauma (in the past), nor can they fully determine when, or if the pain will end" (Dumas, 2014, p. 3). Institutionalized racism has used schools as a location to develop policies and practices that have historically and currently center the preferences of white families over black families, marginalize and disempower Black teachers, all while failing to deliver on the promise of "adequate" education for Black children (Bell, 2004; Dumas, 2014; Morris, 2001; Tillman, 2004). As Dumas aptly put it while discussing the Black experience and observation of the Black schooling dilemma, "education policies and practices (are) complicit with, and reproducing historical patterns of black economic exploitation" (p. 20).

'Risk' and 'Resilience'

The mere presence of systemic, race-based risk factors does not universally predict poor outcomes. Further, environmental or situational factors that may be labeled 'risk' can produce certain individual strengths (i.e., post-traumatic growth; Tedeschi & Calhoun, 1996), or can be the catalyst for engaging resilient processes. Indeed, 40 years ago, Festinger (1983) cautioned against expecting poor outcomes for children simply based on their experience with one or many risk factors or adverse experiences. For example, current conceptualizations of poor, urban, Black children as 'at risk' merely based on their encounters with one or more 'risk factors' can lead to the perpetuation of covertly racist stereotypes that presume maladaptive behavior and poor outcomes. These presumptions have led to disastrous consequences, such as the disproportionate use of Zero-tolerance policies, suspension practices, and the enforcement of more constraining and strict educational environments for Black and Latino/e/x children under the guise of promoting 'higher achievement' (American Psychological Association, 2008; Costenbader & Markson, 1998; Kaeser, 1979; McCarthy & Hoge,1987; McFadden et al., 1992; Raffaele-Mendez & Knoff, 2003; Raffaele-Mendez et al., 2002; Skiba et al., 2002; Wu et al., 1982). Therefore, we may argue that the label of 'at risk' poses a risk factor to children who are its target.

Resilience has been defined as: "a dynamic process encompassing positive adaptation within the context of significant adversity" (Luthar et al., 2000, p. 543) and the "capacity of dynamic systems to withstand or recover from significant disturbances" (Masten, 2007, p. 923). Perhaps the most comprehensive definition comes from the American Psychological Association's Task Force on Resilience and Strength in Black Children and Adolescents (2008): "a dynamic, multidimensional construct that incorporates the bidirectional interaction between individuals and their environments within contexts (family, peer, school and community, and society)" (p. 2). All of the above definitions characterize the concept of resilience as a dynamic process between a person and their environment. Children, however, have limited control over their environment outside of whatever tools they are given and skills they are taught to help themselves cope or adapt. Therefore, children are reliant upon the adults in their lives to shape the environment in ways that help them acquire the skills they need to cope and adapt in the face of adversity.

Nuanced approaches in research, conducted with a process and context orientation, delineates three factors both within and external to the child, that contributes to resilience: (1) personality characteristics, (2) family characteristics, and (3) characteristics of their social environment external to the home (Garmezy, 1985; 1987; 1991; Werner, 1989; 2012). It is the third factor that is the domain of school-based mental health and educational practitioners. We can argue that if it is environmental demands that tax a child's ability to adapt and develop appropriately then environmental solutions must be sought to adequately address these issues. Although schools cannot reduce the risk in the child's familial context, such as parental psychopathology or community violence exposure, they are in the unique position of minimizing harms of structural racism by maximizing a child's exposure to protective factors (Baker, 2008). Across the resilience literature, three major protective factors emerge that directly relate to the school environment: close relationships with supportive adults, access to socially competent adult models, and effective educational environments (Clark, 1983; Doll & Lyon, 1998; Doll et al., 2004; Luthar et al., 2000; Luthar & Zigler, 1991; Masten et al., 2008; Werner, 1995; 2012). Schools are perfectly positioned to use the classroom environment to structurally and systematically include those three factors with the intention of developing a sense of psychological well-being in children (Anderson, 1982; Doll & Cummings, 2008; Doll et al., 2004; Garmezy, 1991; Gregory, 2020; Nastasi, 2004).

Luthar et al. (2000) speak of protective factors as "the location of a *set of processes* that distinguish a substantial proportion of the healthy children from the maladjusted ones" (p. 550, italics ours). In other words, the locus of change is the environment, not the child. Thus, we may transfer the label of 'resilient children' to an environment, such as the 'resilient school', which actively resists individualizing systemic racism. Foundational research highlights the enormous effect of the school environment on child development via shaping social cognition through peer interactions, providing adult role models, and promoting the acquisition of concrete knowledge (Garmezy, 1991). Schools have historically provided long-lasting positive effects on children who may have adverse family and home situations by providing them with a venue where protective processes can take place (Doll & Lyon, 1998; Masten et al., 2008; Rutter, 1979; Werner, 1989; 2012). Doll and colleagues' concept of Resilient Classrooms (2004) centers on the premise that classrooms are the ideal locale to create resilient communities which provide essential supports and guidance to children. In their description of resilient classrooms they draw upon the research in child development, psychology, and education, resulting in the identification of six characteristics of the resilient classroom as places where: (1) children believe that they are effective and competent in their learning skills (academic efficacy), (2) children set their own bars for success and work toward their self-selected goals (academic self-determination), (3) children exhibit appropriate behavior with minimal supervision from adults (behavioral self-control), (4) the teacher is able to engage in an authentic and caring relationship with the children (teacher-child relationships), (5) students are able to have supportive and continuous relationships with other students (peer relationships), and (6) families are informed about and support classroom learning (home-school relationships). Essential to the actualization of these characteristics is the relationship between the teacher and their students.

Bronfenbrenner's Ecological Systems Theory (1979, 1986) posits that processes occurring at and between multiple levels, from the most proximal (micro) to the most distal (macro), all influence a child's development. Specific attention to the multiple contexts of children echoes much of the resilience literature that asserts that the child, as an individual, is not resilient but rather has access to processes that foster their ability to adapt and thrive. Garmezy (1985) suggested that protective processes occur at the three broad levels of the community, family, and child. Schools that consider these multiple contexts are more likely to seek relationships with parents and the community, thus engaging and facilitating protective processes (Doll & Lyon, 1998; Doll et al., 2004; Werner, 2012). Educational systems practicing within an ecological framework are compelled to be aware of various aspects of the ecological systems specific to their student population, to provide well-rounded approaches to teaching and relating to their students. Teacher awareness of the impact of these macrosystemic issues as well as institutionalized racism and privilege, poverty, and lack of access to education can impact how they make meaning of their students' behavior, and risk or protective factors. This awareness can afford the sensitivity to context and awareness of biases that affect practice and school policies (Sosa & Gomez, 2012).

Spencer (2006) expands on Bronfenbrenner's ecological theory with the addition of the subjective experiences of the individual and how they are making meaning of the transactional processes as they are occurring. For younger children, adults who help them make meaning and guide them in appropriate adaptive responses are helping foster resilience through scaffolding the development of positive self-regard and critical thinking. Schools which can offer critical awareness of systemic racism for their students can help them contextualize their circumstances. Developing a critical lens gives Black children a different way to make meaning of their circumstances and the world around them. Knowledge and awareness of the system around them can combat internalized oppression and give students the language to challenge the status quo while restoring or rebuilding a sense of agency (El-Amin et al., 2017; McAdoo et al., 2023).

Awareness and understanding of the effects of multiple systems on the individual child can increase the sensitivity of the teacher to the plight of their students. As teacher awareness of multi-systemic issues affecting their students increases, so may their sensitivity, resulting in improvements in the teacher-student relationship; knowledge of these systemic issues leads to more sensitivity which gives teachers a different lens for viewing their students' coping behaviors (Sosa & Gomez, 2012). Indeed, from the child's perspective, many maladaptive behaviors are the result of coping with stressors (Summerville & Nastasi, 2013). Finally, a public health model of service delivery is the underlying framework for comprehensive mental health programming in schools, and the inclusion of environments that intentionally promote protective factors (Doll & Cummings, 2008; Doll et al., 2004; Hess et al., 2012; Nastasi, 2008). "It is the ethos of the school and the classroom that helps the many rather than focusing on the few" (Garmezy, 1991, p. 427). Garmezy's words embody the principles behind a public health framework, the population-based focus. Schools are an already existing system that can be a useful tool for supporting children's development (Doll et al., 2004). Promoting successful environments on the universal, systemic, and classroom level can positively affect all children (Dorado et al., 2018).

Recommendations and Case Studies for Promoting Healing-Centered, Trauma-Informed Practices for Black Students

The following recommendations are an attempt to demonstrate a range of healing-centered, trauma-informed approaches in schools with marginalized communities. Healing-centered practice, popularized by Dr. Shawn

Ginwright (2018) is a 'forward-looking' orientation, asking and answering the question, how do we establish our current programs, spaces, interventions, and mindsets to not only address trauma, but to also promote healing? We have not identified a single school organization that is incorporating all of the following recommendations into practice. However, we would like to highlight examples of where some of these practices have been attempted in a few different schools. In some of these examples we have been the first-hand actors or doers; others we have observed to embody a recommendation.

Recommendation 1 – Make it contextual. The rationale and approach to healing-centered schools should begin within the context of systemic racism, poverty, and lack of access opportunities. Start the conversation on TIS with a focus on systemic issues, not individual trauma, and then map how the systemic trauma is the root of much of the interpersonal trauma (e.g., community violence, neglect via higher maternal depression rates, emotional trauma, secondary trauma, collective trauma).

Example: Contextual Professional Development Framing. It is the mid-summer professional development training week for new employees, administrative and teaching staff, of a charter network in New Orleans, Louisiana that serves over 3,500 predominantly Black students (upward of 90% of the network's student population), and 93% that qualify for free and reduced cost lunches. Each year there is a track about social-emotional development and this first author, as the Lead Network Psychologist, is usually charged with providing content.

The workshop titled "Fostering Resilience for Urban Black Youth" directly centers the purpose of the workshop and who it is intended to discuss. We intentionally use that title to begin by naming race to acclimate the new employees to normalizing talking about race, racism, and its targets. We ground the workshop in organization mission-aligned statements:

We believe all children can achieve if given the appropriate supports. It's important for us to understand how to support children in order to do our job well.

We believe that building relationships is a key lever in serving our students and our community.

This is followed by a statement of the commitment we are grounding in for the workshop:

We are the safekeepers of our community: I commit to keeping myself and others safe in mind, body, and spirit.

We commit to physical and emotional safety for ourselves and our community. We agree to think about what we do and how it affects others. We assume the best in each other, use non-judgment for self and others, and always offer each other a fresh start.

The workshop continues to illuminate some devastating statistics taken from universal trauma-informed screening at the schools, highlighting the types of traumas experienced by the children within the charter network, and accompanying statistics about the prevalence of trauma in New Orleans at that time. The participants are then led to question why so many Black children in our city have experienced such a staggering amount of adverse experiences. The conclusion is a discussion of systemic racism and intergenerational poverty. We begin every workshop and conversation on trauma in our community by specifically and explicitly naming 'how we got here', so to speak. We believe that providing statistics of marginalized communities, without providing the context of their experiences, is tantamount to unethical practice, as it may result in the perpetuation of harmful stereotypes and reinforce implicit biases. Explicitly naming systemic racism and its far-reaching ecological harms is an essential step for bringing awareness to the systems level and contextualizing the individual traumas that students experience within the collective trauma of racism. Contextualizing the need for trauma-informed care within the framework of social justice and fostering a resilient environment for Black children serves to undo stereotypical victim-blaming of why certain communities have disparate struggles. The conversation starts with systemic racism and its cousin, intergenerational poverty, and then allows the participants to see the resilient factors within the communities that have aided in their survival.

Recommendation 2 – Make it systemic not individualistic. If we truly understand that the context for creating trauma-informed environments is the basis of systemic harm, with schools as the locale for continuing oppression, then we must first intervene at the universal, systemic level. Interventions must first be systemic, ecological, and environmental. We propose that systems change should be three-dimensional: individual, historical, and systemic. This requires that policies and practices should address individual practices and interactions; they actively root out the historical practices and policies that cause harm and replace them with functional solutions; they are systems wide – they become the DNA of the organization, and are explicitly and intentionally addressed in policies and practices, from the human resource department of the school organization to classroom protocols.

Example: Commitments and Organizational Practices. In this section we will provide two models for systemic practices. First, a brief description of developing organizational commitments, then a brief description of shifting to organizational practices in our Training of Trainers model. One of the ways an organization can communicate their commitment to healing-centered practices is by creating Commitments. Commitments embody a statement of what the organization values, and how it is operationalized. One of the most inspiring examples of organizational commitments is the use of the Compass of Valor Academies in Nashville, United States of America, a school organization created on the basis of healing and intentionally fostering the social and emotional capacities of children, with the same emphasis in their curriculum as academics. Through their Compass model, Valor Academies' commitments do not just live within the written word, but are infused into all of their activities and throughout their culture. In school organizations that are not as fortunate to have had these ideas woven into their creation, we have found the following steps useful in their creation. First, we begin with asking a question on every level of the organization, from leadership to the students: "What is it that you need to feel powerful, productive, and emotionally and psychologically safe?" This was completed in focus groups, interviews, and short-answer surveys that were transcribed and analyzed for themes. Those themes were crafted into statements; smaller and succinct headlines that are easy for students to internalize and remember, and more lengthy statements that operationalize the headline. For example, see the 'Commitments' described in the previous section on Recommendation 1.

In New Orleans, when we moved from an embedded staff model to a Train the Trainer (TOT) model of trauma-informed schools implementation, we expanded our focus from the individual classroom teacher to the school and/or Charter Management Organization (CMO) as a whole. Our first year of implementation was the 2019–2020 school year, and while the COVID-19 pandemic is in the rearview mirror for many, the mark it has left on schools and education as a whole cannot be overstated. Schools in the United States were put under extraordinary pressure during the height of the pandemic and most of that pressure has not abated. For example, in New Orleans, where 80% of those who died from COVID-19 were Black, the student population is 94.2% Black, and the teacher population is 53% Black, the school system remains strained. In fact, the school system still does not have the number of substitute teachers as were available pre-pandemic, and so individuals working in schools remain overburdened. Although we offer supportive services, we did not want to caste ourselves as one more organization asking schools to do more. In fact, we needed to find ways for us to ask schools to do less. We reflected that our model should simplify managing multiple relationships with different mental health providers, and include fewer disconnected observations, inventories, and screeners. We worked with our partner schools to either train them to do universal screeners (that they could use for tiered service provision) or have our partner organizations come and do the screeners directly, including tiering and follow-up meetings with school staff. We also made adjustments to our model (including our observation protocol) to make it more responsive to school needs. For example, we give schools the option of focusing on the two domains that seem most relevant at the time rather than forcing them to look at all four domains each time. A school may opt to closely attend to the environment in the first quarter of the year, then teacher-student relationships later on, for example.

Recommendation 3 – Ensure the use of Developmentally Appropriate Practices. Due to the adultification of Black children they are seen as more responsible for their actions and experience less tolerance for age-appropriate behavior (Goff et al., 2014; Koch & Kozhumam, 2022). Not only has this led to more subjective and harsh discipline practices, but it also robs Black children of the same joyous and whimsical experiences of childhood afforded to other children. Increasingly, practices that are not developmentally appropriate, such as shortened recess time, long times in seminar-like classroom settings, and less access to the arts, for example, are more acceptable in Black urban schools. While having 'high expectations' for Black children sounds like an antidote to racist lowered expectations of their innate abilities, in practice, high expectations have been misguided into a justification to employ inappropriate developmental practices, where children are exposed to higher order concepts and accountability for social behavior that they have not yet developed the skills for. Thus, a school that truly works within the zone of proximal development (Vygotsky, 1997) will also become a safer place for children to be children.

Example – Developmentally Appropriate PLAAY. Preventing Long-term Anger and Aggression in Youth (PLAAY) is an intervention developed by Dr. Howard Stevenson at the University of Pennsylvania. This intervention combines social and emotional learning, racial literacy, and physical activity to "[provide] Racial Literacy strategies for managing stress during intense face to face conflicts so they can perform better in the classroom and in their communities" (Stevenson, 2024, p. 1). It has been proven to increase overall school engagement and reduce school assaults and office referrals (Stevenson, 2024). Local implementation has also been successful, though it has not been in place long enough or at a rigorous enough level to show quantitative results. One success story of its implementation is at an alternative Middle School in New Orleans, serving students who have been expelled from their home schools. When the PLAAY Trainer arrived to observe the facilitators as part of their practicum, he noted that while the questions weren't the exact ones from the curriculum, they aligned well enough and were responsive to an event that had happened in the school the previous week. Of particular note was the level of introspection and vulnerability that these students were sharing. "Bear in mind this is 45 minutes squeezed in between Math and English Language

Arts (ELA)," he said, noting that the facilitator shared something personal and appropriately vulnerable with the group, inviting the students to do the same. One student mentioned feeling sad, but did not wish to "scale it." Scaling, a method of describing the intensity of a feeling (typically from 1 to 10) is common practice in PLAAY groups, and a core component of the Calculate, Locate, Communicate, Breathe, and Exhale (CLCBE) skill.

The implementor was quick to point out that what makes this possible is the commitment to making it systemic. The school leaders set aside time for educators, administrators, student support staff, and students to engage in the intervention. Specifically, the chief administrator, clinical director, PLAAY facilitators (and the rest of the teaching staff to a lesser extent) were all trained in the intervention curriculum and mindset. This change in mindset is what we at the CforCS describe as using a 'trauma lens' on student behavior.

Recommendation 4 – Prepare for ongoing assessment. Sustainable systems change requires the recognition that this work is aspirational and ongoing; there is no end to competence. It is not enough that we create systems and policies of care; they must be maintained, they must be flexible and responsive, they must be assessed and interrogated for viability and fidelity. This requires constant revisiting of items on checklists and tools measuring belonging in children, families, and staff; ensuring that student, staff, and parent voice and choice are uplifted and included in decision making; ongoing interrogation to make sure that policies and practices reflect the school as a site of healing.

Ongoing assessment of organizational healing-centered approaches is essential to knowing if and what types of changes are happening due to the intervention or treatment; acknowledging positive or negative unintended effects; testing for relevance of programming and pivots that need to be made in acquiring skills or knowledge, and operationalizing policies through behaviors. Organizations need to position themselves to interrogate neutrality of their systems by probing for who their policies and practices are benefiting and who they may be marginalizing. The goal is systemic integration of healing-centered practices; therefore, assessment practices should include the whole system, including parents, children, teachers, and administrative staff.

Example – Baseline and Ongoing Assessment Tools. There are not many assessments that are made for the specific use of assessing the progress toward healing-centered organizational practices. However, in practice we have found that assessments that test for the belonging of staff and students can give insight into the way that people within the organization are perceiving the climate. Belonging for students has been defined by Panorama Education (2023) as "the extent to which students feel that they are valued members of their school's community. Belonging can include feelings of understanding, respect, connectedness, membership, or mattering. Sense of belonging is influenced by the classroom and school culture, as well as by individual actions taken by adults in the school" (paragraphs 7–8). This definition and description aligns well with our conceptualization of healing-centered approaches for marginalized students, in that it echoes the underlying mechanisms of a systemic approach with the basic needs of humans to be validated and empowered by interconnectedness. Therefore, tools for assessing belongingness can have utility in testing for the baseline and ongoing efforts of healing-centered approaches. Panorama offers a suite of tools that assesses for belongingness in students and staff, and the connectedness of parents and families to the school organization.

Another tool used by the Training of Trainers program of CforCS is the Trauma-Informed Schools Policy, Procedure and Practice Checklist (New Orleans Trauma-Informed Schools Learning Collaborative, 2017). This tool is designed for use by an administrative team to specifically assess for the existence and implementation of specific policies and observable behaviors that indicate the existence of healing-centered approaches in the school building.

An emerging tool set for assessing policies and practices for students' sense of belonging in school are the Adult and Child Agency Inventories (Keig & Swift, 2022). These two complementary tools draw on and synthesize information from multiple sources and direct references from: New Orleans Youth Alliance's Authentic Youth Engagement Checklist (2020), The Trauma-Sensitive School Checklist (Lesley University and Massachusetts Advocates for Children, 2012), Safe Schools NOLA (i.e., New Orleans Louisiana) Policy Checklist (2012), the Collaborative for Academic, Social, and Emotional Learning (CASEL) social-emotional learning competencies, and Gallup's Q12 Index. For students, we also include indicators for evidence of developmentally appropriate practice. The above examples are a few ways of gathering a baseline and ongoing assessment data of efforts toward healing-centered approaches.

Conclusion

This chapter attempts to outline some of the chief concerns and considerations when implementing trauma-informed strategies, specifically within communities of Black students within the United States. However, the recommendations stated within are likely to have utility with other marginalized populations around the world who continue to endure systemic and intergenerational traumatic stresses. It is our hope that these recommendations can lead to sustainable changes within these communities. Specifically, changes that honor the humanity of children within these communities.

References

American Psychological Association, Task Force on Resilience and Strength in Black Children and Adolescents. (2008). *Resilience in African American children and adolescents: A vision for optimal development*. Washington, DC: Author. Retrieved from https://www.apa.org/pi/cyf/resilience.html

Anderson, C. S. (1982). The search for school climate: A review of the research. *Review of Educational Research, 52*, 368–420.

Annie E. Casey Foundation. (2017). *Race for results*. Retrieved from https://www.aecf.org/resources/2017-race-for-results

Avery, J. C., Morris, H., Galvin, E., Misso, M., Savaglio, M., & Skouteris, H. (2020). Systemic review of school-wide trauma-informed approaches. *Journal of Child & Adolescent Trauma*. doi: 10.1007/s40653-020-00326-w

Baker, J. A. (2008). Assessing school risk and protective factors. In B. Doll & J. A. Cummings (Eds.), *Transforming school mental health services: Population-based approaches to promoting the competency and wellness of children* (pp. 43–65). Thousand Oaks, CA: Corwin Press.

Bell, D. (2004). *Silent covenants: Brown v. board of education and the unfulfilled hopes for racial reform*. New York: Oxford.

Bronfenbrenner, U. (1979). *The ecology of human development: Experiments by nature and design*. Cambridge, MA: Harvard University Press.

Bronfenbrenner, U. (1986). Ecology of the family as a context for human development: Research perspectives. *Developmental Psychology, 22*, 723–742. Retrieved from https://web.ebscohost.com/ehost/pdfviewer/pdfviewer?vid=2&sid=8503f9b3-64eb-45d9-900d-da980164579f%40sessionmgr112&hid=113

Carter Andrews, D. J., & Gutwein, M. (2017). "Maybe That Concept Is Still with Us": Adolescents' racialized and classed perceptions of teachers' expectations, *Multicultural Perspectives, 19*(1), 5–15. doi: 10.1080/15210960.2016.1263960

Clark, R. M. (1983). *Family life and school achievement: Why poor Black children succeed or fail*. Chicago, IL: University of Chicago Press.

Costenbader, V., & Markson, S. (1998). School suspension: A study with secondary school students. *Journal of School Psychology, 36*, 59–82. doi: 10.1016/S0022-4405(97)00050-2

Doll, B., & Cummings, J. A. (2008). *Transforming school mental health services: Populations –based approaches to promoting the competency and wellness of children*. Thousand Oaks, CA: Sage Publications.

Doll, B., & Lyon, M. A. (1998). Risk and resilience: Implications for the delivery of educational and mental health services in schools. *School Psychology Review, 27*, 348–363. Retrieved from https://web.ebscohost.com/ehost/detail?vid=2&sid=e82aba41-c229-40f0-abea-1e9a89594a60%40sessionmgr104&hid=113&bdata=JnNpdGU9ZWhvc3QtbGl2ZSZzY29wZT1zaXRl#db=a9h&AN=1188593

Doll, B., Zucker, S., & Brehm, K. (2004). *Resilient classrooms: Creating healthy environments for learning*. New York: Guilford Press.

Dorado, J.S., Martinez, M., McArthur, L.E., & Leibovitz, T. (2016). Healthy Environments and Response to Trauma in Schools (HEARTS): A whole-school, multi-level, prevention and intervention program for creating trauma-informed, safe and supportive schools. *School Mental Health, 8*, 163–176. doi: 10.1007/s12310-016-9177-0

Dumas, M. J. (2014). Losing an arm: Schooling as a site of black suffering. *Race Ethnicity and Education, 17*, 1. doi: 10.1080/13616624.2013.850412

El-Amin, A., Seider, S., Graves, D., Tamerat, J., Clark, S., Soutter, M., Johannsen, J., & Malhotra, S. (2017). Critical consciousness: A key to student achievement. *Phi Delta Kappan, 98*(5), 18–23. doi: 10.1177/0031721717690360

Eng, D. L., & Han, S. (2000). A dialogue on racial Melancholia. *Psychoanalytic Dialogues, 10*(4), 667–700.

Festinger, T. (1983). *No one ever asked us*. New York: Columbia University Press.

Garmezy, N. (1985). Stress-resistant children: The search for protective factors. *Journal of Child Psychiatry and Psychology, 4*, 213–233.

Garmezy, N. (1987). Stress, competence, and development: Continuities in the study of schizophrenic adults, children vulnerable to psychopathology, and the search for stress-resistant children. *American Journal of Orthopsychiatry, 57*, 159–174. Retrieved from https://www.ncbi.nlm.nih.gov/pubmed/3296774

Garmezy, N. (1991). Resilience and vulnerability to adverse developmental outcomes associated with poverty. *American Behavioral Scientist, 34*, 416–430. Retrieved from https://abs.sagepub.com/content/34/4/416.full.pdf

Ginwright, S. (2018). The future of healing: Shifting from trauma informed care to healing centered engagement. *Medium*. Retrieved from https://ginwright.medium.com/the-future-of-healing-shifting-from-trauma-informed-care-to-healing-centered-engagement-634f557ce69c

Goff, P. A., Jackson, M. C., Di Leone, B. A., Culotta, C. M., & DiTomasso, N. A. (2014). The essence of innocence: Consequences of dehumanizing Black children. *Journal of Personality and Social Psychology, 106*(4), 526–545. doi: 10.1037/a0035663

Gregory, J. R. (2020). Whiteness and school shootings: Theorization toward a more critical school social work. *Children & Schools, 42*(3), 153–160. doi: 10.1093/cs/cdaa017

Hess, R. S., Short, R. J., & Hazel, C. E. (2012). *Comprehensive children's mental health services in schools and communities: A public health problem-solving model*. New York: Taylor & Francis Group, LLC.

Kaeser, S. C. (1979). Suspensions in school discipline. *Education and Urban Society, 11*, 465–484. Retrieved from https://eric.ed.gov/?id=EJ210368

Keig, A., & Swift, A. L. (October 2022). *Tools for belonging in Schools: Adult and child development agency cycles & inventories*. Presented at Sustaining Change, Beloved Community National Conference, New Orleans, LA.

Koch, A., & Kozhumam, A. (2022). Adultification of Black children negatively impacts their health: Recommendations for health care providers. *Nurses Forum, 57*(5), 963–967. doi: 10.1111/nuf.12736

Lesley University and Massachusetts Advocates for Children. (2012). *The trauma-sensitive school checklist*. Retrieved from https://www.learningforjustice.org/sites/default/files/general/trauma%20sensitive%20school%20checklist%20(1).pdf

Luthar, S. S., Cicchetti, D., & Becker, B. (2000). The construct of resilience: A critical evaluation and guidelines for future work. *Child Development, 71*, 543–562. doi: 10.1111/1467-8624.00164

Luthar, S. S., & Zigler, E. (1991). Vulnerability and competence: A review of research on resilience in childhood. *American Journal of Orthopsychiatry, 61*, 6–12. Retrieved from https://www.ncbi.nlm.nih.gov/pubmed/2006679

Malone, L., Seeberg, V., & Yu, X. (2023). "The soft bigotry of low expectations": Perceptions of teacher expectations among Black families in a suburban school. *Educational Studies: Journal of the American Educational Studies Association, 59*(3), 247–263.

Masten, A., Herbers, J. E., Cutulu, J. J., & Lafavor, T. L. (2008). Promoting competence and resilience in the school context. *Professional School Counseling, 12*, 76–84. Retrieved from https://web.ebscohost.com/ehost/detail?vid=2&sid=aa6c9ea5-e794-43da-b1c8-e8791b9abecd%40sessionmgr198&hid=113&bdata=JnNpdGU9ZWhvc3QtbGl2ZSZzY29wZT1zaXRl#db=a9h&AN=35895616

Masten, A.S. (2007). Resilience in developing systems: Progress and promise as the fourth wave rises. *Development and Psychopathology, 19*(3), 921–930. doi: 10.1017/S0954579407000442

Maynard, B. R., Farina, A., Dell, N. A., & Kelly, M. S. (2019). Effects of trauma-informed approaches in schools: A systematic review. *Campbell Systematic Reviews, 15*(1–2), e1018. doi: 10.1002/cl2.1018

McAdoo, G., Williams, K., & Howard, T. C. (2023). Racially just, trauma-informed care for black students. *Urban Education, 60*(3), 1–28. doi: 10.1177/00420859231175668

McCarthy, J. D., & Hoge, D. R. (1987). The social construction of school punishment: Racial disadvantage out of universalistic process. *Social Forces, 65*, 1101–1120. Retrieved from https://web.ebscohost.com/ehost/pdfviewer/pdfviewer?sid=1b8ff3b2-323c-4ae9-815b-b787abf995e5%40sessionmgr110&vid=2&hid=113

McFadden, A. C., Marsh, G. E., Price, B. J., & Hwang, Y. (1992). A study of race and gender bias in the punishment of school children. *Education & Treatment of Children, 15*, 140–146. Retrieved from https://web.ebscohost.com/ehost/detail?vid=2&sid=c66e4fb5-acca-4414-940d-8c88ea2659cc%40sessionmgr104&hid=113&bdata=JnNpdGU9ZWhvc3QtbGl2ZSZzY29wZT1zaXRl#db=a9h&AN=9608010108

Morris, J. E. (2001). Forgotten voices of black educators: Critical race perspectives on the implementation of a desegregation plan. *Educational Policy, 15*(4), 575–600.

Nastasi, B. K. (2004). Meeting the challenges of the future: Integrating public health and public education for mental health promotion. *Journal of Educational and Psychological Consultation, 15*, 295–312. doi: 10.1207/s1532768xjepc153&4_6

Nastasi, B. K. (2008). Social justice and school psychology. *School Psychology Review, 37*, 487–492. Retrieved from https://web.ebscohost.com/ehost/pdfviewer/pdfviewer?sid=24eca980-5417-4a2c-a644-b5a71d6fb6cf%40sessionmgr114&vid=2&hid=113

National Education Association. (2024). *Trauma informed schools*. Retrieved from https://www.nea.org/professional-excellence/student-engagement/trauma-informed-schools.

National Center for Education Statistics. (2017). *The condition of education*. Retrieved from https://nces.ed.gov/pubsearch/pubsinfo.asp?pubid=2017144

National Child Traumatic Stress Network, Schools Committee. (2017). *Creating, supporting, and sustaining trauma-informed schools: A system framework*. Los Angeles, CA, and Durham, NC: National Center for Child Traumatic Stress.

New Orleans Trauma-Informed Schools Learning Collaborative. (2017). *Trauma-informed schools policy, procedure & practice checklist.*

New Orleans Youth Alliance. (2020). *Authentic youth engagement check-list*. New Orleans, LA. Retrieved from https://static1.squarespace.com/static/5a5fb5adb1ffb6cb741dbee5/t/5defe8618594a9745b8f273e/1576003809004/NOYA+Authentic+Youth+Engagement+Checklist

Panorama Education. (2023). https://www.panoramaed.com/

Raffaele-Mendez, L. M., & Knoff, H. M. (2003). Who gets suspended from school and why: A demographic analysis of schools and disciplinary infractions in a large school district. *Education & Treatment of Children, 26*, 30–51. Retrieved from https://web.ebscohost.com/ehost/pdfviewer/pdfviewer?vid=2&sid=7bbd57fe-827d-4a53-8673-390542aeb287%40sessionmgr111&hid=113

Raffaele-Mendez, L. M., Knoff, H. M., & Ferron, J. F. (2002). School demographic variables and out-of-school suspension rates: A quantitative and qualitative analysis of a large, ethnically diverse school district. *Psychology in the Schools, 39*, 259–277. doi: 10.1002/pits.10020

Rutter, M. (1979). Protective factors in children's responses to stress and disadvantage. *Annals of the Academy of Medicine, Singapore, 8*(3), 324–338.

Same, M. R., Guarino, N. I., Pardo, M., Benson, D., Fagan, K., & Lindsay, J. (2018). *Evidence-supported interventions associates with Black students' educational outcomes; Findings from a systemic review of research*. Regional Education Laboratory Midwest, American Institute for Research. https://eric.ed.gov/?id=ED581117

Skiba, R. J., Michael, R. S., Nardo, A. C., & Peterson, R. (2002). The color of discipline: Sources of racial and gender disproportionality in school punishment. *Urban Review, 34*, 317–342. doi: 10.1023/A:1021320817372

Sosa, T., & Gomez, K. (2012). Conneting teacher efficacy beliefs in promoting resiliens to support of Latino Students. *Urban Education, 47*, 876–909. doi: 10.1177/0042085912446033

Spencer, M. B. (2006). Phenomenology and ecological systems theory: Development of diverse groups (Chapter 15). In W. Damon, & R. Lerner (Eds.), *Handbook of child psychology*, vol. 1 (R. Lerner, Ed.): *Theoretical models of human development* (6th ed., pp.829–893). New York: Wiley.

Stevenson, (2024). *PLAAY*. The Racial Empowerment Collaborative. https://www.recastingrace.com/research/plaay

Summerville, M., & Nastasi, B. K. (2013, August). The ecomap as self-report mental health screener for early elementary students. *Paper presentation at the American Psychological Association's Annual Convention*, August 3rd, Honolulu, HI.

Tedeschi, R. G., & Calhoun, L. G. (1996). The posttraumatic growth inventory: Measuring the positive legacy of trauma. *Journal of Traumatic Stress, 9*, 455–469. doi: 10.1002/jts.2490090305

Thomas, M. S., Crosby, S., & Vanderhaar, J. (2019). Trauma-informed practices in schools across two decades: An interdisciplinary review of research. *Review of Research in Education, 43*, 422–452.

Tillman, L. C. (2004). (Un)Intended consequences? The impact of the Brown v. Board of Education decision on the employment status of black educators. *Education and Urban Society, 36*(3), 280–303.

U.S. Government Accountability Offices. (2016). *K-12 education: Better use of information could help agencies identify disparities and address racial discrimination*. Retrieved from https://www.gao.gov/products/gao-16-345

Vygotsky, L. S. (1997). The historical meaning of the crisis in psychology: A methodological investigation. In R. W. (Ed.), *The Collected Works of L. S. Vygotsky. Vol. 3. Problems of the theory and history of psychology* (pp. 233–344).

Werner, E. E. (1989). High-risk children in young adulthood: A longitudinal study from birth to 32 years. *American Journal of Orthopsychiatry, 59*, 72–81. doi: 10.1111/j.1939-0025.1989.tb01636.x

Werner, E. E. (1995). Resilience in development. *Current Directions in Psychological Science, 3*, 81–85. Retrieved from https://www.jstor.org/stable/20182335

Werner, E. E. (2012). Risk, resilience, and recovery. *Reclaiming Youth and Children,* 21, 18–23. Retrieved from https://web.ebscohost.com/ehost/pdfviewer/pdfviewer?vid=2&sid=cb1f46f3-09f7-48e7-8721-0eccd6161f55%40sessionmgr111&hid=113

Wu, S. C., Pink, W. T., Crain, R. L., & Moles, O. (1982). Student suspension: A critical reappraisal. *Urban Review, 14,* 245–303. doi: 10.1007/BF02171974

8 Parents, Caregivers, and School Trauma-Informed Practice

Angela Gazey, Karen E. Martin, and Andrea Reupert

Introduction

Parents and/or carers as well as schools play an important role in supporting children impacted by trauma. This chapter describes parent/caregiver understanding of trauma and how their involvement and interaction with schools is an important component of trauma-informed practice. After outlining the potential role for schools to educate parents/carers about trauma-informed practice, this chapter highlights the need for schools to understand cultural considerations and intergenerational trauma within its community. This chapter also discusses existing literature about trauma-informed parenting interventions and the importance of building strong relationships which feature genuine engagement and communication between parent/carers and schools. This chapter concludes with a summary of practice recommendations to assist schools to identify strategies for engaging parents/carers in embedding trauma-informed practice within their community.

Parents' and Carers' Knowledge and Awareness about the Impacts of Trauma

A child's most important and influential relationships are with their parents/carers (Reupert et al., 2022) who can play a crucial role in mitigating the impacts of trauma (Cobham et al., 2016; Miller et al., 2018; Lindstrom Johnson et al., 2018). Parent/carer involvement is important in developing children's social communication skills, capacity to regulate and express

DOI: 10.4324/9781003436034-8

emotions, and form healthy attachments (Sullivan et al., 2015). Despite this, there remains little published research on parents'/carers' knowledge about the impacts of trauma on children. Existing research has primarily focused on parents' knowledge about the impacts of trauma in the context of trauma-informed parenting interventions and situations in which parents/carers have adopted children, or are providing kinship or out of home care (Miller et al., 2018; Strolin-Goltzman et al., 2018; Sullivan et al., 2015). There is a need for more research involving parent/carers from a broader range of socioeconomic, cultural, and ethnic groups to ensure findings and subsequent implications are generalizable and inclusive.

Trauma-Informed Practice in Schools

The potential benefits of a trauma-informed approach in schools have been increasingly recognized (Chafouleas et al., 2016; Dorado et al., 2016; Howard, 2019; Perry & Daniels, 2016). Despite inconsistencies in definitions and characteristics of trauma-informed practice, a systematic review of multi-tiered trauma-informed practice approaches in schools found that most programs were associated with positive changes for students and school staff (Berger, 2019). Dorado and Martinez et al. (2016) evaluated a trauma-informed practice intervention and found increased student engagement and a decrease in negative behavioral incidents. Another study found that students involved in trauma-informed practice programs reported an increased capacity to self-regulate their emotions (Perry & Daniels, 2016). Importantly, and with relevance to this chapter, a recent synthesis of core concepts from 18 trauma-informed practice school-based programs found that involving the community, families, and parents/carers is a core principle of a trauma-informed school (Martin et al., 2023).

Role of the School in Educating Parents/Carers about Trauma-Informed Practice

The sustainability and long-term success of school-based trauma-informed practice requires support from parents/carers as well as the wider community (Langley et al., 2010; Jaycox et al., 2014; Kataoka et al., 2018). Trauma-informed practice in schools also appears to prevent and mitigate the negative impacts of trauma beyond the school setting (Ijadi-Maghsoodi et al., 2017; Kataoka et al., 2018; Langley et al., 2010). Accordingly, Chafouleas et al. (2016) referred to the need to create trauma-informed systems that extend beyond the educational sector. Typically, trauma-informed practice in schools encompasses changes beyond immediate school polices, practices, and the environment (Kataoka et al., 2018). The process of creating a school environment that is trauma-informed and that supports parents and the broader community involves developing an awareness amongst all stakeholders of the impacts of trauma and adversity (Kataoka et al., 2018) and then having the school follow up with appropriate trauma-informed responses to children and parents/carers (Chafouleas et al., 2016).

However, notwithstanding the need to expand trauma-informed systems beyond the immediate school setting, many school-based trauma-informed programs have not involved parents/carers or the wider community. Likewise, despite the need for engagement with parents/carers and the community, information about the potential benefits of a trauma-informed school is unlikely to have been disseminated to them (Berger, 2019). The lack of parent/carer involvement in many school-based trauma-informed practice approaches may present barriers to the success and sustainability of trauma-informed approaches. It is possible that parents/carers of children at schools in the early stages of implementing trauma-informed practice may have concerns about the potential impact changes to classroom and behavior management strategies and policies will have on their child. It is therefore important that schools implement trauma-informed practice with parents/carers and develop tailored education with, and for, parents/carers on the potential benefits of a trauma-informed approach (Romero et al., 2018).

There is limited published literature evaluating the involvement of parents in trauma-informed practice programs within educational settings (Berger, 2019). One of the few programs in this area comes from Kataoka et al. (2018) who described a school-based trauma-informed practice program that specifically engages parents/carers with the aim of promoting a sense of community and trust in the school. The program also provided parents/carers with education about the impacts of trauma on children (Kataoka et al., 2018). As parents/carers and community members identified the lack of physical safety in the neighborhood surrounding the school as a key barrier to engaging with the program, the school worked with community-based Organizations to increase safety (Kataoka et al., 2018). As a consequence, there were substantial increases in the engagement of parents/carers in the program which led to a reduction in students' negative behavioral incidents and school suspensions (Kataoka et al., 2018). Another study by Fleming (2019), described the outcomes of adopting a trauma-informed approach in school which included a focus on strengthening relationships between staff, students, and their parents/caregivers. This included the use of policies that promoted respectful relationships as well as trauma-informed communication protocols that would strengthen teacher-student and teacher-family relationships. The authors reported benefits from this approach including positively influencing the family dynamics and parent/caregiver relationship with teacher/school, increasing the likelihood that the student would trust the teacher, encouraging the development of caring relationship with adults within the school and that understanding the difficulties the students were experiencing at home, and enabling teachers to express affection and motivate students to achieve.

Parents' Experiences of Trauma and Intergenerational Consequences

The intergenerational consequences of trauma are well established and it is important schools are aware of these when implementing trauma-informed practice (Cerdeña et al., 2021; Menzies, 2019). Parents'/carers' experiences of trauma, particularly experiences associated with school or educational institutions, are likely to impact their connection and relationships with the school and ability to engage with school-based trauma-informed practice initiatives (Langley et al., 2013; Piper et al., 2021). Schools also need to be aware of the potential that training or education programs they provide may cause distress for participants with current or prior trauma and ensure evidence-based strategies are in place to support participants.

Trauma-Informed Parenting Interventions

Trauma-informed parenting practices refer to broad parenting approaches that recognize the impact of traumatic experiences on children and prevent re-traumatisation (Lindstrom Johnson et al., 2018; Miller et al., 2018; Sullivan et al., 2015). There is growing evidence that trauma-informed parenting approaches positively impact family functioning and mitigates some of the intergenerational sequelae of trauma and adversity (Champine et al., 2018; Lindstrom Johnson et al., 2018; Razuri et al., 2016; Traub & Boynton-Jarrett, 2017). Accordingly, parents/carers play a substantial role in helping children manage the impacts of trauma and reduce the negative consequences associated with traumatic and adverse experiences (Cabaj et al., 2014; Champine et al., 2018; Collishaw et al., 2007; Traub & Boynton-Jarrett, 2017; Wu et al., 2020). Despite substantial growth in the field of trauma-informed practice, evidence related to trauma-informed parenting practice, especially those delivered in school settings or in conjunction with school-based programs, remains small (Champine et al., 2018).

The majority of the existing literature on parents and trauma-informed practice has focused on specific interventions aimed at parents/carers providing kinship care or those with adoptive or foster children and whose children are known to have experienced trauma (Sullivan et al., 2015; Miller et al., 2018; Strolin-Goltzman et al., 2018). The characteristics of these programs and interventions vary considerably in terms of content, setting, delivery mode, and intensity, as do the types (and quality) of evaluations undertaken to ascertain the impact of these interventions. The interventions and evaluations for a select number of trauma-informed parenting interventions are described below.

The Trauma-Informed Behavioral Parenting 'Smart Start' program aims to support parents and caregivers meet the social and emotional needs of young children in a trauma-informed manner. Participants involved in the program receive eight weekly training sessions on positive parenting practices and behavior management strategies to avoid re-traumatisation (Agazzi et al., 2019). A pre-post evaluation of the program found significant decreases in parenting stress scores, although there was no significant change in child behavior scores (Agazzi et al., 2019). Other results showed increased parent and caregiver knowledge about the impact and symptoms of trauma in children and an increase in knowledge about positive parenting strategies (Agazzi et al., 2019).

Sullivan et al. (2015) evaluated a training program for caregivers fostering children from birth to 15 years of age. The program was intended to educate parents about the impact of traumatic experiences on children's behavior and increase parents' knowledge about trauma-informed responses to challenging behaviors (Sullivan et al., 2015). After the program, participants reported increased knowledge about the impact of trauma on children and higher parenting self-efficacy (Sullivan et al., 2015). These findings are consistent with a subsequent evaluation of a larger training program for foster parents, developed to support the use of trauma-informed parenting strategies amongst people providing foster, adoptive, and kinship care (Strolin-Goltzman et al., 2018). A pre-post evaluation design found increased awareness of the impact of traumatic experiences on children, reduced parental stress, and increased knowledge about how to manage children's challenging behaviors (Strolin-Goltzman et al., 2018). Consistent with these findings, Miller et al. (2018) found that, after completion of a trauma-informed parenting intervention, kinship carers' understanding of potential behavioral consequences for children who have experienced trauma improved, as did their willingness to tolerate difficult behaviors displayed by children in their care. Similarly, another evaluation of a trauma-informed parenting program for foster parents in the Netherlands reported increased parental knowledge and awareness of the impacts of trauma, which persisted 12 months post-training (Konijn et al., 2020). Parents who reported the greatest increase in knowledge as a result of the training had reduced parental stress (Konijn et al., 2020). Many of these results are summarized in a systematic review of parenting interventions for these carers and found that parenting interventions reduced carers' perceived stress and enhanced carers' perceptions of their parenting competency (Wu et al., 2020). Similarly, Fein et al. (2021), evaluated a school-based trauma-informed education program for parents of culturally diverse children, and found that completing the program enhanced family functioning and parents' perceptions of social connectedness and support.

Other program evaluations have reported increases in parents' and caregivers' knowledge and awareness of the impacts of traumatic experiences on children. For example, Razuri et al. (2016) evaluated the impact of an online trauma-informed parent training intervention for parents whose adoptive children had experienced of trauma prior to their adoption and reported a decrease in trauma-related behavioral challenges in their children with no change recorded in the incidence of behavioral challenges in the control group (Razuri et al., 2016).

These evaluations demonstrate that programs aimed at promoting the knowledge and skill of parents and caregivers in trauma-informed parenting practices may be effective in positively impacting on children's outcomes. Whether and how they can be delivered through school settings is unclear. Nonetheless, delivering parenting and carer programs through schools can strengthen community ties and create a bridge between home and school, thereby promoting consistency. For some parents and carers, schools may be more accessible than community-based resources, especially for families who face barriers such as transportation issues, geographical isolation, or financial constraints. Moreover, given that schools are a universal service which most children attend, it can also provide a non-stigmatizing site to access support and psychoeducation. Thus, it is important to investigate further the acceptability and effectiveness of school-based parenting programs in this field.

Parent/Carer Connection and Engagement with Schools

Parent/carer engagement with schools is influenced by both school and parent characteristics (Feuerstein, 2000; Hornby & Lafaele, 2011). Literature on parent/carer engagement with schools, and the importance and impact of this engagement has expanded substantially in the last two decades (Reupert & Minke, 2021; Toren & Seginer, 2015). Generally, parent/carer engagement with their child's school is associated with improvements in student engagement, motivation, and educational outcomes (Annunziata et al., 2006; Fan & Williams, 2010; Mo & Singh, 2008; Wilder, 2014).

Parent engagement is highest when the school culture is perceived as welcoming and supportive of parent involvement (Povey et al., 2016; Rattenborg et al., 2019; Schueler et al., 2014). High levels of parental engagement have been found to be associated with a positive school environment and mental wellbeing amongst students (Kataoka et al., 2018; Suldo et al., 2012). Likewise, Povey et al. (2016) in Queensland, Australia, found that parent engagement was strongest where the school was perceived by parents to have a culture that emphasized collaboration, trust and respect. However, parent engagement differed significantly according to their socioeconomic circumstances; parents with higher socioeconomic advantage were more likely to be engaged with their child's school (Povey et al., 2016). Despite the development of recent guidelines, for example, the Family-School Partnerships Framework (Department of Skills Education and Employment, 2020), there remains a paucity of evidence about how parents/carers engage and collaborate with schools regarding school responses to trauma.

The Importance of Cultural Considerations

Underlying systemic racism, a negative school culture and their own experiences of trauma can present substantial barriers to culturally diverse parents'/carers' relationship with their child's school (Blitz et al., 2016; Cooper, 2009; Piper et al., 2022). Differences in language and culture between parents, caregivers, and school staff can result in less frequent communication or communication that is perceived as negative or disrespectful by parents (Kataoka et al., 2018; Langley et al., 2013; Rattenborg et al., 2019). Trauma-informed practice requires that schools actively identify and address barriers to engagement for the parents/carers of culturally diverse students (Cooper, 2009; Ijadi-Maghsoodi et al., 2017; Langley et al., 2013; Piper et al., 2022).

Communication between School and Parents and Caregivers

Strong communication between parents and schools is an important aspect of parent engagement and a core component of creating a positive school culture (Rattenborg et al., 2019; Toren & Seginer, 2015). School culture can be shaped by parent and caregiver engagement and communication with the school, and conversely, impact the willingness of parents and caregivers to engage and communicate (Toren & Seginer, 2015). Frequent respectful and genuine communication between parents and school staff increases parents' and caregivers' perceptions of the school culture as positive and promotes greater parent engagement (Kataoka et al., 2018; Langley et al., 2013; Povey et al., 2016; Toren & Seginer, 2015).

The type of communication between parents, caregivers, and schools is important; Toren (2013) observed that communication, particularly when children transition to middle or high school, is often only initiated when problems occur which require parent/caregiver and staff input. Moreover, differing expectations between parents, caregivers, and school staff can create barriers to parent engagement in schools (Kataoka et al., 2018; Toren & Seginer, 2015). Other systematic barriers to parent engagement include conflicting parent and school agendas and logistical challenges (Donnelly et al., 2019; Hornby & Lafaele, 2011). There appears to be little literature describing how parents, caregivers, and teachers communicate about student trauma, nor the enablers and barriers to these conversations.

Recommendations

Schools are ideal sites for engaging with parents due to their central location, regular interaction opportunities, access to resources, community-building functions, established communication channels, staff expertise, and support networks (Reupert et al., 2021). They are ideally placed to disseminate information to, and educate parents and caregivers about trauma and trauma-informed practice. Schools serve as a central hub in most communities, making them convenient places for parents, caregivers, and other community members to meet. Parents and caregivers are already accustomed to dropping off and picking up their children from school and may already be interacting with the school through assemblies and parent/teacher meetings, so prompting them to further engage with schools regarding trauma-informed approaches may be a natural progression if managed in a culturally sensitive manner.

However, the majority of existing research has focused on the impact of trauma-informed parenting interventions outside of school settings and amongst particular groups of parents, primarily those who have adopted children or are providing out of home care (Jay Miller et al., 2018; Miller et al., 2018; Strolin-Goltzman et al., 2018; Sullivan et al., 2015). Despite an emerging body of evidence supporting the benefits of a whole community approach to trauma-informed practice, there remains an important gap in terms of what we know about how schools might support and work with parents and others who care for children impacted by trauma. Another gap is how schools might support a wide group of parents and caregivers outside of kinship carers, those who have adopted children, and those who are providing out of home care. Accordingly, on the basis of the research conducted to date, the following research and practice recommendations include:

- Future research is needed to examine the knowledge about the potential impact of trauma on children amongst a broad sample of parents and children including those from diverse backgrounds, family structures, and regions.
- Children and young people should be engaged in developing strategies for how their parents/carers might be involved in school-based trauma-informed practice interventions. A recent study by Berger et al. (2024) asked young people what parents/carers can do to support children impacted by trauma. Young people reported that parents should provide

non-judgmental and caring responses to young people, and support them to access mental health support without pressuring young people.

- Parents involvement in developing and facilitating school-based trauma-informed practice interventions and strategies should be encouraged and evaluated.
- Evidence-based models of school, parent/caregiver, and community collaboration should be developed and evaluated, especially those that can be replicated across different settings.
- Professional development programs aimed at promoting the capacity of teachers and school staff to effectively engage with parents and caregivers needs to be developed and evaluated.
- Longitudinal studies might be conducted to understand how parent, caregiver, and school engagement related to trauma impacts student academic and social-emotional development over time.

Conclusion

This chapter has described the importance of involving parents/carers in school-based trauma-informed practice. It emphasized how parents play a substantial role in interacting with schools to help children impacted by trauma. The importance of parents/carers and schools collaborating in regard to approaches to transform environments for children to be trauma-informed is clear, however further research identifying best strategies to achieve this is required. Moving forward with increased knowledge and effective, evidence-based action is likely to lead to many short- and long-term community benefits.

References

Agazzi, H., Adams, C., Ferron, E., Ferron, J., Shaffer-Hudkins, E., & Salloum, A. (2019). Trauma-informed behavioral parenting for early intervention. *Journal of Child and Family Studies, 28*(8), 2172–2186. https://doi.org/10.1007/s10826-019-01435-3

Annunziata, D., Hogue, A., Faw, L., & Liddle, H. A. (2006). Family functioning and school success in at-risk, inner-city adolescents. *Journal of Youth and Adolescence, 35*(1), 100–108. https://doi.org/10.1007/s10964-005-9016-3

Berger, E. (2019). Multi-tiered approaches to trauma-informed care in schools: A systematic review. *School Mental Health, 11*, 650–664. https://doi.org/10.1007/s12310-019-09326-0

Berger, E., Marston, N., Faragher, B. C., Allen, K. A., Martin, K., & O'Donohue, K. (2024). Young people's perspectives on parents helping young people exposed to trauma. *Child & Youth Care Forum*. https://doi.org/10.1007/s10566-024-09807-7

Blitz, L. V., Anderson, E. M., & Saastamoinen, M. (2016). Assessing perceptions of culture and trauma in an elementary school: Informing a model for culturally responsive trauma-informed schools. *The Urban Review, 48*(4), 520–542. https://doi.org/10.1007/s11256-016-0366-9

Cabaj, J. L., McDonald, S. W., & Tough, S. C. (2014). Early childhood risk and resilience factors for behavioural and emotional problems in middle childhood. *BMC Pediatrics, 14*(1), 166. https://doi.org/10.1186/1471-2431-14-166

Cerdeña, J. P., Rivera, L. M., & Spak, J. M. (2021). Intergenerational trauma in Latinxs: A scoping review. *Social Science & Medicine, 270*, 113662. https://doi.org/10.1016/j.socscimed.2020.113662

Chafouleas, S. M., Johnson, A. H., Overstreet, S., & Santos, N. M. (2016). Toward a blueprint for trauma-informed service delivery in schools. *School Mental Health, 8*(1), 144–162. https://doi.org/10.1007/s12310-015-9166-8

Champine, R. B., Matlin, S., Strambler, M. J., & Tebes, J. K. (2018). Trauma-informed family practices: Toward integrated and evidence-based approaches. *Journal of Child and Family Studies, 27*(9), 2732–2743. https://doi.org/10.1007/s10826-018-1118-0

Cobham, V. E., McDermott, B., Haslam, D., & Sanders, M. R. (2016). The role of parents, parenting and the family environment in children's post-disaster mental health. *Current Psychiatry Reports, 18*(6), 53. https://doi.org/10.1007/s11920-016-0691-4

Collishaw, S., Pickles, A., Messer, J., Rutter, M., Shearer, C., & Maughan, B. (2007). Resilience to adult psychopathology following childhood maltreatment: Evidence from a community sample. *Child Abuse & Neglect, 31*(3), 211–229. https://doi.org/10.1016/j.chiabu.2007.02.004

Cooper, C. W. (2009). Parent involvement, African American mothers, and the politics of educational care. *Equity & Excellence in Education, 42*(4), 379–394. https://doi.org/10.1080/10665680903228389

Department of Skills Education and Employment. (2020). *The family-school partnerships framework*. Australian Government. https://www.education.gov.au/supporting-family-school-community-partnerships-learning/family-school-partnerships/family-school-partnerships-framework

Donnelly, S., Buchan, D. S., Gibson, A.-M., McLellan, G., & Arthur, R. (2019). An insight into the involvement of mothers of low socioeconomic status in Scottish primary school health education activities. *Health Education & Behavior, 47*(1), 111–122. https://doi.org/10.1177/1090198119871329

Dorado, J. S., Martinez, M., McArthur, L. E., & Leibovitz, T. (2016). Healthy environments and response to trauma in schools (HEARTS): A whole-school, multi-level, prevention and intervention program for creating trauma-informed, safe and supportive schools. *School Mental Health, 8*(1), 163–176. https://doi.org/10.1007/s12310-016-9177-0

Fan, W., & Williams, C. M. (2010). The effects of parental involvement on students' academic self-efficacy, engagement and intrinsic motivation. *Educational Psychology, 30*(1), 53–74. https://doi.org/10.1080/01443410903353302

Fein, E. H., Kataoka, S., Aralis, H., Lester, P., Marlotte, L., Morgan, R., & Ijadi-Maghsoodi, R. (2021). Implementing a school-based, trauma-informed resilience curriculum for parents. *Social Work in Public Health, 36*(7–8), 795–805. https://doi.org/10.1080/19371918.2021.1958116

Feuerstein, A. (2000). School characteristics and parent involvement: Influences on participation in children's schools. *The Journal of Educational Research, 94*(1), 29–40. https://doi.org/10.1080/00220670009598740

Fleming, S. (2019). A mixed methods multiple case study of the initial implementation of the trauma-sensitive schools model in an elementary and middle school (Publication No. 27794903) [Doctoral dissertation, North Carolina State University]. ProQuest One Academic; Social Science Premium Collection ProQuest Dissertation.

Hornby, G., & Lafaele, R. (2011). Barriers to parental involvement in education: An explanatory model. *Educational Review, 63*(1), 37–52. https://doi.org/10.1080/00131911.2010.488049

Howard, J. A. (2019). A systemic framework for trauma-informed schooling: Complex but necessary! *Journal of Aggression, Maltreatment & Trauma, 28*(5), 545–565. https://doi.org/10.1080/10926771.2018.1479323

Ijadi-Maghsoodi, R., Marlotte, L., Garcia, E., Aralis, H., Lester, P., Escudero, P., & Kataoka, S. (2017). Adapting and implementing a school-based resilience-building curriculum among low-income racial and ethnic minority students. *Contemporary School Psychology, 21*(3), 223–239. https://doi.org/10.1007/s40688-017-0134-1

Jay Miller, J., Niu, C., & Moody, S. (2018). Investigating the child trauma knowledge of adoptive parents: An exploratory study. *Adoption Quarterly, 21*(4), 229–246. https://doi.org/10.1080/10926755.2019.1579134

Jaycox, L., Stein, B., & Wong, M. (2014). School intervention related to school and community violence. *Child and Adolescent Psychiatric Clinics of North America, 23*(2), 281–293.

Kataoka, S. H., Vona, P., Acuna, A., Jaycox, L., Escudero, P., Rojas, C., Ramirez, E., Langley, A., & Stein, B. D. (2018). Applying a trauma informed school systems approach: Examples from school community-academic partnerships. *Ethnicity and Disease, 28*(2), 417–226.

Konijn, C., Colonnesi, C., Kroneman, L., Liefferink, N., Lindauer, R. J. L., & Stams, G.-J. J. M. (2020). 'Caring for children who have experienced trauma' – an evaluation of a training for foster parents. *European Journal of Psychotraumatology, 11*(1), 1756563. https://doi.org/10.1080/20008198.2020.1756563

Langley, A., Santiago, C. D., Rodríguez, A., & Zelaya, J. (2013). Improving implementation of mental health services for trauma in multicultural elementary schools: Stakeholder perspectives on parent and educator engagement. *The Journal of Behavioral Health Services & Research, 40*(3), 247–262. https://doi.org/10.1007/s11414-013-9330-6

Langley, A. K., Nadeem, E., Kataoka, S. H., Stein, B. D., & Jaycox, L. H. (2010). Evidence-based mental health programs in schools: Barriers and facilitators of successful implementation. *School Mental Health*, *2*(3), 105–113. https://doi.org/10.1007/s12310-010-9038-1

Lindstrom Johnson, S., Elam, K., Rogers, A. A., & Hilley, C. (2018). A meta-analysis of parenting practices and child psychosocial outcomes in trauma-informed parenting interventions after violence exposure. *Prevention Science*, 19(7), 927–938. https://doi.org/10.1007/s11121-018-0943-0

Martin, K., Dobson, M., Fitzgerald, K., Ford, M., Lund, S., Egeberg, H., Walker, R., Milroy, H., Wheeler, K., Kasten-Lee, A., Bayly, L., Gazey, A., Falconer, S., Platell, M., & Berger, E. (2023). *International trauma-informed practice principles for schools (ITIPPS): Expert consensus of best-practice principles*. The Australian Educational Researcher. https://doi.org/10.1007/s13384-023-00648-2

Menzies, K. (2019). Understanding the Australian Aboriginal experience of collective, historical and intergenerational trauma. *International Social Work*, 62(6), 1522–1534. https://doi.org/10.1177/0020872819870585

Miller, J. J., Niu, C., Sauer, C., Bowman, K., Segress, M., & Benner, K. (2018). Foster parents' knowledge of child trauma: An exploratory study. *Journal of Aggression, Maltreatment & Trauma*, *27*(5), 505–522. https://doi.org/10.1080/10926771.2017.1422839

Mo, Y., & Singh, K. (2008). Parents' relationships and involvement: Effects on students' school engagement and performance. *RMLE Online*, 31(10), 1–11. https://doi.org/10.1080/19404476.2008.11462053

Perry, D. L., & Daniels, M. L. (2016). Implementing trauma—Informed practices in the school setting: A pilot study. *School Mental Health*, *8*(1), 177–188. https://doi.org/10.1007/s12310-016-9182-3

Piper, K. N., Elder, A., Renfro, T., Iwan, A., Ramirez, M., & Woods-Jaeger, B. (2022). The importance of anti-racism in trauma-informed family engagement. *Administration and Policy in Mental Health and Mental Health Services Research*, *49*(1), 125–138. https://doi.org/10.1007/s10488-021-01147-1

Povey, J., Campbell, A. K., Willis, L.-D., Haynes, M., Western, M., Bennett, S., Antrobus, E., & Pedde, C. (2016). Engaging parents in schools and building parent-school partnerships: The role of school and parent organisation leadership. *International Journal of Educational Research*, *79*, 128–141. https://doi.org/10.1016/j.ijer.2016.07.005

Rattenborg, K., MacPhee, D., Walker, A. K., & Miller-Heyl, J. (2019). Pathways to parental engagement: Contributions of parents, teachers, and schools in cultural context. *Early Education and Development*, *30*(3), 315–336. https://doi.org/10.1080/10409289.2018.1526577

Razuri, E. B., Howard, A. R., Parris, S. R., Call, C. D., DeLuna, J. H., Hall, J. S., Purvis, K. B., & Cross, D. R. (2016). Decrease in behavioral problems and trauma symptoms among at-risk adopted children following web-based trauma-informed parent training intervention. *Journal of Evidence-Informed Social Work*, *13*(2), 165–178.

Reupert, A., & Minke, K. (2021). Family engagement. In *Building Better Schools with Evidence-based Policy: Adaptable Policy for Teachers and School Leaders* (pp. 192–197). Routledge.

Reupert, A., Straussner, S. L., Weimand, B., & Maybery, D. (2022). It takes a village to raise a child: Understanding and expanding the concept of the "village." *Frontiers in Public Health, 10*, 756066. https://doi.org/10.3389/fpubh.2022.756066

Romero, V. E., Robertson, R., & Warner, A. N. (2018). *Building resilience in students impacted by adverse childhood experiences: A whole-staff approach*. Corwin Press.

Schueler, B., Capotosto, L., Sofia, B., McIntyre, J., & Gehlbach, H. (2014). Measuring parent perceptions of school climate. *Psychological Assessment, 26*(1), 314–320.

Strolin-Goltzman, J., McCrae, J., & Emery, T. (2018). Trauma-informed resource parent training and the impact on knowledge acquisition, parenting self-efficacy, and child behavior outcomes: A Pilot of the resource parent curriculum parent management training (RPC+). *Journal of Public Child Welfare, 12*(2), 136–152. https://doi.org/10.1080/15548732.2017.1352555

Suldo, S. M., McMahan, M. M., Chappel, A. M., & Loker, T. (2012). Relationships between perceived school climate and adolescent mental health across genders. *School Mental Health, 4*(2), 69–80. https://doi.org/10.1007/s12310-012-9073-1

Sullivan, K. M., Murray, K. J., & Ake, G. S. (2015). Trauma-informed care for children in the child welfare system: An initial evaluation of a trauma-informed parenting workshop. *Child Maltreatment, 21*(2), 147–155. https://doi.org/10.1177/1077559515615961

Toren, N. K. (2013). Multiple dimensions of parental involvement and its links to young adolescent self-evaluation and academic achievement. *Psychology in the Schools, 50*(6), 634–649. https://doi.org/10.1002/pits.21698

Toren, N. K., & Seginer, R. (2015). Classroom climate, parental educational involvement, and student school functioning in early adolescence: A longitudinal study. *Social Psychology of Education, 18*(4), 811–827. https://doi.org/10.1007/s11218-015-9316-8

Traub, F., & Boynton-Jarrett, R. (2017). Modifiable resilience factors to childhood adversity for clinical pediatric practice. *Pediatrics, 139*(5), e20162569. https://doi.org/10.1542/peds.2016-2569

Wilder, S. (2014). Effects of parental involvement on academic achievement: A meta-synthesis. *Educational Review, 66*(3), 377–397. https://doi.org/10.1080/00131911.2013.780009

Wu, Q., Zhu, Y., Ogbonnaya, I., Zhang, S., & Wu, S. (2020). Parenting intervention outcomes for kinship caregivers and child: A systematic review. *Child Abuse & Neglect, 106*, 104524. https://doi.org/10.1016/j.chiabu.2020.104524

9

Trauma-Informed Partnerships with Aboriginal and Torres Strait Islander Peoples

Emily Hall, Sharon Louth, Murray Phillips, John Cairney, and Kai Wheeler

Introduction

This chapter takes a strengths-based approach to health, wellbeing, and educational excellence of Aboriginal and Torres Strait Islander students in schools consistent with Prehn (2024). A growing body of evidence supports health, wellbeing, and education practitioners using the Social Determinants of Health to better inform Aboriginal and Torres Strait Islander partnerships. It is only recently however, that research has begun to consider the Cultural Determinants of Health and how these impact the health, wellbeing, and education outcomes of Aboriginal and Torres Strait Islander peoples and communities. Aboriginal and Torres Strait Islander Elders and leaders have for many years emphasized that health and wellbeing are all-encompassing, including physical, social, emotional, spiritual, and ecological factors, grounded in strong collectivist support networks through extended kinship and community. A question remains as to how the Cultural Determinants of Health can best be utilized in broader fields such as education and applied in schools. In understanding the Cultural Determinants of Health, teachers and school-leaders can better co-design culturally safe and culturally responsive trauma-informed partnerships that facilitate excellence. This chapter explores the key health and wellbeing aspects that impact Aboriginal and Torres Strait Islander engagement within schools. Specifically, this chapter outlines the advantages of a trauma-informed care approach

DOI: 10.4324/9781003436034-9

for Aboriginal and Torres Strait Islander children, and then continues with highlighting application of this approach for Aboriginal and Torres Strait Islander children in schools.

Background to Trauma-Informed Practice for Aboriginal and Torres Strait Islander Students

Aboriginal and Torres Strait Islander peoples experience ongoing trauma from colonization, dispossession from Country, and removal from families and kinship. This impacts educational and school engagement and is a central feature justifying the importance of trauma-informed practice in schools in partnership with Aboriginal and Torres Strait Islander peoples (Miller & Berger, 2020). Teachers and school-leaders must approach this complex issue with an in-depth understanding of the wider drivers behind participation, retention, and excellence of Aboriginal and Torres Strait Islander students in schools. The Yumbin Program is an example of a school success story which employs this strategy within the schooling system, centering belonging and collaboration for inclusivity. Eidsvold State School's Wakka Wakka language reclamation program (Yumbin) has strengthened ties between the school and the local Aboriginal community, enhancing student wellbeing and learning experiences. The initiative, recognised as a state finalist for the Queensland Teachers' Union Showcase Award for Excellence in Aboriginal and Torres Strait Islander Education in 2019, allows community members and Elders to share their unique knowledges and perspectives with students and staff to promote engagement across the school and as part of the community.

These successes often feature a strength-based approach when working in partnership with Aboriginal and Torres Strait Islander students, with a strong emphasis on self-determination and reciprocity.

It is proposed that schools with a comprehensive understanding of how the Social Determinants of Health (Wilkinson & Marmot, 2003) impact Aboriginal and Torres Strait Islander health and wellbeing will be better placed to meet the challenges they experience in attaining educational excellence (Anderson et al., 2007). In addition, thorough consideration of the Cultural Determinants of Health will further strengthen the abilities of schools to respond to the needs of Aboriginal and Torres Strait Islander students (Verbunt et al., 2021). Both frameworks emphasize the central role of community in the lives of Aboriginal and Torres Strait Islander students, and schools incorporating a collectivist approach will be better equipped to engage in genuine and meaningful ways with these students and their communities.

Adopting a holistic health, wellbeing, and educational engagement approach will no doubt cater to diverse learners within contemporary schools. Caring for Aboriginal and Torres Strait Islander students' social and emotional health and wellbeing builds on the Social Determinants of Health and the Cultural Determinants of Health and has been described extensively through nine guiding principles (Dudgeon et al., 2014). These principles outline that self-determination for Aboriginal and Torres Strait Islander peoples is a fundamental right and that schools must recognize the cultural diversity among Aboriginal and Torres Strait Islander students. Recognition of the impact of racism and stigma, along with the history of trauma and loss among Aboriginal and Torres Strait Islander students and families, is acknowledged as key features of Aboriginal and Torres Strait Islander health and wellbeing, and this can be applied to school settings (Dudgeon et al., 2014). Schools must employ culturally safe and culturally responsive learning environments using strengths-based approaches to better promote Aboriginal and Torres Strait Islander excellence (Ayre et al., 2022).

Trauma-informed practice incorporates cultural responsiveness which caters to colonized histories and supports diversity among Aboriginal and Torres Strait Islander students (Huang et al., 2014). Trauma-informed practice is a foundational element of Aboriginal and Torres Strait Islander engagement in schools, providing teachers and school-leaders with a range of strategies that empower students and their communities (Miller & Berger, 2020). Despite this, trauma-informed practice that specifically empowers Aboriginal and Torres Strait Islander students is not well understood in education, and this can sometimes be placed into the 'too hard' category for teachers (Louth et al., 2023). Some educators feel that they lack knowledge around Aboriginal and Torres Strait Islander ways of knowing, being, and doing within a trauma-informed context. However, with greater understanding of the key drivers promoting Aboriginal and Torres Strait Islander excellence, teachers and schools can be in a prime position to enrich the lives of Aboriginal and Torres Strait Islander students and their communities.

The aim of this chapter is to explore the key health and wellbeing aspects that impact Aboriginal and Torres Strait Islander engagement within schools and how trauma-informed approaches can create culturally reflexive environments to increase their engagement. The first objective is to highlight the application of the Social Determinants of Health in an educational context. The second objective is to define how the Cultural Determinants of Health apply to Aboriginal and Torres Strait Islander community engagement with schools. The third objective is to delineate how trauma-informed practice can be implemented when working in partnership with Aboriginal and Torres Strait Islander students to co-design culturally responsive learning environments. Thorough consideration of the Social Determinants of Health and Cultural Determinants of Health, within a trauma-informed practice framework, will help address the ongoing impacts from colonization, dispossession from Country, and dislocation of families and kinship structures for Aboriginal and Torres Strait Islander students.

Social Determinants of Health

The Social Determinants of Health model (shown in Table 9.1) (Wilkinson & Marmot, 2003) supports the notion that the concept of health and wellbeing is shaped by more than medical factors. The Social Determinants of Health are an important consideration when engaging holistically with Aboriginal and Torres Strait Islander students at school. This is because social aspects have a significant impact on health and wellbeing, beyond just a primary health perspective, which impacts a student's ability to flourish and socialize in a school setting (Braveman & Gottlieb, 2014). Previous research has shown that the Social Determinants of Health can be more impactful than primary healthcare or lifestyle choices in influencing health and wellbeing outcomes (Braveman & Gottlieb, 2014; Organization). There are many different domains identified as social determinants, but not all of these apply to a student's health and wellbeing directly. Indirect influences include education level, socioeconomic status (i.e., social gradient), and social exclusion, and these are influencers that are often observed in a school learning environment. Whether direct or indirect drivers, social determinants are an important consideration when considering the health and wellbeing of Aboriginal and Torres Strait Islander students in school.

It is important to consider the specific Social Determinants of Health that apply to Aboriginal and Torres Strait Islander students who have a

Table 9.1 Applying the social determinants of health to students within a school environment

Determinant	Example for students in school
Social gradient	Students higher on the social gradient tend to be healthier
Stress	Stressful circumstances make students feel anxious and unable to cope and can be damaging to their health
Early life	The health impacts of early nurturing and education last a lifetime for students
Social exclusion	Students experiencing hardship, poverty, social exclusion, and discrimination on average have poorer quality of life
Work	Students who have more self-determination in their studies tend to experience better health
Unemployment	Higher family health and wellbeing is experienced by students whose parents have job security
Social support	Friendship, good social relations, and strong supportive networks are associated with improved health for students
Addiction	Students may use alcohol, tobacco, and/or other drugs during development which negatively impacts on health
Food	Students may experience food supply issues that impact healthy nutrition and family food security
Transport	Adequate transport promotes students' capacity to engage in school and learning activities

Adapted from Wilkinson and Marmot (2003)

history of trauma, because of colonization, dispossession from Country, and dislocation of kinship and families. While the Social Determinants of Health hold relevance and impact on health outcomes for Aboriginal and Torres Strait Islander students, they fail to frame health from a First Nations viewpoint, which contributes to the dominant deficit discourse of health (Ian et al., 2004). The Social Determinants of Health for Aboriginal and Torres Strait Islander students (shown in Table 9.2) reflect on health determinants which are specific to the lives and experiences of Aboriginal and Torres Strait Islander peoples. Each of these determinants requires consideration in education programs. In addition, these determinants should be considered when establishing resources aimed at increasing the health and wellbeing, along with the education engagement of Aboriginal and Torres Strait Islander peoples.

Table 9.2 Defining the social determinants of health that apply to Aboriginal and Torres Strait Islander peoples

Determinant	Application to Aboriginal and Torres Strait Islander peoples
History of health	Acknowledgment of the historical and colonial origins of Aboriginal and Torres Strait Islander ill-health
Racism and marginalization	Acknowledgment of not only the multilayered occurence and effects of racism, but also the physical and mental impacts that occur as a result
Poverty and social class	Low socioeconomic status can present barriers to engagement in health and education
Control over own health	Right to continuation of traditional health practices and decision-making in health
Powerlessness	Impact of compounding socioeconomic disadvantage that has occurred because of colonization, often resulting in feelings of being unable to escape this cycle
Employment and income	Employment is a major factor determining economic security
Education and training	Acknowledges the central role education plays in health as both a determinant of health and as an active driver to address health inequalities
Incarceration and the justice system	Acknowledges the over-representation of incarcerated Aboriginal and Torres Strait Islander peoples and the high instances of discrimination within the legal system
Housing and infrastructure	Acknowledges the multiple aspects of living conditions that may contribute to ill-health, including both the physical conditions as well as the accessibility, appropriateness, and safety of the structure and its surrounds
Family separation	The ongoing impact of the disruption of family and kinship systems due to government policies and practices
Place, land, and reconciliation	Health cannot be separated from land rights, dispossession from Country, loss, and grief

Adapted from Anderson et al. (2007)

Cultural Determinants of Health

Recent discussions have focused on the Cultural Determinants of Health, which have been defined to ensure that health is viewed more holistically

Table 9.3 The Cultural Determinants of Health applied to Aboriginal and Torres Strait Islander students

Determinant	Example
Family/community	Generations and kinship systems connect custodians of traditional knowledge, history, culture, and language to learners. This is a vital component of knowledge transfer and cultural continuation
Country and place	Engagement with Country provides a significant source of social cohesion and space for spirituality for Aboriginal and Torres Strait Islander peoples
Cultural identity	Culture is an integral component of Aboriginal and Torres Strait Islander peoples' identity and wellbeing
Self-determination	Allowing Aboriginal and Torres Strait Islander peoples to pursue their cultural, social, and economic rights. Self-determination requires Aboriginal and Torres Strait Islander peoples leading decision-making

Adapted from Verbunt et al. (2021)

with respect to Aboriginal and Torres Strait Islander peoples and cultures (shown in Table 9.3). This offers educators a practical framework to work in partnership with Aboriginal and Torres Strait Islander students in schools. Embedding the Cultural Determinants of Health center the school community around giving students, families, and community the ability to draw strength, resilience, and empowerment from culturally responsive strategies and engagement methods (Verbunt et al., 2021). The Cultural Determinants of Health provide considerable opportunity in a school environment to promote educational engagement, health, and wellbeing.

Nine Guiding Principles of Aboriginal and Torres Strait Islander Health

The Social and Cultural Determinants of Health have provided the grounding for understanding health and wellbeing outcomes for Aboriginal and Torres Strait Islander peoples, and direct teachers and schools on ways to better empower Aboriginal and Torres Strait Islander students. The focus on self-determination as a key factor in the health of Aboriginal and Torres Strait Islander peoples has resulted in the development of socioemotional wellbeing (SEWB) principles for Aboriginal and Torres Strait Islander people (shown in Table 9.4) (Dudgeon et al., 2014). These nine guiding principles address long-standing issues in Aboriginal and Torres Strait Islander SEWB (Brockman & Dudgeon, 2020; Swan, 1995). The principles also strengthen the application of health and wellbeing-based programs when delivered and designed in reference to the social and cultural determinants, allowing for schools to scaffold their engagement with Aboriginal and Torres Strait Islander students.

The nine guiding principles acknowledge the continued unmet needs of Aboriginal and Torres Strait Islander peoples in Western-focused health and wellbeing strategies. These principles can be extrapolated to education and learning contexts involving Aboriginal and Torres Strait Islander students. Comparatively, the guiding principles acknowledge parts of the Social and Cultural Determinants of Health, but go further to represent the complexities of SEWB for Aboriginal and Torres Strait Islander peoples. The conceptualization of the guiding principles has occurred in conjunction with an understanding of colonization and its ongoing effects on Aboriginal and Torres Strait Islander peoples. Culturally responsive application of the guiding principles will impact education outcomes for Aboriginal and Torres Strait Islander peoples and lead to high-impact, community-led partnerships centered on self-determination and reciprocity for Aboriginal and Torres Strait Islander peoples. Consideration of the relevant social and Cultural Determinants of Health in the guiding principles positions schools to better promote excellence in SEWB with First Nations people.

It is recommended that teachers embed protocols and outcomes to align with the social and cultural determinants of Aboriginal and Torres Strait Islander health, as well as the nine guiding principles of SEWB. Emphasis must be placed on the key cultural inclusions required for genuine and meaningful education engagement with Aboriginal and Torres Strait Islander students. As such, schools must seek to connect each educational program element with the specific social and cultural determinant, along with the nine guiding principles of Aboriginal and Torres Strait Islander SEWB. An example of this approach may include facilitation of programs prioritizing delivery of education in Country to promote Aboriginal and Torres Strait Islander ways of knowing, being, and doing. Teachers, guided by the nine principles of Aboriginal and Torres Strait Islander SEWB, should ensure long-term SEWB for community, including for Aboriginal and Torres Strait Islander students and communities with a trauma background. Curriculum and strategic engagement approaches must acknowledge the right to

Table 9.4 Nine guiding principles of Aboriginal and Torres Strait Islander SEWB

Principle	Example
1. Health as a holistic concept	Aboriginal and Torres Strait Islander health is viewed in a holistic context that encompasses mental health and physical, cultural, and spiritual health. Land is central to wellbeing. Crucially, it must be understood that when the harmony of these interrelations is disrupted, Aboriginal and Torres Strait Islander ill-health will persist
2. Self-determination	Self-determination is central to the provision of Aboriginal and Torres Strait Islander health services
3. Cultural reflective learning	Culturally responsive understandings must shape the provision of services and guide assessment, and care associated with Aboriginal and Torres Strait Islander peoples' health
4. History of trauma and loss	It must be recognized that the experiences of trauma and loss are a direct outcome of the disruption to cultural wellbeing. Trauma and loss of this magnitude continue to have intergenerational effects
5. Recognition of human rights	The human rights of Aboriginal and Torres Strait Islander peoples must be recognized and respected
6. Impact of racism and stigma	Racism, stigma, environmental adversity, and social disadvantage constitute ongoing stressors and have negative impacts on Aboriginal and Torres Strait Islander peoples' health and wellbeing
7. Centrality of kinship	The centrality of Aboriginal and Torres Strait Islander family and kinship must be recognized, as well as the broader concepts of family and the bonds of reciprocal affection, responsibility, and sharing
8. Recognition of cultural diversity	There is no single Aboriginal or Torres Strait Islander culture or group, but numerous groupings, languages, and kinships, as well as ways of living. Aboriginal and Torres Strait Islander peoples may reside in various settings, including urbanized, traditional, or other lifestyles, and frequently move between these ways of living
9. Strengths-based approach	Recognition of Aboriginal and Torres Strait Islander peoples' strengths, creativity, and endurance, as well as a deep understanding of the relationships between people and their environment

Adapted from Dudgeon et al. (2014)

self-determination through culturally responsive co-design, whereby these methods place control of the program and its direction within the hands of the Aboriginal and Torres Strait Islander community.

Trauma and Aboriginal and Torres Strait Islander Peoples

The impacts of colonization for Aboriginal and Torres Strait Islander peoples is well documented, continuing, and widespread (Atkinson, 2002). Previous research has highlighted the considerable extent that Aboriginal and Torres Strait Islander peoples have experienced trauma over a long period, and as such culturally safe and culturally responsive trauma-informed programs must be co-designed to counter the impacts of colonization (Miller & Berger, 2020). This is true for education, health, and wellbeing, whereby programs aimed at partnering with Aboriginal and Torres Strait Islander students must be designed by Aboriginal and Torres Strait Islander peoples and stakeholders. This will ensure the greatest uptake of subsequent programs and promote high-impact school and community-level outcomes.

Trauma may re-occur (re-traumatization) through the sharing of past trauma through generations (intergenerational trauma) (Miller & Berger, 2020). Research using epigenetics has demonstrated that trauma can be passed on through the expression of genes from one generation to the next, which highlights the importance of employing decolonized methodology to overcome colonization when working in partnership with Aboriginal and Torres Strait Islander peoples (Gapp et al., 2016). The long-term, multi-generational impact of colonization, and numerous government agendas aimed at the genocide of Aboriginal and Torres Strait Islander peoples has caused inter-generational traumatic outcomes (Atkinson, 2002). Atkinson (2002) unpacks the trauma of cultural genocide felt by Aboriginal and Torres Strait Islander peoples:

> Genocide not only works to destroy the cultures of the oppressed peoples, it also eradicates the sense of self, of self-worth, and of well-being in individuals and groups so that they are unable to function

> from either their own cultural relatedness or from the culture of the oppressors. They feel in a world between devalued, and devaluing who they are.
>
> (p. 71)

Significant trauma may impact a person's health and influence the outcomes of educational interventions (Huang et al., 2014). For students who experience such trauma, negative impacts may include adverse education outcomes (Miller & Berger, 2020), as well as increased risks of mental and substance misuse (Huang et al., 2014). Further to this, unresolved childhood trauma has potential to increase experiences of health concerns in adulthood (Miller & Berger, 2020).

When working to provide education programs for Aboriginal and Torres Strait Islander students who experience ongoing trauma, consideration must be made to limit situations which risk re-traumatization (Huang et al., 2014). The reduction of re-traumatization risk can be achieved by utilizing trauma-informed practice through decolonized methodology.

Trauma-Informed Practice with Aboriginal and Torres Strait Islander Peoples

Trauma-informed practice is a multifaceted approach that will empower students in a school setting (Huang et al., 2014). The purpose of following trauma-informed practice is to minimize the long-term impact of trauma, while simultaneously reducing the risk of re-traumatization for students exposed to trauma (Huang et al., 2014). The approach is designed to include the physical, psychological, and emotional safety of the participant (Hopper et al., 2010). By prioritizing these multiple aspects of health and wellbeing, trauma-informed practice aligns with the need to address education holistically for Aboriginal and Torres Strait Islander students, as it aligns with the key engagement drivers and community excellence. The Substance Abuse and Mental Health Services Administration (SAMHSA) National Center for Trauma-Informed Care has outlined a framework which includes six key principles of a trauma-informed approach (shown in Table 9.5). The framework can be used when working in partnership with Aboriginal and Torres Strait Islander peoples (Huang et al., 2014).

Table 9.5 Principles of trauma-informed practice with students

Principle	Example
Safety	All students and families involved of all ages should feel physically and psychologically safe. This includes the physical setting, and all interpersonal interactions
Trustworthiness and transparency	Organizational operations and decisions are transparently conducted with the goal of building and maintaining trust with students and family members, as well as teachers and other participants
Collaboration and mutuality	Importance is placed on partnering and reducing power differences between teachers and students. This is prioritized to demonstrate that healing occurs in social relationships and in the meaningful sharing of power and decision-making. The school recognizes that everyone has a role to play in a trauma informed approach
Peer support	Peer support and mutual self-help are prioritized to establish safety and hope, build trust, enhance collaboration, and utilize student and family stories and lived experience to promote recovery and healing. The term Peers refers to individuals with lived experience of trauma, or in the case of children this may be family members of children who have experienced traumatic events and are key caregivers in their recovery
Empowerment, voice, and choice	Community strengths and experiences are recognized and built upon. The school fosters a belief in the prioritization of the people served, in resilience, and in the ability of children, families, and other stakeholders to heal and promote recovery from trauma. There is an understanding that the trauma may be a unifying aspect in the lives of those who run the school, who provide their services, and/or those who come for assistance and support. Therefore, empowerment must be given to staff and students alike. Schools should understand the importance of power differentials and how historically this may have impacted students. There is support for shared decision-making, choice, and goal setting to determine a plan of action to move forward and heal
Cultural, historical, and gender issues	The school actively moves past cultural stereotypes and biases, leverages the healing value of traditional cultural connection, incorporates policies, protocols, and processes that are responsive to the racial, ethnic, and cultural needs of students and families, and recognizes and addresses historical trauma

Adapted from SAMHSA (Huang et al., 2014)

Applying the Principles of Trauma-Informed Practice with Aboriginal and Torres Strait Islander Students

Trauma-informed practice when working in partnership with Aboriginal and Torres Strait Islander peoples should focus on an Indigenist Methodological approach (Rigney, 1999). This will center Aboriginal and Torres Strait Islander ways of knowing, being, and doing, entwined with the SAMHSA guiding principles (see Table 9.5) (Huang et al., 2014). By combining these methods, the school can apply trauma-informed practice to drive outcomes for and by Aboriginal and Torres Strait Islander peoples. By embedding trauma-informed practice, the school can not only acknowledge and anticipate that students may have histories of trauma, but also highlight that a trauma-informed approach is effective for most learners, no matter their history.

It should also be noted that a strengths-based approach is a central attribute to trauma-informed practice and a requirement when working in partnership with Aboriginal and Torres Strait Islander peoples. This approach seeks to promote healing through a positivist framework, and when applied to students, it works particularly well in developing a strong sense of self and SEWB (Hopper et al., 2010; Miller & Berger, 2020). For Aboriginal and Torres Strait Islander peoples, the acknowledgment and recognition of collective strengths has been identified as a pivotal theme to empowering education, health, and wellbeing (Dudgeon et al., 2014).

Safety, Trustworthiness, and Transparency

Safety, trustworthiness, and transparency privilege reciprocal partnerships built within community. Ultimately this creates a space of trust, cultural safety, and cultural responsiveness. The uptake of trauma-informed practice will promote strong commitment to transparency through every aspect of a student's education, which in turn will promote collaboration, engagement, and authentic relationships with the Aboriginal and Torres Strait Islander community. By partnering with community, the structure and delivery of the education program will be entwined with Aboriginal and Torres Strait Islander ways of knowing, being, and doing that will function to empower student excellence.

Collaboration and Mutuality

Implementing Aboriginal and Torres Strait Islander methods of communication, such as Dadirri and Yarning, will promote the SAMSHSA guiding principle of collaboration and mutuality (Huang et al., 2014). Reciprocity is fundamental to the application of these methods (Atkinson, 2002; Ungunmerr-Baumann et al., 2022). This responsibility guides the educators in community engagement and co-design to better facilitate learning. Meaningful partnerships occur in Aboriginal and Torres Strait Islander communities when equal or greater value is placed on the community's cultures, knowledge systems, and ways of knowing, being, and doing (Tamwoy et al., 2022). A partnership built on respect and reciprocity will assist in delivering high-quality, trauma-informed educational practices and learning environments.

Peer Support

Previous research has discussed the importance of connection to peers and kin as a dominant health consideration for Aboriginal and Torres Strait Islander peoples (Dudgeon et al., 2014). This is displayed in the Cultural Determinants of Health for Aboriginal and Torres Strait Islander peoples, prioritizing family/community connection for positive health and wellbeing (Verbunt et al., 2021). These ideas are also evident through the centrality of family and kinship, which is recognized as a source of providing reciprocal affection, responsibility, and sharing in Aboriginal and Torres Strait Islander communities (Dudgeon et al., 2014). Education programs must promote peer support by embedding socioemotional skills through teamwork and emotional regulation, as well as positive relationship building as part of engagement. This will create an environment that nourishes the social relationships for Aboriginal and Torres Strait Islander students (Dudgeon et al., 2020).

Empowerment, Voice, and Choice

The impact of Aboriginal and Torres Strait Islander trauma is linked to a feeling of powerlessness (Huang et al., 2014). Continual government-based interventions have failed to encourage empowerment or instill agency of Aboriginal and Torres Strait Islander people. This has resulted in further dependencies and dysfunctions, can have a re-traumatizing effect on Aboriginal and Torres Strait Islander peoples and communities. Schools must include community voice and decision-making at all stages of program development and delivery. This empowerment of community will be displayed through a co-design protocol, with community decision-making guiding the direction of the outcomes. Further to this, schools must embed Aboriginal and Torres Strait Islander agency through decision-making opportunities and leadership which features meaningful and genuine engagement with Elders and Knowledge Holders. Elders play a central and revered role in Aboriginal and Torres Strait Islander communities, acting as the custodians of cultural knowledges, traditions, and histories. They are entrusted with the responsibility of passing down wisdom through storytelling, ceremonies, and teachings, ensuring the preservation of rich heritage. Elders provide guidance and leadership, helping to maintain social cohesion and cultural continuity. Their insights and experiences are invaluable in decision-making processes, conflict resolution, and the education of younger generations. The respect afforded to Elders highlights the deep appreciation for their contributions to the community's identity, resilience, and ongoing connection to ancestral lands and traditions. Knowledge Holders are vital to Aboriginal and Torres Strait Islander communities, serving as the keepers and transmitters of specialized cultural, ecological, and spiritual knowledges. Unlike Elders, who are often recognized for their wisdom, age, and experience, Knowledge Holders may be of any age and are respected for their deep understanding of specific cultural practices, languages, rituals, and lore. They play a crucial role in educating the community, in various aspects of traditional life, such as medicinal plant use, navigation, and cultural ceremonies. Knowledge Holders ensure the continuity and application of traditional knowledge in contemporary contexts, aiding in the preservation of cultural identity and the promotion of community wellbeing. Their expertise complements the broader guidance provided by Elders, creating a rich tapestry of knowledge and leadership within Aboriginal and Torres Strait Islander communities.

Cultural, Historical, and Gender Issues

Recovery approaches informed by Aboriginal and Torres Strait Islander cultures can have positive outcomes for healing. Implementation strategies that recognize the healing value of traditional cultural connections as well as responsiveness to cultural needs will have a better chance of sustained success in schools (Huang et al., 2014). This approach aligns with the Cultural Determinants of Health for Aboriginal and Torres Strait Islander peoples, ensuring that appropriate perspectives and ways of knowing, being, and doing are included in schools (Verbunt et al., 2021).

Case Study: Marigurium Yan Partnerships with Schools

In establishing a culturally safe and culturally responsive learning environment within schools, it is crucial to cultivate meaningful, respectful partnerships with community that are transparent, founded on trust, and focus on strengths of all stakeholders. The Marigurium Yan (Strong Walk in Butchulla) program is an example of a strength-based approach that takes a collaborative and community-driven model of engagement to build students' educational aspirations. This project engages meaningfully with Aboriginal and Torres Strait Islander students by ensuring community voices provide the foundations for the project, validating Aboriginal and Torres Strait Islander knowledges and perspectives. The following is a case study illustrating the central tenets of the Marigurium Yan program and how it aligns with provision of culturally safe and responsive trauma-informed practice with Aboriginal and Torres Strait Islander students.

Through co-conceptualization and collaboration with multiple stakeholders, including Aboriginal and Torres Strait Islander Elders and Knowledge Holders, community representatives, government agencies, industries, and not-for-profit organizations, the development of strength-based relationships and common understandings led to the formation of robust partnerships, enriching the program with a sense of cultural safety for all of those involved.

A series of culturally responsive workshops was developed to widen educational aspirations of Aboriginal and Torres Strait Islander students. The delivery of the workshops privileged Elders, Knowledge Holders, and community members, along with educators, to build a sense of belonging and connection to community. Partners worked together to showcase a wide range of opportunities available to young

Aboriginal and Torres Strait Islander students, while fostering a growth mindset and applying these ideals to their schoolwork.

The combination of building self-efficacy through growth mindsets and adapting problem-solving skills to learning provided a strong foundation for higher educational aspirations and excellence. The program embraced the principles of trauma-informed practice and assisted schools to move past cultural stereotypes and biases into a more culturally responsive approach that demonstrated the importance of cultural connections, reciprocity, and shared decision-making. This developed genuine partnerships that focused on educational outcomes and aspirations of Aboriginal and Torres Strait Islander students.

The ongoing co-design of the program, including feedback and leadership in the Marigurim Yan program, celebrated Aboriginal and Torres Strait Islander success in education and industry, and recognized the achievements of participants and facilitators in the project. Active and engaged community members reinforced the value of educational aspirations in a culturally responsive and developmentally informed way, ensuring the project became part of a positive home-school-career conversation.

The support elicited from a variety of educational and employment providers enabled Aboriginal and Torres Strait Islander students and their communities to develop a greater understanding of the opportunities that exist in education. The productive partnerships established through this program led to sustainable, collaborative partnerships that enhanced educational opportunities and aspirations for Aboriginal and Torres Strait Islander students, their families, and kinship networks and met the high ambitions of community.

The Marigurim Yan project was significant in that community had a central voice in the project and was meaningfully engaged in the development and implementation of the project throughout every stage. Building strong and robust partnerships with key local stakeholders from a wide range of fields provided the cornerstones for a strength-based approach to improve educational aspirations for all of those involved in the program. Ongoing dialogues with Elders, Knowledge Holders, and community representatives created a culturally safe, culturally responsive, and sustainable program that other Aboriginal and Torres Strait Islander communities could adapt to their own needs and aspirations to build stronger futures for Aboriginal and Torres Strait Islander students.

Recommendations for Building Trauma-Informed Schools for Aboriginal and Torres Strait Islander Students

1. Teachers and school-leaders must build their understanding of the Social Determinants of Health and the Cultural Determinants of Health and apply the key elements to the implementation of genuine and meaningful engagement in partnership with Aboriginal and Torres Strait Islander students and their communities.
2. Schools should approach health, wellbeing, and education engagement from a holistic viewpoint using the nine guiding principles of Aboriginal and Torres Strait Islander social and emotional wellbeing to inform culturally safe and culturally responsive practices.
3. Schools and educators should seek to deliver culturally responsive trauma-informed practice to promote self-determination and reciprocity, both of which are essential when working in partnership with Aboriginal and Torres Strait Islander students. This environment will be created through purposeful and ongoing engagement with each of the six SAMHSA attributes of trauma-informed care.

Conclusion

The health of Aboriginal and Torres Strait Islander peoples is a factor of both the Social Determinants of Health and Cultural Determinants of Health and must be considered when co-designing education programs in schools. These determinants, if embedded with careful consideration, can assist in the development of culturally safe and culturally responsive learning environments that take into consideration the drivers of overall health and wellbeing of Aboriginal and Torres Strait Islander people. The Social Determinants of Health model not only recognizes pivotal contributors to the success of a student's educational outcomes, but is also important to Aboriginal and Torres Strait Islander perspectives and decision-making.

The Cultural Determinants of Health specifically address considerations that impact the social and emotional health and wellbeing of Aboriginal and Torres Strait Islander peoples. This model privileges Aboriginal and Torres Strait Islander ways of knowing, being, and doing, and must be a fundamental consideration for schools in co-designing curriculum and culturally responsive engagement methods. The Cultural Determinants of Health specifically address considerations that impact social and emotional wellbeing, understanding that approaches must be co-designed based on the collectivist nature of Aboriginal and Torres Strait Islander communities, and embedding community decision-making at all stages of program design and delivery.

Educational settings that empower Aboriginal and Torres Strait Islander students must acknowledge not only the Social Determinants of Health and the Cultural Determinants of Health, but also the nine guiding principles of SEWB for Aboriginal and Torres Strait Islander peoples. The application of the guiding principles of SEWB in partnership with Aboriginal and Torres Strait Islander students within a school setting moves more effectively toward holistic practice that recognizes the many facets of Aboriginal and Torres Strait Islander social and emotional wellbeing. This approach will demonstrate greatest benefit for Aboriginal and Torres Strait Islander students and the school when embedded with community-led partnerships and ultimately prioritizing self-determination and reciprocity of First Nations peoples.

Following on from these sociocultural perspectives, trauma-informed practice is essential when working in partnership with Aboriginal and Torres Strait Islander students in education settings due to ongoing colonization, dispossession from Country, and dislocation of families and kinship. To align effectively with trauma-informed practice for Aboriginal and Torres Strait Islander students, each of the six SAHMSA elements of safety, trustworthiness and transparency, collaboration and mutuality, peer support, empowerment, voice, and choice, and cultural, historical, and gender issues must be considered within the unique schooling context and within the setting of collectivist cultures. The application of trauma-informed practice in partnership with Aboriginal and Torres Strait Islander students in schools ensures that learning environments are co-constructed and focus on the strengths and experiences of community, endeavoring to empower Aboriginal and Torres Strait Islander students in the education system. Opportunities exist to better design and evaluate trauma-informed practice in schools in partnership with Aboriginal and Torres Strait Islander communities, to ensure that this practice is continually embedding Aboriginal and Torres Strait Islander ways of knowing, being, and doing.

References

Anderson, I., Baum, F., & Bentley, M. (2007). Beyond Bandaids: Exploring the underlying social determinants of Aboriginal health: Papers from the social determinants of Aboriginal Health workshop, Adelaide, July 2004. CRC for Aboriginal Health.

Atkinson, J. (2002). *Trauma trails, recreating song lines: The transgenerational effects of trauma in Indigenous Australia*. Spinifex Press.

Ayre, K., Krishnamoorthy, G., Rees, B., & Berger, E. (2022). Balancing the needs of the school community: Implementing trauma-informed behaviour supports in an Australian Regional Primary School. *Australian Journal of Teacher Education, 47*, 43–61. https://doi.org/10.14221/ajte.2022v47n9.3

Braveman, P., & Gottlieb, L. (2014). The social determinants of health: It's time to consider the causes of the causes. *Public Health Reports, 129*(1_suppl2), 19–31. https://doi.org/10.1177/00333549141291s206

Brockman, R., & Dudgeon, P. (2020). Indigenous clinical psychology in Australia: A decolonising social–emotional well-being approach. In P. Rhodes (Ed.), *Beyond the psychology industry: How else might we heal?* (pp. 83–93). Springer International Publishing. https://doi.org/10.1007/978-3-030-33762-9_8

Dudgeon, P., Bray, A., Smallwood, G., Walker, R., & Dalton, T. (2020). *Wellbeing and healing through connection and culture*. Lifeline Australia.

Dudgeon, P., Milroy, H., & Walker, R. (2014). *Working together: Aboriginal and Torres Strait Islander mental health and wellbeing principles and practice*. Telethon Kids Institute, Kulunga Aboriginal Research Development Unit, Department of the Prime Minister and Cabinet (Australia).

Gapp, K., Bohacek, J., Grossmann, J., Brunner, A. M., Manuella, F., Nanni, P., & Mansuy, I. M. (2016). Potential of environmental enrichment to prevent transgenerational effects of paternal trauma. *Neuropsychopharmacology, 41*(11), 2749–2758. https://doi.org/10.1038/npp.2016.87

Hopper, E., Bassuk, E., & Olivet, J. (2010). Shelter from the storm: Trauma-informed care in homelessness services settings. *The Open Health Services and Policy Journal, 3*, 80–100. https://doi.org/10.2174/1874924001003010080

Huang, L. N., Flatow, R., Biggs, T., Afayee, S., Smith, K., Clark, T., & Blake, M. (2014). *SAMHSA's concept of trauma and guidance for a trauma-informed approach*.

Ian, A., Fran, B., & Michael, B. (2004). *Beyond bandaids: Exploring the underlying social determinants of Aboriginal health: Papers from the Social Determinants of Aboriginal Health Workshop, Adelaide, July 2004* (0734037449 9780734037442).

Louth, S., Wheeler, K., Jamieson-Proctor, R., & Sanderson, T. (2023). Stoking the fires of pre-service educators through Aboriginal and Torres Strait islander ways of learning. *International Journal of Educational Innovation and Research, 2*(2), 104–113.

Miller, J., & Berger, E. (2020). A review of school trauma-informed practice for Aboriginal and Torres Strait Islander children and youth. *Educational and Developmental Psychologist, 37*(1), 39–46. https://doi.org/10.1017/edp.2020.2

Prehn, J. (2024). An indigenous strengths-based theoretical framework. *Australian Social Work, 78*(2), 145–158. https://doi.org/10.1080/0312407X.2024.2340464

Rigney, L.-I. (1999). Internationalization of an indigenous anticolonial cultural critique of research methodologies: A guide to indigenist research methodology and its principles. *Wicazo Sa Review, 14*(2), 109–121. https://doi.org/10.2307/1409555

Substance Abuse and Mental Health Services Administration (SAMHSA). (2014). *SAMHSA's concept of trauma and guidance for a trauma-informed approach* (HHS Publication No. (SMA) 14-4884). https://store.samhsa.gov/shin/content/SMA14-4884/SMA14-4884.pdf

Swan, P. (1995). *"Ways forward": National consultancy report on Aboriginal and Torres Strait Islander mental health / by P. Swan and B. Raphael*. Australian Govt. Publishing Service.

Tamwoy, N., Rosas, S., Davis, S., Farthing, A., Houghton, C., Johnston, H., Maloney, C., Samulkiewicz, N., Seaton, J., & Tuxworth, G. (2022). Co-design with aboriginal and torres strait islander communities: A journey. *Australian Journal of Rural Health, 30*(6), 816–822.

Ungunmerr-Baumann, M.-R., Groom, R. A., Schuberg, E. L., Atkinson, J., Atkinson, C., Wallace, R., & Morris, G. (2022). Dadirri: An Indigenous place-based research methodology. *AlterNative: An International Journal of Indigenous Peoples, 18*(1), 94–103. https://doi.org/10.1177/11771801221085353

Verbunt, E., Luke, J., Paradies, Y., Bamblett, M., Salamone, C., Jones, A., & Kelaher, M. (2021). Cultural determinants of health for Aboriginal and Torres Strait Islander people – A narrative overview of reviews. *International Journal for Equity in Health, 20*(1), 181. https://doi.org/10.1186/s12939-021-01514-2

Wilkinson, R. G., & Marmot, M. (2003). *Social determinants of health: The solid facts*. World Health Organization.

10

Effects of Music, Music Interventions, and Trauma

Alysha Kramer, Katrina Skewes Ferran, and Louise Jenkins

Introduction

Human interest and involvement in music is not a recent phenomenon. Engagement with music has been found in every known human culture, with evidence dating back over 40, 000 years (Zatorre & Peretz, 2001). Music can entertain us, helps us commemorate or commiserate important life events, create atmosphere while we shop, and motivate us while we exercise. Music is a popular leisure activity (Schäfer et al., 2013) and an important component in everyday life (Lonsdale & North, 2011; Rentfrow, 2012). Given its prevalence and prominence in human cultures, it is no wonder that attention has increased over the past decades as to how and why music affects us.

Neurosciences have become invested in the complex neural networks and cognitive functioning involved in receiving and producing music (Castro et al., 2015; Koelsch, 2015; O'Kelly et al., 2016; Zatorre, 2005). Psychological sciences have explored the relationships between music and personality traits (Chamorro-Premuzic & Furnham, 2007), identity (Boer et al., 2013; North et al., 2000), behavior (North et al., 1999; North et al., 2004; Yalch & Spangenberg, 2000), social connection (Boer et al., 2011; Gabriel & Paravati, 2021; Joseph & Human, 2020), and cognitive processes (Mizener, 2008; Roden et al., 2014). While the field of biological sciences has investigated music and physiological responses; music has been shown to influence the autonomic nervous system (Ellis & Thayer, 2010; Thoma et al., 2013), the immune system (Chanda & Levitin, 2013; Kreutz et al., 2004), and induce various endocrine outcomes (Koelsch et al., 2016), even in individuals without music training (McCraty et al., 1996).

This chapter discusses what is currently known about music interventions for children and adolescents, how music is used within educational

DOI: 10.4324/9781003436034-10

settings, and how music interventions can be applied within a trauma-informed framework. A case study to demonstrate how trauma-informed music-interventions can be applied with children and adolescents within educational settings, will additionally be provided.

Music Use in Children and Adolescents

Music plays a meaningful role in contemporary youth culture (Laughey, 2006; McFerran, 2010). Research reports that children and adolescents engage in music for a variety of reasons, such as self-regulation (Phillips et al., 2019), to connect with others (Travis & Bowman, 2012), enhance mood (Saarikallio et al., 2020), and to assist in identity formation (Chittenden, 2013; McFerran, 2010). Over the past two decades, research has grown regarding the use of music and music interventions with children and adolescents (Belski et al., 2021; Facchini & Ruini, 2021; Geipel et al., 2018; Ye et al., 2021; Yinger & Gooding, 2014). Literature has investigated the value of playing a musical instrument during childhood and adolescence (Bergman-Nutley et al., 2014; Forgeard et al., 2008), with some studies linking it to improved cognitive health and well-being (Dingle et al., 2021; Rose et al., 2019). Using music therapeutically, (i.e., music therapy and other music interventions), has been demonstrated to assist children and adolescents in processing grief (Rosner et al., 2010; McFerran & Crooke, 2016), reduce emotional and behavioral problems (McFerran, 2010), support children experiencing mental illness (McFerran, 2010), and reduce psychological distress and increase wellbeing in pediatric oncology patients (Facchini & Ruini, 2021). Additionally, music can be a useful way to communicate and engage children and adolescents who may not necessarily respond to other traditional therapeutic methods, such as talking therapies (Keen, 2005; Kimbel & Protivnak, 2010).

Music Interventions to Support Mental Health and Socio-Emotional Development in Children and Adolescents

A number of studies report that music interventions have been favored over other evidence-based interventions when working with younger population groups (who present with mental health and social-emotional concerns), as music can be perceived as a less confronting intervention compared to traditional talking therapies (Davis, 2010; Keen, 2005; Kimbel & Protivnak, 2010). Much of the literature within this area uses case studies to draw attention to children and young people's experiences of music interventions. However, there has been a trend over the past two decades to examine the efficacy and evidence for music interventions in child and adolescent populations, through experimental studies, meta-analyses, and systematic reviews.

Ye et al. (2021) conducted a meta-analysis to investigate the effects of music interventions on aggressive behaviors in children and adolescents, and found that music interventions were generally more effective in decreasing aggressive behaviors and increasing self-control when compared to control groups. According to a meta-analysis and systematic review conducted by van der Heijden et al. (2015), music interventions may produce statistically significant effects in minimizing post-operative pain, anxiety, and distress in pediatric patients undergoing surgery. While a meta-analysis conducted by Geipel et al. (2018) examined the effectiveness of music-based interventions in decreasing internalizing symptoms (i.e., depression and anxiety) in children and adolescents, and found that music-based interventions may be effective in decreasing internalizing symptoms. They also recommended that more rigorous research is required to replicate existing results and strengthen evidence.

Similar results were observed in a recent systematic review by Belski et al. (2021), which aimed to examine the efficacy of music therapy in decreasing symptoms of depression and/or anxiety in children and adolescents. Belski et al. found evidence for music therapy interventions improving depressive symptoms at short- and intermediate-term follow-ups, when compared to control groups, however only one study was found to demonstrate the effectiveness of music therapy in improving anxiety symptoms (at short-term follow-up) in comparison to the control group. Belski et al. additionally concluded that limited evidence exists to indicate that music therapy is an effective treatment for improving depression and/or anxiety symptoms in children and adolescents and that higher quality studies are required.

It is important to recognize that not all music activities will induce beneficial outcomes or help to regulate the mood of people in positive ways. Music can also induce negative moods (Stack et al., 2012), and negatively impact behavior and attitudes (Drew, 2020; Mast & McAndrew, 2011).

A study by Tanner et al. (2009) found that adolescents who listened to rap music reported significantly more antisocial behavior and greater feelings of inequality compared to their peers who listened to other music genres. While a study by Felsenstein (2013) reported that particular sounds and use of musical instruments made of seashells, enhanced trauma symptoms within displaced preschoolers, as it evoked memories of their previous community and homes by the coast.

The effectiveness of music interventions can also be influenced by the qualifications of the facilitator administering the intervention. For example, Ye et al. (2021) found that music therapy delivered by registered music therapists was more effective in reducing aggressive behaviors in children and adolescents compared to music interventions administered by music teachers, music professionals, or other health experts. Therefore, when using music as an intervention, it is vital that the type of music is carefully selected, and essential considerations are made around who the facilitator is (e.g., what are their qualifications), and what music activities are delivered. This is particularly true when working with children and adolescents who have been exposed to a potentially traumatic event, as re-traumatization may unintentionally occur.

Trauma, Music Interventions, and Music Therapy

Using music to manage trauma symptomology is at the core of music therapy; music therapy was officially established as a health therapy after music was observed to therapeutically support veterans with posttraumatic stress disorder (PTSD) after World War II (Beyers, 2016). Since this time, research has been building to demonstrate the effects of music interventions for trauma-related symptoms (Eyre, 2007; Hillman et al., 2022; Slotoroff, 1994). Studies have been conducted across various settings to better understand the effectiveness of music interventions within child and adolescent population groups who have been exposed to a potentially traumatic event. Within hospital settings, music interventions (i.e., music therapy) have been found to act as a protective factor against PTSD in pediatric surgical patients (Wallace et al., 2013), and reduced the risks of PTSD in severely unwell and hospitalized children (Uggla et al., 2016). A randomized controlled trial conducted by Alemán et al. (2017) found that participation in a community-based youth orchestra program enhanced self-control and reduced antisocial behaviors in children exposed to violence. Similar results were observed by Kang (2017) who found an improvement in self-expression and emotion regulation in children who had been exposed to domestic violence after participation in a music, imagery, and sand play intervention. However, currently, the trauma and music literature reportedly lack sufficient high quality and rigorous studies necessary for music to be recognized as an evidence-based trauma intervention, with many studies conducting case studies or using qualitative methods (Hillman et al., 2022; Kramer & Berger, 2025; McFerran et al., 2020).

Music Interventions and the Polyvagal Theory

Recent interest in music interventions for managing trauma has drawn renewed attention through the emergence of neuroscience theories that link trauma symptomology with primitive human responses and brain networks, such as Porges' (2011) Polyvagal Theory and Perry's (2009) Neurosequential Model of Therapeutics (McFerran et al., 2020). These theories suggest that repetitive and patterned neural input, such as music, can help to organize and regulate dysfunctional neural pathways that have developed through trauma exposure, and have the potential to reduce anxiety, impulsivity, and other symptoms that may occur due to experiencing a traumatic event (Perry, 2009; Porges, 2011). Van der Kolk (2007) has also proposed that rhythmic and repetitive activities (such as music) could promote neurological healing that has been disturbed through trauma exposure. Through a Polyvagal Theory lens, Williamson et al. (2015) suggest that trauma interventions ought to target the parasympathetic nervous system, further adding that interventions which involve slow and paced breathing, such as singing or playing a musical instrument that requires controlled breathing (i.e., wind or brass instruments), could offer the opportunity to enhance the parasympathetic tone. However, as this is a relatively new area of exploration, there are limited studies that examine the effects of music upon trauma symptomology within a Polyvagal Theory framework (McFerran et al., 2020).

Music Use Within Educational Settings

Current Role of Music in School Systems

Globally, many schools provide children and adolescents with the opportunity to engage in music education (Garvis et al., 2017). Music education reviews and research support the inclusion of music in schools, evidencing the benefits to students' academic and personal development (Collins et al., 2020; Government of South Australia, 2019; Masson, 2013; Päivi-Sisko Eerola & Tuomas Eerola, 2014; Parliament of Victoria, 2013). The benefits of music education in schools for children and adolescents include, among others, increasing a sense of belonging, developing effective social skills, improving the ability to work as part of a team, lifting self-esteem, creating feelings of achievement, nurturing confidence, honing fine motor skills, and developing ongoing identity construction (Goopy, 2022; Jenkins & Crawford, 2022; Hallam, 2010; Powell, 2019). Overall, a good quality music education contributes to academic success at school as well as success as a member of society and throughout one's life (Parliament of Victoria, 2013).

Despite recognition of the benefits of a good music education, the extent and quality of music learning provided in schools globally are somewhat variable (Garvis et al., 2017). For example, in Australia, all primary school students who are studying the Australian Curriculum learn music as a classroom activity, with either a specialist music teacher or increasingly over the last 20 years, with their generalist classroom teacher (de Vries, 2015; Holden & Button, 2006; Government of South Australia, 2019; Wiggins & Wiggins, 2008). In contrast, Thailand's elementary to secondary school students attend weekly 30-minute music lessons with qualified teachers (Chandransu, 2019).

Role of School Music to Support Children Therapeutically

Given the wide availability of classroom and extra-curricular music programs offered to students in schools, some have argued that music is currently an underused resource for the purpose of addressing school students' health and wellbeing (Dingle et al., 2021). In Germany, Italy, the UK, and the US, music therapy has been used in mainstream schools as an intervention for children with emotional, social, or behavioral problems, those from culturally diverse backgrounds, and as part of the process of integrating students with disabilities into mainstream schools. Orff-based music therapy has been identified as a support for bereaved children in elementary schools (Hilliard, 2007; McFerran et al., 2010), and in Australian schools, music therapy has been used to support students from refugee backgrounds (Carr & Wigram, 2009).

Music therapists are specially trained to use music to improve peoples' social skills, communication, academic outcomes, physical health, mental health, and spiritual wellbeing. They do this by working with the elements of music, drawing on their own expertise as to how these elements affect people, and the ways in which musical associations impact and influence behavior and thinking (Swanson, 2020). Assessment of musical interests and psycho-social-emotional needs is a critical part of music therapy practice processes, with cycles of referral, assessment, goal setting, program planning, implementation, and evaluation providing the typical structure of their work (Thompson, 2022). This structure is reflected in the illustrative example contained within this chapter and is typical of allied health interventions generally, with music therapists often working as part of an allied health team (Allied Health Professions Australia, 2023).

Specific music therapy programs for schools are not an embedded part of Australian schools, but in 2022 in Victoria (a South-eastern state of Australia), a government-funded Schools Mental Health Fund was developed which included a provision for music therapy programs in schools. The intended outcomes of this program are to assist students to regulate their emotions, build emotional literacy, sustain positive relationships, develop students' interest and motivation, nurture positive coping resources and strategies, and develop students' sense of self and identity (Victorian Department of Education, 2023). It has been suggested that this program will allow schools to work more effectively and positively with students exposed to trauma such as "community violence, natural disasters, divorce, death of a loved one, neglect or abuse" (van Klompenberg, 2023, p. 56).

Considerations for Trauma-Informed Music Education and Music Use within Classroom Settings: Practical Applications

While music therapy is one way to provide trauma-informed musical interventions in schools, consideration of the way music activities can be included and accessed within the classroom environment, as well as other musical activities and events in schools (e.g., instrumental lessons, musical productions) should be considered. It is important for music teachers, classroom teachers, and other professionals who use music when working with students to prioritize effective classroom management practices that support traumatized children's healing. For example, a welcoming and safe classroom environment provides a space in which a teacher can get to know their students and be a responsible and caring adult in their lives. Positive teacher and student relationships and engaging musical activities which students enjoy have been proposed to help "trauma-affected students repair disrupted attachment styles" (Bauman-Field, 2023, p. 1). A well-structured and predictable classroom, with clearly understood and adhered to expectations for behavior and routine, implementing praise as a regular part of teacher feedback, and avoiding punishments that have the potential to trigger a traumatized student, can contribute to a classroom experience which supports healing from trauma (Bauman-Field, 2023; van Klompenberg, 2023).

It is also helpful for teachers and those working with students to have knowledge of a child's musical background as this can inform lesson planning that includes musical performances and simultaneously enables positive communication with the child's family and carers. Asking parents about what kind of music their child enjoys, as well as gently enquiring about whether there is any music that might have negative associations for the child, can be an important, insightful, and often enjoyable conversation. If trauma-informed music education is to be considered as a more embedded part of school music programs, then there is a need for classroom teachers, music teachers, and instrumental teachers to be appropriately trained to lower the chances of triggering traumatized students through particular performances or music activities, and to ensure quality teaching and learning (Kramer & Berger, 2025).

For some children exposed to trauma it might be that loud music is overwhelming and triggers a traumatic reaction. For others it might be that a certain repertoire of music is associated with traumatic experiences. Musical triggers cannot be generalized, since they uniquely reflect the child's particular situation, however they can be managed with appropriate consultation with the child's parents and caregivers, and importantly with the student themselves, and through warnings such as 'this next section is going to be loud, does anyone need to prepare for that?', or 'we are studying a new style of music today. If this style is troubling for you, please feel free to let me know'. These and other examples are illustrated in the case example within this chapter.

The extent of trauma-informed musical experience in schools globally is currently limited (Kramer & Berger, 2025), however research suggests that wider inclusion of trauma-informed musical activities would be a valuable addition to the school curriculum because of the potential positive benefit to student's mental health and wellbeing. The following section illustrates how this can look as part of a music therapy intervention, drawing on an anonymized, composite case study designed to protect the privacy of participants.

Case Study Illustration of Music Intervention

Eight primary-school-aged children experiencing homelessness and family violence are referred to a music therapy group program due to reported challenges they are experiencing in their respective schools. Each of the children is described as having difficulty with the social expectations of the classroom resulting in either their exclusion from class or being isolated from their peers. This is also impacting their academic performance.

The qualified music therapist conducts individual assessments with each of the children, comprising between two and four sessions. This allows them to assess their musical interests and comfort levels, build trust between themselves and each child, develop insights into the ways that music and noise might be triggering for them, and also identify whether they need support in managing their arousal levels. Two of the children withdraw from their school before the assessments are completed and are lost to follow up. One family struggle with the time required to travel to the venue and decide not to attend the program. Three of the children are neurodiverse, one child appears to have poor mental health, and the other has a mild intellectual disability.

The first child, named Jordan, is diagnosed as being on the autism spectrum and is hyper-sensitive to noise. They are comfortable when the level of noise is under their control, however they enjoy playing on drums and other large instruments, such as the piano when feeling safe and comfortable, but do not enjoy unplanned changes.

The second child, named Jesiah, has an ADHD diagnosis and is comfortable with noise and fun. They love hip-hop beats and dancing as well as playing drums and other handheld percussion. They are very focused when engaging in 1:1 music activities, such as song writing and playing games with beats in the background, and engage enthusiastically with new ideas.

The third child, named Jules, is socially withdrawn and reluctant to play on the instruments at first. They do agree to draw while listening to their favorite music by the heavy metal band, Metallica, and gradually start to express a willingness to play along with the music on the drumkit and other instruments. They do not speak very often, but do increasingly make eye contact and even smile on occasion.

The fourth child, name Jru, is easily overwhelmed if things do not go exactly their way. They enjoy musical games with clear rules and can play for extended periods of time with high levels of engagement on the instruments.

The fifth child, Jalani, has a mild intellectual disability and a friendly, easy-going personality. They bring their favorite music to sessions, and enjoy singing along with their favorite pop, hip-hop, and rock songs. They also enjoy playing on the instruments and drawing to peaceful music.

An extended and individual assessment period is considered helpful for these children in order to establish safety before commencing the group. Each of the five children remains engaged for the two, three, or four sessions they are able to attend before the group starts. Jesiah, Jru, and Jalani all write songs as part of the individual assessment and engagement process, with lyrics that they have generated after brainstorming about the strengths and resources that help them cope with challenges in their lives. They share their songs with the support person who has traveled with them to the session, often a parent, and appear proud of their creations and excited for the group. Jordan and Jules choose not to create a song during their individual sessions, but both are able to express themselves using either instrumental play or drawing, and are not opposed to the idea of joining the group. Overall, the children seem comfortable with the idea of using music and art for expressive purposes, and seem to trust the music therapist, as seen by their enthusiasm to enter the room at the start of sessions, eye contact and facial expression, as well as the comments some make to their support person. The music therapist also has a strong sense of each child's musical interests and triggers and is able to manage the conditions to support optimal arousal in the 1:1 sessions. However, coming together for a group program will significantly increase the social challenges for each child and the chances of each child being triggered by the musical interests and behavior of the other children.

The music therapist carefully constructs goals and a session plan for a ten-week group program, taking into account what is known about each child. The intention is to gradually work towards a performance by the group, whether that is live or recorded, in order for them to have an output of their time together that will serve as a reminder of the group. In the meantime, they will meet regularly for 60-minute sessions that begins with 15 minutes for snacks and settling in, and concludes with a gentle music and relaxation time during which each child departs when they are ready.

The program goals are for each group member to have a positive experience of being in the music therapy group together, as seen by:

- Attending sessions regularly and being able to regulate their arousal levels enough to stay in the room for the full duration
- Playing music together on percussion instruments such as drums without being overwhelmed and needing to withdraw from the group activities
- Joining in with structured games while strong rhythmic tracks are playing in the background
- Contributing to a song that expresses something about their shared experience of traveling through the homelessness and family violence system.

The session plan is structured to enable the successful achievement of these goals and is flexibly adapted and extended each week depending on the presenting needs and abilities of the various group members on different days. Within this safety-focused structure, other goals related to the trauma experiences of the children emerge and are addressed. These included:

For individual group members to develop self-understanding through:

- Building a repertoire of emotion-focused words that reflect embodied experience of emotions (see Instrumental Play below)
- Reflecting on strengths they have developed through trauma experiences (See Song Creation below)
- Identifying self-soothing strategies that can be used in a range of environments (see Music and Drawing below).

The session structure for the ten-week group program is detailed below:

Welcome and Settling In (15 minutes) – gentle music playing in background, healthy snacks and drinks available, tables set up with individual activities such as coloring in, dominoes, and other simple sensory objects.

Warm Up (10 minutes) – Invitation to form a circle and sway or move to the backing track which is electronic and beat-based, with a subtle bass line but no other embellishments. When everyone has joined, the music therapist describes a structured game that will be played and provides clear directions about what to do. Games include:

- Walking in a circle to the music
- Passing balloons to the music
- Tossing bean bags to the music
- Taking turns to suggest a movement to the music (option to pass)
- Bust-a-move and taking a solo to the music (option to pass).

Transition (five minutes) – all the children sit in a circle and the music therapist puts pictures and word cards in the middle of the circle. Children are invited to choose how they're feeling today and share about their choice if they want to.

Song Creation Time (between 5 and 20 minutes depending on comfort levels) – the music therapist plays a well-known song that has been deemed tolerable to all group members, usually of a soft pop, rock, or hip-hop style. Group members are invited to sing or dance along while the song plays, but are asked to listen while they do. Soft toys are also provided as sensory objects for those who would like to do something with their hands while listening.

The music therapist then asks the group to help change the words to the song. In the first week it is just a couple of words from the chorus which they then sing back to one another. The topic is light and is about having fun. This task increases in complexity across the weeks until the group begins to work on changing all the words to the song that has proven to be most mutually acceptable. The topic they are writing lyrics about is what strengths they have developed through their experience of homelessness.

Instrumental Play (between 5 and 15 minutes depending on capacity) – The group take part in structured games using the instruments, slowly moving towards slower and calmer games as the end of group time comes closer. Games include:

- Playing This is how I'm feeling on the instruments – words given as prompts (happy, sad, angry, excited, peaceful)
- Stop and Go, with people taking turns at being the leader
- Playing along with the music therapist, with people taking turns then being the leader
- Copy my sound, with people taking turns then being the leader
- Last chance to play your favorite instrument.

Music and Drawing/Relaxation (between 5 and 10 minutes as needed) – drawing materials, and cushions are provided for people to take some time to chill out and then leave the group, saying or waving goodbye, when they are ready. Gentle instrumental music playing in background with minimal variation in volume, timbre, and a steady structure.

Evaluation is twofold, first based on what is observable about the children's experience of the group in relation to the program goals. The music therapist also visits each child's school to discuss the group outcomes with staff and to offer advice about any strategies that worked well for the child either in the group or the individual sessions. This often involves suggestions about how to use down time for music listening, what kind of music might be calming for each child, and also any instruments or games that were calming for them.

Recommendations

Based on the current evidence, the following recommendations for implementing trauma-informed music interventions for children and adolescents within school settings are provided:

- Consider engaging a registered music therapist. Registered music therapists are currently recognized as the most appropriate professional group to implement and administer therapeutic music interventions in vulnerable population groups. Schools would likely benefit from employing or consulting with a registered music therapist to implement trauma-informed music interventions with their students.
- Teachers and those working with students would benefit from sufficient knowledge of a child's background (e.g., their home situation, mental and physical health status, etc.), particularly when assessing behavior, as trauma-informed practice shifts the emphasis from what is wrong with you to 'what happened to you'. This knowledge would also help to target appropriate interventions and to avoid potential re-traumatization.
- Consider asking the student and/or the parents or carers about what kind of music the student enjoys and whether there is any music that might have negative associations. It is important to keep in mind that musical triggers cannot be generalized among students and are dependent upon the student's unique situation.
- Provide students with clear expectations around music interventions to reduce any potential distress, for example, 'this next section is going to be loud, does anyone need to prepare for that?'.

- Ensure that the environment is welcoming and safe (e.g., consider comfortability of physical environment), encourage positive relationships (e.g., provide praise as regular feedback to the students, avoid punishment), and provide clear direction around structure, routine, and behavior.
- If considering trauma-informed music education more broadly. Classroom teachers, music teachers, and instrumental teachers need to be appropriately trained to reduce the risks of triggering traumatized students through particular performances or music activities.

Conclusion

Music is currently an underused resource for addressing school students' overall wellbeing (Dingle et al., 2021). The benefits of music interventions for children and adolescents have been demonstrated across multiple disciplinaries' (e.g., psychology, neurosciences, education, etc.) and have been shown to influence social connection, mood regulation, and sense of identity (Phillips et al., 2019; Saarikallio et al., 2020; Travis & Bowman, 2012). More recently, interest has increased around using music therapeutically to support children and adolescents who have experienced trauma (Kramer & Berger, 2025). This phenomenon has grown alongside the emergence of various trauma theories (e.g., Polyvagal Theory, Neurosequential Model of Therapeutics), which imply repetitive and patterned neural input, such as music, could positively influence neural pathways that have been disrupted through trauma exposure (McFerran et al., 2020). This interest has led to discussion around the potential benefits of (and in some cases, application of) music interventions within school settings to support students who may have been exposed to trauma. While there are some promising results for the use of trauma-informed music interventions for children and adolescents within school settings, further rigorous research is required to better understand the potential benefits and limitations of this form of support (Kramer & Berger, 2025). It is important that those wishing to use music interventions to support students within a trauma-informed framework understand that this is an emerging area and therefore a careful and considered approach is vital to ensure a positive experience for all involved.

References

Alemán, X., Duryea, S., Guerra, N. G., McEwan, P. J., Muñoz, R., Stampini, M., & Williamson, A. A. (2017). The effects of musical training on child development: A randomized trial of El Sistema in Venezuela. *Prevention Science, 18*(7), 865–878. https://doi.org/10.1007/s11121-016-0727-3

Allied Health Professions Australia. *Music therapy*. https://ahpa.com.au/allied-health-professions/music-therapy/

An, S., Capraro, M. M., & Tillman, D. A. (2013). Elementary teachers integrate music activities into regular mathematics lessons: Effects on students' mathematical abilities. *Journal for Learning through the Arts*. *9*(1), 1–19.

Australian Curriculum Assessment and Reporting Authority. Australian Curriculum, Learning Areas. https://www.australiancurriculum.edu.au/

Barrett, M., Flynn, L. M., & Welch, G. (2018). Music value and participation: An Australian case study of music provision and support in Early Childhood Education. *Research Studies in Music Education*, *40*(2), 226–243. https://doi.org/10.1177/1321103X18773098

Bauman-Field, B. (2023). Trauma-informed classroom management in music education: A literature review. *Update: Applications of Research in Music Education, 42*(3), 43–51. https://doi.org/10.1177/87551233231173149

Belski, N., Abdul-Rahman, Z., Youn, E., Balasundaram, V., & Diep, D. (2021). Review: The effectiveness of musical therapy in improving depression and anxiety symptoms among children and adolescents – A systematic review. *Child and Adolescent Mental Health*. https://doi.org/10.1111/camh.12526

Bergman-Nutley, S., Darki, F., & Klingberg, T. (2014). Music practice is associated with development of working memory during childhood and adolescence. *Frontiers in Human Neuroscience, 7*, 926. https://doi.org/10.3389/fnhum.2013.00926

Beyers, K. L. (2016). *A history of the music therapy profession: Diverse concepts and practices* (1st ed.). Barcelona Publishers.

Boer, D., Fischer, R., González Atilano, M. L., de Garay Hernández, J., Moreno García, L. I., Mendoza, S., Gouveia, V. V., Lam, J., & Lo, E. (2013). Music, identity, and musical ethnocentrism of young people in six Asian, Latin American, and Western cultures. *Journal of Applied Social Psychology, 43*(12), 2360–2376. https://doi.org/10.1111/jasp.12185

Boer, D., Fischer, R., Strack, M., Bond, M. H., Lo, E., & Lam, J. (2011). How shared preferences in music create bonds between people: Values as the missing link. *Personality and Social Psychology Bulletin, 37*(9), 1159–1171. https://doi.org/10.1177/0146167211407521

Carr, C., & Wigram, T. (2009). Music therapy with children and adolescents in mainstream schools: A systematic review. *British Journal of Music Therapy, 23*(1), 3–18. https://doi.org/10.1177/135945750902300102

Castro, M., Tillmann, B., Luauté, J., Corneyllie, A., Dailler, F., André-Obadia, N., & Perrin, F. (2015). Boosting cognition with music in patients with disorders of consciousness. *Neurorehabilitation and Neural Repair, 29*(8), 734–742. https://doi.org/10.1177/1545968314565464

Chamorro-Premuzic, T., & Furnham, A. (2007). Personality and music: Can traits explain how people use music in everyday life? *British Journal of Psychology, 98*(2), 175–185. https://doi.org/10.1348/000712606X111177

Chanda, M. L., & Levitin, D. J. (2013). The neurochemistry of music. *Trends in Cognitive Sciences, 17*(4), 179–193. https://doi.org/10.1016/j.tics.2013.02.007

Chandransu, N. (2019). Integrating multicultural music education into the public elementary school curricula in Thailand. *International Journal of Music Education, 37*(4), 547–560. https://doi.org/10.1177/0255761419855827

Chittenden, T. (2013). In my rearview mirror. *Journal of Children and Media, 7*(2), 186–200. https://doi.org/10.1080/17482798.2012.673500

Collins, A., Dwyer, R., & Date, A. (2020). *Music education a sound investment.* Alberts: The Tony Foundation. https://www.alberts.co/wp-content/uploads/2020/10/Alberts_Music-Education-Report_A4.pdf

Creech, A., Hallam, S., M., Gaunt, H., McQueen, H., Pincas, A & Varvarigou, M. (2014). The role of musical possible selves in supporting subjective wellbeing in later life. *Music Education Research, 16*(1), 32–49. https://doi.org/10.1080/14613808.2013.788143

Davis, K. M. (2010). Music and the expressive arts with children experiencing trauma. *Journal of Creativity in Mental Health, 5*(2), 125–133. https://doi.org/10.1080/15401383.2010.485078

De Vries, P. (2015). Music without a music specialist: A primary school story. *International Journal of Music Education, 33*(2), 210–221. https://doi.org/10.1177/0255761413515818

Dingle, G. A., Sharman, L. S., Bauer, Z., Beckman, E., Broughton, M., Bunzli, E., Davidson, R., Draper, G., Fairley, S., Farrell, C., Flynn, L. M., Gomersall, S., Hong, M., Larwood, J., Lee, C., Lee, J., Nitschinsk, L., Peluso, N., Reedman, S. E., Vidas, D., Walter, Z. C., & Wright, O. R. L. (2021). How do music activities affect health and well-being? A scoping review of studies examining psychosocial mechanisms. *Frontiers in Psychology*. https://doi.org/10.3389/fpsyg.2021.713818. PMID: 34566791; PMCID: PMC8455907.

Doebler, G. (2021) "Ukulele in music class: Teachers' perspectives". *Visions of Research in Music Education, 38*(2). https://opencommons.uconn.edu/vrme/vol38/iss1/2

Drew, A. M. (2020). *Consuming rap: An examination of exposure to substance use lyrics, lived experiences, and attitudes toward substance use*. ProQuest Dissertations Publishing.

Ellis, R. J., & Thayer, J. F. (2010). Music and autonomic nervous system (dys)function. *Music Perception, 27*(4), 317–326. https://doi.org/10.1525/mp.2010.27.4.317

Eyre, L. (2007). Music, music therapy and trauma: International perspectives. *Canadian Journal of Music Therapy, 13*(1), 61.

Facchini, M., & Ruini, C. (2021). The role of music therapy in the treatment of children with cancer: A systematic review of literature. *Complementary Therapies in Clinical Practice, 42*, Article 101289. https://doi.org/10.1016/j.ctcp.2020.101289

Felsenstein, R. (2013). From uprooting to replanting: On post-trauma group music therapy for pre-school children. *Nordic Journal of Music Therapy, 22*(1), 69–85. https://doi.org/10.1080/08098131.2012.667824

Forgeard, M., Winner, E., Norton, A., & Schlaug, G. (2008). Practicing a musical instrument in childhood is associated with enhanced verbal ability and nonverbal reasoning. *PLoS One, 3*(10), Article e3566. https://doi.org/10.1371/journal.pone.0003566

Gabriel, S., & Paravati, E. (2021). If music be the food of love, play on: Four ways that music may lead to social connection. *The Behavioral and Brain Sciences, 44*, Article e71. https://doi.org/10.1017/S0140525X20001430

Garvis, S., Barton, G., & Hartwig, K. (2017). Music education in school – what is taught? A comparison of cirriculum in Sweden and Australia. *Australian Journal of Music Education, 51*(1), 3–12.

Geipel, J., Koenig, J., Hillecke, T. K., Resch, F., & Kaess, M. (2018). Music-based interventions to reduce internalizing symptoms in children and adolescents: A meta-analysis. *Journal of Affective Disorders, 225*, 647–656. https://doi.org/10.1016/j.jad.2017.08.035

Good, A., & Russo, F. A. (2016). Singing promotes cooperation in a diverse group of children. *Social Psychology, 47*(6), 340–344. https://doi.org/10.1027/1864-9335/a000282

Goopy, J. (2022). Children's identity work in daily singing-based music classes: A case study of an Australian boys' school. *Research Studies in Music Education, 44*(3), 570–588. https://doi.org/10.1177/1321103X22110948

Government of South Australia, Department of Education. (2019). *Music Education Strategy* 2019–2029. https://www.education.sa.gov.au/schools-and-educators/strategies-and-initiatives/music-education-strategy-and-innovation-fund/music-education-strategy-and-music-innovation-fund

Hallam, S. (2010). The power of music: Its impact on the intellectual, social and personal development of children and young people. *International Journal of Music Education, 28*(3), 269–289. https://doi.org/10.1177/0255761410370658

Heinrich, J. (2012). The provision of classroom music programs to regional Victorian primary schools. *Australian Journal of Music Education, 2*, 45–58.

Hilliard, R. E. (2007). The effects of Orff-based music therapy and social work groups on childhood grief symptoms and behaviors. *Journal of Music Therapy, 44*(2), 123–138. https://doi.org/10.1093/jmt/44.2.123

Hillman, K. B., Bolger, L., & McFerran, K. S. (2022). Deconstructing trauma narratives: A critical interpretive synthesis of research into music therapy and psychological trauma in adults. *The Arts in Psychotherapy, 77*, 101863. https://doi.org/10.1016/j.aip.2021.101863

Holden, H., & Button, S. (2006). The teaching of music in the primary school by the nonmusic specialist. *British Journal of Music Education, 23*(1), 23–38.

International Baccalaureate. https://www.ibo.org/

Jenkins, L., & Crawford, R. (2022). Interview ready: A student-led artistic project as an authentic experience to support pre-service music teachers' pathways to employment. *International Journal of Music Education, 40*(3), 328–339. https://doi.org/10.1177/02557614211050992

Jenkins, L., & Southcott, J. E. (2016). When I see a note I like, I play it: Musical identity enacted in a community orchestra. *International Journal of Community Music, 9*(3), 273–289. https://doi.org/10.1386/ijcm.9.3.273_1

Joseph, D., & Human, R. (2020). "It Is More Than Just about Music": Lifelong learning, social interaction and connection. *Muziki: Journal of Music Research in Africa, 17*(1), 72–93. https://doi.org/10.1080/18125980.2020.1855082

Kang, H. (2017). Supportive music and imagery with sandplay for child witnesses of domestic violence: A pilot study report. *The Arts in Psychotherapy, 53*, 72–79. https://doi.org/10.1016/j.aip.2017.01.009

Kang, J., Scholp, A., & Jiang, J. J. (2018). A review of the physiological effects and mechanisms of singing. *Journal of Voice, 32*(4), 390–395. https://doi.org/10.1016/j.jvoice.2017.07.008

Keen, A. W. (2005). Using music as a therapy tool to motivate troubled adolescents. *Social Work in Health Care, 39*(3–4), 361–373. https://doi.org/10.1300/J010v39n03_09

Kimbel, T. M., & Protivnak, J. J. (2010). For those about to rock (with your high school students), we salute you: School counselors using music interventions. *Journal of Creativity in Mental Health, 5*(1), 25–38. https://doi.org/10.1080/15401381003626857

Koelsch, S. (2015). Music-evoked emotions: Principles, brain correlates, and implications for therapy. *Annals of the New York Academy of Sciences, 1337*(1), 193–201. https://doi.org/10.1111/nyas.12684

Koelsch, S., Boehlig, A., Hohenadel, M., Nitsche, I., Bauer, K., & Sack, U. (2016). The impact of acute stress on hormones and cytokines and how their recovery is affected by music-evoked positive mood. *Scientific Reports, 6*(1), 23008. https://doi.org/10.1038/srep23008

Kramer, A., & Berger, E. (2025). An integrative review of trauma-informed music interventions in educational settings. *Journal of Music Therapy, 62*(2), thaf011. https://doi.org/10.1093/jmt/thaf011

Kreutz, G., Bongard, S., Rohrmann, S., Hodapp, V., & Grebe, D. (2004). Effects of Choir singing or listening on secretory immunoglobulin A, cortisol, and emotional state. *Journal of Behavioral Medicine, 27*(6), 623–635. https://doi.org/10.1007/s10865-004-0006-9

Laughey, D. (2006). *Music and youth culture*. Edinburgh University Press.

Lonsdale, A. J., & North, A. C. (2011). Why do we listen to music? A uses and gratifications analysis. *British Journal of Psychology, 102*(1), 108–134. https://doi.org/10.1348/000712610X506831

Masson, A. (2013). *Summary of the victorian parliamentary inquiry into school music education*. Music Australia Website Advocacy Resources, Policy Submissions. https://musicaustralia. org.au/publications/summary-of-the-victorianparliamentary-inquiry-into-school-music-education/

Mast, J. F., & McAndrew, F. T. (2011). Violent lyrics in heavy metal music can increase aggression in males. *North American Journal of Psychology, 13*(1), 63–64.

McCraty, R., Atkinson, M., Rein, G., & Watkins, A. (1996). Music enhances the effect of positive emotional states on salivary IgA. *Stress Medicine, 12*, 167–175. https://doi.org/10.1002/(SICI)1099-1700(199607)12:3<167::AID-SMI697>3.0.CO;2-2

McFerran, K. (2010). *Adolescents, music, and music therapy*. Jessica Kingsley Publishers.

McFerran, K., Roberts, M., & O'Grady, L. (2010). Music therapy with bereaved teenagers: A mixed methods perspective. *Death Studies, 34*(6), 541–565. https://doi.org/10.1080/07481181003765428

McFerran, K. S., & Crooke, A. (2016). Music therapy and mourning. In J. W. Davidson & S. Garrido (Eds.), *Music and mourning: Interdisciplinary investigations* (pp. 97–113). Routledge. https://doi.org/10.4324/9781315596648

McFerran, K. S., Lai, H. I. C., Chang, W., Acquaro, D., Chin, T. C., Stokes, H., & Crooke, A. H. D. (2020). Music, rhythm and trauma: A critical interpretive synthesis of research literature. *Frontiers in Psychology, 11*, Article 324. https://doi.org/10.3389/fpsyg.2020.00324

Mizener, C. P. (2008). Enhancing language skills through music. *General Music Today, 21*(2), 11–17. https://doi.org/10.1177/1048371308316414

NAMM Foundation. (2015). *Striking a chord: The public's hopes and beliefs for k-12 education in the United States*. https://www.nammfoundation.org/EDUCATOR-RESOURCES/STRIKING-CHORD-PUBLICS-HOPES-AND-BELIEFS-K-12-EDUCATION-UNITED-STATES-2015

New South Wales Education Standards Authority. (2023). *New South Wales Curriculum*, https://curriculum.nsw.edu.au/

North, A. C., Hargreaves, D. J., & McKendrick, J. (1999). The influence of in-store music on wine selections. *Journal of Applied Psychology, 84*(2), 271–276. https://doi.org/10.1037/0021-9010.84.2.271

North, A. C., Hargreaves, D. J., & O'Neill, S. A. (2000). The importance of music to adolescents. *British Journal of Educational Psychology, 70*(2), 255–272. https://doi.org/10.1348/000709900158083

North, A. C., Tarrant, M., & Hargreaves, D. J. (2004). The effects of music on helping behavior: A field study. *Environment and Behavior, 36*(2), 266–275. https://doi.org/10.1177/0013916503256263

O'Kelly, J., Fachner, J. C., & Tervaniemi, M. (2016). Editorial: Dialogues in music therapy and music neuroscience: Collaborative understanding driving clinical advances. *Frontiers in Human Neuroscience, 10*, Article 585. https://doi.org/10.3389/fnhum.2016.00585

Päivi-Sisko, E., & Tuomas, E. (2014). Extended music education enhances the quality of school life. *Music Education Research, 16*(1), 88–104. https://doi.org/10.1080/14613808.2013.829428

Pan, Y. Y., Sun, X. Y., Dang, Y. N., Chen, M., Wang, L., & Shen, L. (2021). *Music Education Research, 23*(1), 41–49. https://doi.org/10.1080/14613808.2020.1847058

Parliament of Victoria. (2013). Inquiry into the extent, benefits and potential of music *education in Victorian schools.* www.parliament.vic.gov.au/etc

https://www.parliament.vic.gov.au/4962eb/contentassets/d1918e5623274f879784943338fb5f49/music_education_final_041113.pdf

Perry, B. D. (2009). Examining child maltreatment through a neurodevelopmental lens: Clinical applications of the neurosequential model of therapeutics. *Journal of Loss and Trauma, 14*(4), 240–255. https://doi.org/10.1080/15325020903004350

Phillips, S. P., Reipas, K., & Zelek, B. (2019). Stresses, strengths and resilience in adolescents: A qualitative study. *The Journal of Primary Prevention, 40,* 631–642. https://doi.org/10.1007/s10935-019-00570-3

Porges, S. W. (2009). The polyvagal theory: New insights into adaptive reactions of the autonomic nervous system. *Cleveland Clinic Journal of Medicine, 76*(Suppl 2), S86–S90. https://doi.org/10.3949/ccjm.76.s2.17

Porges, S. W. (2011). *The polyvagal theory: Neurophysiological foundations of emotions, attachment, communication, and self-regulation* (1st ed.). W. W. Norton.

Powell, S. (2019). Singing with young children: Empowering early childhood teachers to sing Orff-style. *Musicworks: Journal of the Australian Council of Orff Schulwerk, 24*(1), 23–30. https://search.informit.org/doi/10.3316/informit.857737270279646

Powell, S. (2022). The power of singing with young children: Teacher skill and confidence. *Rattler (Sydney), 137,* 6–8. https://search.informit.org/doi/10.3316/informit.516947487023819

Rentfrow, P. J. (2012). The role of music in everyday life: Current directions in the social psychology of music. *Social and Personality Psychology Compass, 6*(5), 402–416. https://doi.org/10.1111/j.1751-9004.2012.00434.x

Roden, I., Könen, T., Bongard, S., Frankenberg, E., Friedrich, E. K., & Kreutz, G. (2014). Effects of music training on attention, processing speed and cognitive music abilities-findings from a longitudinal study. *Applied Cognitive Psychology, 28*(4), 545–557. https://doi.org/10.1002/acp.3034

Rose, D., Jones-Bartoli, A., & Heaton, P. (2019). Measuring the impact of musical learning on cognitive, behavioural and socio-emotional wellbeing development in children. *Psychology of Music, 47*(2), 284–303. https://doi.org/10.1177/0305735617744887

Rosner, R., Kruse, J., & Hagl, M. (2010). A meta-analysis of interventions for bereaved children and adolescents. *Death Studies, 34*(2), 99–136. https://doi.org/10.1080/07481180903492422

Saarikallio, S. H., Randall, W. M., & Baltazar, M. (2020). Music listening for supporting adolescents' sense of agency in daily life. *Frontiers in Psychology, 10,* Article 2911. https://doi.org/10.3389/fpsyg.2019.02911

Schäfer, T., Sedlmeier, P., Städtler, C., & Huron, D. (2013). The psychological functions of music listening [Original Research]. *Frontiers in Psychology, 4*(511). https://doi.org/10.3389/fpsyg.2013.00511

Slotoroff, C. (1994). Drumming technique for assertiveness and anger management in the short-term psychiatric setting for adult and adolescent survivors of trauma. *Music Therapy Perspectives, 12*(2), 111–116. https://doi.org/10.1093/mtp/12.2.111

Stack, S., Lester, D., & Rosenberg, J. S. (2012). Music and suicidality: A quantitative review and extension. *Suicide & Life-Threatening Behavior, 42*(6), 654–671. https://doi.org/10.1111/j.1943-278X.2012.00120.x

Swanson, A. L. (2020). Music therapy in schools: Stimulating the mind and body to create positive change. In C. Maykel & M. A. Bray (Eds.), *Promoting mind–body health in schools: Interventions for mental health professionals* (pp. 233–244). American Psychological Association. https://doi.org/10.1037/0000157-016

Tanner, J., Asbridge, M., & Wortley, S. (2009). Listening to rap: Cultures of crime, cultures of resistance. *Social Forces, 88*(2), 693–722. https://doi.org/10.1353/sof.0.0271

Thoma, M. V., La Marca, R., Brönnimann, R., Finkel, L., Ehlert, U., & Nater, U. M. (2013). The effect of music on the human stress response. *PLoS one, 8*(8), Article e70156. https://doi.org/10.1371/journal.pone.0070156

Thompson, G. (2022). *Goal processes in music therapy practice*. Jessica Kingsley Publishers.

Travis, R., & Bowman, S. W. (2012). Ethnic identity, self-esteem, and variability in perceptions of rap music's empowering and risky influences. *Journal of Youth Studies, 15*(4), 455–478. https://doi.org/10.1080/13676261.2012.663898

Uggla, L., Bonde, L. O., Svahn, B. M., Remberger, M., Wrangsjö, B., & Gustafsson, B. (2016). Music therapy can lower the heart rates of severely sick children. *Acta Paediatrica, 105*(10), 1225–1230. https://doi.org/10.1111/apa.13452

Van der Heijden, M., Oliai-Araghi, S., van Dijk, M., Jeekel, J., & Hunink, M. (2015). The effects of perioperative music interventions in pediatric surgery: A systematic review and meta-analysis of randomized controlled trials. *PLoS One, 10*(8), Article e0133608. https://doi.org/10.1371/journal.pone.0133608

Van der Kolk, B. A. (2007). The developmental impact of childhood trauma. In L. J. Kirmayer, R. Lemelson, & M. Barad (Eds.), *Understanding trauma: Integrating biological, clinical and cultural perspectives* (pp. 224–241). Cambridge University Press. https://doi.org/10.1017/CBO9780511500008.

Van Klompenberg, A. (2023). Trauma-informed practices in the music classroom. *Teaching Music*, 30(3), 56. https://www.proquest.com/trade-journals/trauma-informed-practices-music-classroom/docview/2779156556/se-2

Victorian Department of Education. (2023). *Music therapy*. https://www.education.vic.gov.au/school/teachers/health/mentalhealth/mental-health-menu/Pages/Menu-Item.aspx?queryid=25

Wallace, M., Puryear, A., & Cannada, L. K. (2013). An evaluation of posttraumatic stress disorder and parent stress in children with orthopaedic injuries. *Journal of Orthopaedic Trauma, 27*(2), 38–41. https://doi.org/10.1097/BOT.0b013e318250c837

Wiggins, R. A., & Wiggins, J. (2008). Primary music education in the absence of specialists. *International Journal of Education & the Arts, 9*(12). http://www.ijea.org/

Williamson, J. B., Porges, E. C., Lamb, D. G., & Porges, S. W. (2015). Maladaptive autonomic regulation in PTSD accelerates physiological aging [Review]. *Frontiers in Psychology, 5*. https://doi.org/10.3389/fpsyg.2014.01571

Yalch, R. F., & Spangenberg, E. R. (2000). The effects of music in a retail setting on real and perceived shopping times. *Journal of Business Research, 49*(2), 139–147. https://doi.org/10.1016/S0148-2963(99)00003-X

Ye, P., Huang, Z., Zhou, H., & Tang, Q. (2021). Music-based intervention to reduce aggressive behavior in children and adolescents: A meta-analysis. *Medicine (Baltimore), 100*(4), Article e23894. https://doi.org/10.1097/MD.0000000000023894

Yinger, O. S., & Gooding, L. (2014). Music therapy and music medicine for children and adolescents. *Child and Adolescent Psychiatric Clinics of North America, 23*(3), 535–553. https://doi.org/10.1016/j.chc.2013.03.003

Zatorre, R. (2005). Music, the food of neuroscience? *Nature, 434*(7031), 312–315. https://doi.org/10.1038/434312a

Zatorre, R. J., & Peretz, I. (Eds.). (2001). *The biological foundations of music: Annals of the New York academy of sciences.* New York Academy of Sciences.

11

Multi-Disciplinary Partnering in School-Based Trauma-Informed Active Play

Ellie Lawson, Jaime Barratt, Emily Hall, John Cairney, and Kai Wheeler

Introduction

Empowering learning environments for children include opportunities for play and engagement with other children and adults. Play which includes gross bodily movements (active play) can have additional benefits and thus is prevalent within the school day, particularly in the early years. However, few summaries are available which explore the potential role active play may have in assisting students impacted by trauma, as well as the need for a trauma-informed approach to the facilitation of active play. In this chapter, trauma-informed practice is explored with specific reference to children participating in play as a physical activity (active play). Active play has previously been described as a form of physical activity that involves unstructured, freely chosen gross motor movement (Truelove et al., 2017). Active play is a developmentally appropriate process for children that can build physical activity along with vital socioemotional skills (Ginsburg & Committee on Psychosocial Aspects of Child and Family Health, 2007). The potential benefits of active play are particularly relevant when active play experts (for example, an exercise physiologist or physical education teacher) work with generalist educators to develop and implement appropriate active play sessions during the school day. This chapter outlines the important relationship between active play and increasing opportunities for children to process emotions, build resilience, and regain a sense of mastery

DOI: 10.4324/9781003436034-11

of their bodies and surroundings. Finally, this chapter guides the integration of trauma-informed active play within practices in the school setting to support positive student health and wellbeing, and potentially assist with the healing of trauma.

Importance of Play for Children

Play is seen as an exploratory process that allows children to learn and process emotions and make meaning of their world (Parker et al., 2020). When working with children, a play-based approach is fundamental to a child's success in reaching several different developmental milestones (Bunker, 1991; Olive et al., 2021; Stegelin, 2005; Stevens-Smith & Stegelin, 2015). A systematic review indicates that play therapy, using unstructured materials (especially based on movement) is an influential positive mental health and wellbeing intervention for children (Parker et al., 2020). Play can also function as a physical activity which brings the added benefit of physical movement to the development of social and emotional health and wellbeing (Brockman et al., 2011). Play has been identified as a highly rewarding activity that is fundamental to the developing child (Nijhof et al., 2018). In 2002, the Association for Childhood Education International (ACEI) published a pivotal position statement on the importance of play, affirming its essential role within a child's life (Isenberg & Quisenberry, 2002). Play serves a significant role in all aspects and developmental domains, including physical, emotional, social, and cognitive development (Brockman et al., 2011).

Play can be used with children to support the development of imagination, ingenuity, and physical, cognitive, and emotional skills (Stenman et al., 2019). Play can enable children to practice physical and communication skills, through experimenting with their behavioral and social interactions (Nijhof et al., 2018). Through negotiation during play, children can learn cooperation and leadership skills, which help to develop their social and emotional literacy and skills (Frost, 1998). Founding psychological and developmental theorists, Erikson, Piaget, Vygotsky, and Montessori, stressed the importance of learning through play in schools (Alharbi & Alzahrani, 2020). These theorists agreed that education should be child-centered, be both active and interactive, and should involve the social world of the child and their community (Alharbi & Alzahrani, 2020). As an example, Piaget's theory focuses on play as a means of facilitating learning by exposing children to new experiences and activities to prepare "a child for new experiences and new possibilities of physical and mental activities for dealing with the world" (as cited in Burris & Tsao, 2002, p. 231). Play allows children to meet psychological and physical needs by helping the child to transform reality and develop symbolic representations of the world (Burris & Tsao, 2002).

As a child's period of dependence and motor immaturity is relatively long, parents and caregivers are encouraged to interact with their child through play during this period (Frost, 1998). Parents initiating play, as well as structuring and giving directions, are thought to act as the scaffolding for future development (Frost, 1998). Evidence has shown that 75% of brain development occurs after birth, with play being a crucial aspect, as it stimulates connections between nerve cells (Anderson-McNamee & Bailey, 2010). Play facilitates the development of fine and gross motor skills, which are crucial for physical activity, and is an example of the physical development that comes from play (Sutapa et al., 2021).

Play and Trauma

What is less known about play is that play-based approaches emphasize and promote autonomy and decision-making, which has been shown to empower and support self-determination for those who have experienced trauma (Day et al., 2022; Ley & Barrio, 2019). Trauma-informed active play, such as autonomous free play, offers an approach to support positive changes and outcomes for students experiencing trauma or high stress. While parents and caregivers are important in facilitating development, some may be emotionally unavailable due to their own trauma, with 30% of Australians aged 16–65 years and over reporting experiences of physical or emotional abuse, or domestic violence in childhood (Haslam et al., 2023). This may ultimately lead to children having limited opportunities to heal from trauma in their home environments due to a lack of interaction and play from their parents and caregivers. In some cases, the lack of interaction available from parents and caregivers may also create attachment problems and increase stress through neglect or insufficient emotional support of the child. This emphasizes the importance of other adults in children's lives being available to facilitate play and provide other developmental opportunities for children exposed to trauma.

Active Play and Trauma

Active play involves physical movements and activities that require moderate to vigorous bursts of energy in varying play scenarios. The communicative function of active play is an integral part of the lives of children, and thus play therapy is proven to be a developmentally sensitive treatment modality for trauma (Findling et al., 2006; Parker et al., 2020). Active play allows for the symbolic expression of inner conflict, with children using symbols to communicate ideas and emotions (Parker et al., 2020). There is some evidence that there is a role for active play in assisting children who have experienced trauma. One review of literature exploring Play Therapy and Trauma noted that the use of toys and loose parts in active play enables children to process their emotions and heal from traumatic experiences, as they attain mastery of events by using imagination to modify their story (Parker et al., 2020). As trauma is associated with explicit impacts on the brain, it is important to consider potential neurological impacts of active play to help counteract negative impacts from traumatic experiences and ongoing stress on children. Neural networks which are repeatedly activated will adapt to the specific stimulus causing activation (MacKinnon, 2012). Patterned repetitive sensory activity in active play may be important in neurophysiological process, as the sensation may modify neural networks involved in the stress response (MacKinnon, 2012).

Repetitive and rhythmic somatosensory active play is an evocative cue that elicits a sensation of safety (MacKinnon, 2012). Patterned repetitive movement includes a host of everyday physical activities such as free dancing, jumping on a trampoline, and swinging, which all provide rhythm which when combined with elements such as feelings of safety and assist with soothing dysregulation (MacKinnon, 2012). There are several powerful associations to rhythmic somatosensory activity stored in the brainstem and diencephalon (the thalamus, subthalamus, hypothalamus, and epithalamus), which are created in utero and reinforced early in life (MacKinnon, 2012). Enabling a child to be involved in a form of active play that is both repetitive and rhythmic may enhance their feelings of safety.

Child-Centered Play Therapy

Child-centered play therapy (CCPT) has been identified as a developmentally responsive, mental health intervention for young children between the ages of 3 and 10 years (Ray et al., 2022). CCPT includes the use of purposely selected materials to be utilized during unstructured or 'free play' activities (Baggerly et al., 2010). These activities may see a child participating in a form of free play that encourages emotional expression and decision-making, and occurs while CCPT facilitators are providing encouragement (Baggerly et al., 2010). This type of intervention provides children with an environment characterized by safety and acceptance, and thus enforces the freedom for self-exploration, empowering children to build self-concept, personal responsibility, and self-direction (Ray et al., 2022). Ray et al. (2022) have identified play therapy to be well-suited for children who have experienced trauma, and relevant to incorporate in the development and facilitation of trauma-informed active play programs.

Trauma-informed active play programs which take into consideration a sensorimotor framework have resulted in positive change for children exposed to trauma (Fraser et al., 2017). A sensorimotor framework in therapy, as described by Wolan et al. (2015), focuses on helping children access positive bodily experiences and re-establish somatic attunement, that emphasizes sensory processing and integration. By teaching children to identify and modulate their arousal states, and providing them with language to understand their experiences, the framework fosters healthier responses and social engagement in a supportive sensory environment (Wolan et al., 2015). Wolan et al. (2015) utilized the work of Ogden et al. (2006) to develop a sensorimotor psychotherapy treatment approach for children aged 7–12 who have experienced trauma. The approach is known as Cool Moves for Kids and is a body and movement-based group program designed using a sensorimotor framework. Interventions such as this enable children to experience their bodies as a source of positivity and fun, allowing them to feel a greater sense of control, and have been suggested to show great potential when applied to early childhood (Wolan et al., 2015). Additionally, group interventions such as these can assist traumatized children with identifying and then changing habitual ways of relating to others in the world (Wolen et al., 2015). Researchers have emphasized the importance of using this active play approach, which uses less language and is more sensory-based, as it helps the child to increase their ability to regulate emotions (Fraser et al., 2017).

Educators as Enablers of Trauma-Informed Active Play

It is important to consider the multi-disciplinary professionals who may be involved in supporting trauma-informed practice in the school setting. In trauma-informed school initiatives, a couple of aims include increasing compassion and improving relationships (Lacey & Minnis, 2020). To effectively implement educational programs in schools, it is important for different service providers to work together (Vericat & Ruitenberg, 2019). Professionals, such as educators, have extensive opportunities to observe and identify trauma experiences and support referrals, thus representing a significant point of entry for early intervention (Vericat & Ruitenberg, 2019). By integrating active play into their daily routines, educators can create empowering learning environments that align with using active play to assist students impacted by trauma.

Supportive and nurturing relationships have been identified as critical for healing from trauma, with every person who has contact with a child contributing to this process (Goddard, 2021). Early caregiving relationships provide the context in which children are able to better understand themselves, others, and themselves in relation to others (Green & Myrick, 2014). For children, when attachment relationships are secure, they can see themselves as more lovable and the world as a more positive and predictable place (Green & Myrick, 2014). Additionally, opportunities for safe eye contact, proximity, and relational closeness have been identified in adult-supported, child-directed, and strength-based play (Tandon et al., 2015; Ryan et al., 2017). Active play facilitated by educators offers these opportunities, helping children process emotions, build resilience, and regain a sense of mastery over their bodies and surroundings (Parker et al., 2020). This is suggested to lead to neural changes which promote greater adaptive attachments and regulation skills (Ryan et al., 2017).

Educators who work in schools can provide children with consistent and familiar stimuli, as children will often have the same educator for an extended period of time. Due to the amount of contact time that educators have with children, it is clear that after a traumatic experience, they play an essential role in helping a child re-establish a sense of safety and security (Martin et al., 2021). By integrating trauma-informed active play into their teaching practices, educators can support positive student health and wellbeing, through positive and nurturing interactions (Perry & Hambrick, 2008), potentially assisting students to heal from trauma. Educators have a prominent role in supporting the integration of active play within trauma-informed practice. It is recommended that they implement trauma-informed strategies as part of health and care interventions focused on creating safe and trustworthy learning environments (Darroch et al., 2020). By doing so, they enhance opportunities for children to process emotions, build resilience, and regain a sense of mastery over their bodies and surroundings through active play (Darroch et al., 2020).

Creating and Implementing Trauma-Informed Active Play

Active play experts, such as accredited exercise physiologists (AEPs) or physical education (PE) teachers specialize in the assessment, design, and delivery of exercise (Lederman et al., 2016). They are respectively responsible for formulating and designing exercise programs and activities for individuals with chronic diseases and other health conditions (Franklin et al., 2009), as well as physical activity and education activities for children within school settings. Exercise physiology interventions are movement and activity-based strategies, incorporating health and physical activity education, advice, support, and lifestyle modifications. Within schools, PE teachers provide physical activity and long-term healthy lifestyle educational outcomes for children within an education and play-based context. The implementation of health-related activities, such as active play, has been identified as a key intervention with regard to addressing trauma, and it falls within the scope of practice for both AEPs and PE teachers.

Active play trauma-informed interventions focused on socioemotional development in children are recommended to target the child's ability to communicate with emotions in effective ways, solve problems, build positive relationships with peers and adults, as well as engage in challenging tasks (Hemmeter et al., 2006). This is because trauma and chronic stress in childhood are associated with difficulty with emotional regulation due to the adverse impacts of stress on the developing brain (Parker et al., 2020). Active play experts are equipped with a scope of practice which can deliver interventions or implement trauma-informed play-based activities for this population both safely and effectively as part of a multi-disciplinary team. When providing multi-disciplinary interventions for students exposed to trauma specific care should be considered to ensure positive, safe, and meaningful interactions during the healing process. It has been identified that when dealing with people who experience mental illness, access to specialist exercise support and structured supervised health-related activities help to improve cognitive function (Furness et al., 2018). Pediatric trauma-informed practice with active play is an emerging area for active play experts working in partnership with teachers and as part of a multi-disciplinary team (Johnstone et al., 2018).

Active play experts can enhance both physical and mental health outcomes and are well positioned to deliver holistic multi-disciplinary approaches to education (Furness et al., 2018; Lederman et al., 2016). There is common ground between educators and active play experts, in the sense that both roles focus on supporting children's physical development and facilitate active play opportunities for children. Recognizing this connection helps to understand the positive impact that active play experts can have on children who have experienced trauma and who are engaged in the educational system. Working in partnership expands the network of trustworthy and reliable service providers for the child and promotes the regulation of stress responses.

The Phased Approached to Reducing Re-Traumatization

Addressing trauma involves empowering a child to participate in trauma-informed interventions through a phase-oriented approach (Fraser et al., 2017). Trauma-informed active play is a strategy that embeds an understanding of trauma and violence in all phases of program design and delivery (Darroch et al., 2020). More specifically, active play programs emphasize approaches that are relevant, relational, repetitive, rewarding, and guided by two basic principles which are considered the fundamental building blocks of development (Ryan et al., 2017). The first building block is the fact that the brain changes in response to patterned repetitive experiences (Ryan et al., 2017). The second states that arousal of the child organizes their perceptions and behaviors (Ryan et al., 2017). It has been identified that the implementation of active play programs is necessary for helping children who have experienced trauma through regulated and repetitive physical movements (Devereaux & Harrison, 2022).

It is also important to consider that the autonomic nervous system must be calmed before progressing through different phases of active play (Green & Myrick, 2014). It is recommended that active play experts in partnership with educators start trauma-informed programs with activities to help children transition between activities, such as guided imagery or yoga (Green & Myrick, 2014).

The phase-oriented approach takes into consideration the 4Rs of a trauma-informed approach. The 4Rs consist of: realize, recognize, respond, and resist re-traumatization (Goddard, 2021).

Realize signifies the widespread nature of childhood trauma and its impacts on a child's emotional, social, behavioral, cognitive, and physical development, as well as mental health (Bartlett & Steber, 2019). It is crucial that before the implementation of any trauma-informed active play activities that the teachers understand how trauma can affect child development and consequent long-term effects into adulthood (Goddard, 2021).

Recognize relates to the different signs of trauma, including how trauma reactions may represent within the classroom or school-based setting, and how they may vary depending on demographic, environmental, or social factors (Bartlett & Steber, 2019). In addition, educators and active play experts must understand and be able to identify potential re-traumatizing situations (Goddard, 2021). Active play experts and teachers must be able to identify that a child's challenging behaviors are self-protective and adaptive (Bartlett & Steber, 2019). Research has identified that attention issues, aggressive behavior, and delinquency are the internalizing symptoms that are associated with difficult or highly emotional temperament in children (Price et al., 2013). It is during this phase that educators and active play experts may refer the child on for further screening by the appropriate health professionals and that moving forward within a multi-disciplinary team may be important.

Responding is the referral process and knowing which health care and educational systems are required to provide trauma-informed practice (Goddard, 2021). Active play experts can provide children with opportunities for active play that is based around the approach of trauma-informed practice in a safe and supportive education environment.

Resisting re-traumatization is about actively shaping the children's environment to avoid triggers (Bartlett & Steber, 2019). It refers to critically thinking about the approach of the school and the support that needs to be provided to protect them from further trauma (Goddard, 2021).

Avoiding Triggers and Re-Traumatization in Active Play

While play offers opportunities for exploration and self-expression, it can also expose children to situations or themes that evoke fear, anxiety, or distress. For instance, imaginative play scenarios or exposure to media content can inadvertently introduce children to violence, loss, or other traumatic experiences. Moreover, competitive or overly structured play environments can induce stress and pressure, potentially leading to emotional harm. Recognizing the potential for re-traumatization in play underscores the importance of providing safe, supportive environments where children can engage in play while receiving guidance and reassurance from caregivers to navigate challenging content or experiences.

Case Study: Active Play

Asher is a 6-year-old child who has experienced multiple ACEs and uses play as a form of communication and language (Frost, 1998). While Asher's parents talk about fears and experiences, Asher processes the same situations through play and physical activity. This is because the physical movements associated with play are a means by which Asher learns to cope. Active play facilitates their expression of feelings and reactions in stressful situations. It provides a physiological understanding of the body as it responds to physical activity and the repetitive nature of bodily movements (Stenman et al., 2019). Active play also has therapeutic qualities for Asher in their development, as Asher lacks words and cognitive abilities to understand complex situations or resolve conflicts. This allows Asher to play out the conflicts and move to position their body so that they can better resolve their tensions and express how they are feeling. It is understood by Asher's multi-disciplinary team that a major function of play for them is changing what may be unmanageable, to manageable situations through symbolic representations, and through physiological response to stress that are controllable and not overwhelming (Frost, 1998). This emphasizes the importance of play to Asher's narrative and how active play can be positioned to assist them in their development.

Recommendations

Multi-disciplinary Interventions: Implementing multi-disciplinary interventions for children exposed to trauma involves active play experts working in collaboration with educators. This partnership enhances both physical and mental health outcomes by creating trauma-informed active play programs. These programs are designed to support the child's ability to communicate emotions, solve problems, build positive relationships, and engage in challenging tasks.

Phase-oriented Approach: Adopting a phase-oriented approach to trauma-informed active play is crucial. This approach includes stages that help regulate the child's stress response and promote healing through repetitive and rhythmic physical movements. Starting with activities like guided imagery or yoga can calm the autonomic nervous system, fostering a safe environment for building healthy relationships and enhancing emotional regulation.

Avoiding Triggers and Re-traumatization: When designing active play environments, it is essential to avoid potential triggers that may cause re-traumatization. Providing safe, supportive environments where children can engage in play without fear, anxiety, or distress is critical. Caregivers and educators should guide children through challenging content and experiences, ensuring a nurturing atmosphere that supports healing and development.

Conclusion

Schools need to create active play programs that incorporate an understanding of how the brain develops and in collaboration with active play experts. Active play is a developmentally sensitive trauma-informed treatment modality which can be embedded into multi-disciplinary trauma-informed approaches.

Multi-disciplinary interventions must be targeted toward the specific needs of the child. This chapter argues that play and physical activity are a significant part of a child's life, and can provide a powerful catalyst for recovery after trauma. Active play interventions are beneficial for children who have experienced trauma, and when implemented through trauma-informed practice, can support children in their development. The delivery of such programs requires significant consideration of factors such as committed, stable care from nurturing service providers such as active play experts and educators within the multi-disciplinary team.

Due to the knowledge, skills, and abilities of active play experts, and the trauma-informed environments that these professionals can provide, it is important that they are involved in the care of children exposed to trauma, in partnership with teachers. Active play experts will not only be able to assist in the functional evaluation of the children but are able to provide valuable education and behavior modification strategies centered around active play.

References

Alharbi, M. O., & Alzahrani, M. M. (2020). The importance of learning through play in early childhood education: Reflection on the "bold beginnings" report. *International Journal of the Whole Child, 5*(2), 9.

Anderson-McNamee, J. K., & Bailey, S. J. (2010). The importance of play in early childhood development. *Montana State University Extension, 4*(10), 1–4.

Baggerly, J. N., Ray, D. C., & Bratton, S. C. (Eds.). (2010). *Child-centered play therapy research: The evidence base for effective practice.* John Wiley & Sons.

Bartlett, J. D., & Steber, K. (2019). How to implement trauma-informed care to build resilience to childhood trauma Child Trends. https://www.childtrends.org/publications/how-to-implement-trauma-informed-care-to-build-resilience-to-childhood-trauma.

Brockman, R., Jago, R., & Fox, K. R. (2011). Children's active play: Self-reported motivators, barriers and facilitators. *BMC Public Health, 11,* 1–7. https://doi.org/10.1186/1471-2458-11-461

Bunker, L. K. (1991). The role of play and motor skill development in building children's self-confidence and self-esteem. *The Elementary School Journal, 91*(5), 467–471. https://doi.org/10.1086/461669

Darroch, R. C., Varcoe, C., Oliffe, J., & Gonzalez Montaner, G. (2020). Trauma-informed approaches to physical activity: A scoping study. *Complementary Therapies in Clinical Practice, 41,* 101224. https://doi.org/10.1016/j.ctcp.2020.101224

Day, N., Paas, F., Kervin, L., & Howard, S. J. (2022). A systematic scoping review of pre-school self-regulation interventions from a self-determination theory perspective. *International Journal of Environmental Research and Public Health, 19*(4), 2454.

Findling, J. H., Bratton, S. C., & Henson, R. K. (2006). Development of the trauma play scale: An observation-based assessment of the impact of trauma on the play therapy behaviours of young children. *International Journal of Play Therapy, 15*(1), 7–36. https://doi.org/10.1037/h0088906

Franklin, B., Fern, A., Fowler, A., Spring, T., & de Jong, A. (2009). Exercise physiologist's role in clinical practice. *British Journal of Sports Medicine, 43*(2), 93–95. https://doi.org/10.1136/bjsm.2008.055202

Fraser, K., MacKenzie, D., & Versnel, J. (2017). Complex trauma in children and youth: A scoping review of sensory-based interventions. *Occupational Therapy in Mental Health, 33*(3), 199–216. https://doi.org/10.1080/0164212X.2016.1265475

Frost, J. L. (1998). Neuroscience, play, and child development. *ERIC*, 1–18. https://eric.ed.gov/?id=ED427845

Furness, T., Hewavasam, J., Barnfield, J., McKenna, B., & Joseph, C. (2018). Adding an accredited exercise physiologist role to a new model of care at a secure extended care mental health service: A qualitative study. *Journal of Mental Health, 27*(2), 120–126.

Ginsburg, K. R., & Committee on Psychosocial Aspects of Child and Family Health. (2007). The importance of play in promoting healthy child development and maintaining strong parent-child bonds. *Pediatrics, 119*(1), 182–191.

Goddard, A. (2021). Adverse childhood experiences and trauma-informed care. *Journal of Pediatric Health Care, 35*(2), 145–155. https://doi.org/10.1016/j.pedhc.2020.09.001

Green, E. J., & Myrick, A. C. (2014). Treating complex trauma in adolescents: A phase-based, integrative approach for play therapists. *International Journal of Play Therapy, 23*(3), 131–145. https://doi.org/10.1037/a0036679

Haslam, D., Mathews, B., Pacella, R., Scott, J. G., Finkelhor, D., Higgins, D. J., Meinck, F., Erskine, H. E., Thomas, H. J., Lawrence, D., & Malacova, E. (2023). *The prevalence and impact of child maltreatment in Australia: Findings from the Australian Child Maltreatment Study: Brief Report*. Australian Child Maltreatment Study, Queensland University of Technology.

Hemmeter, M. L., Ostrosky, M., & Fox, L. (2006). Social and emotional foundations for early learning: A conceptual model for intervention. *School Psychology Review, 35*(4), 583–601.Isenberg, J. P., & Quisenberry, N. (2002). A position paper of the Association for Childhood Education International PLAY: Essentials for all children. *Childhood Education, 79*(1), 33–39.

Johnstone, A., Hughes, A. R., Martin, A., & Reilly, J. J. (2018). Utilising active play interventions to promote physical activity and improve fundamental movement skills in children: A systematic review and meta-analysis. *BMC Public Health, 18*, 1–12. https://doi.org/10.1186/s12889-018-5687-z

Lacey, R. E., & Minnis, H. (2020). Practitioner review: Twenty years of research with adverse childhood experience scores – advantages, disadvantages and applications to practice. *Journal of Child Psychology and Psychiatry, 61*(2), 116–130. https://doi.org/10.1111/jcpp.13135

Lederman, O., Grainger, K., Stanton, R., Douglas, A., Gould, K., Perram, A., … Rosenbaum, S. (2016). Consensus statement on the role of accredited exercise physiologists within the treatment of mental disorders: A guide for mental health professionals. *Australasian Psychiatry, 24*(4), 347–351. https://doi.org/10.1177/1039856216632400

Ley, C., & Barrio, M. R. (2019). Promoting health of refugees in and through sport and physical activity: A psychosocial, trauma-sensitive approach. In T. Wenzel & B. Drožđek (Eds.), *An uncertain safety* (pp. 301–343). Springer. https://doi.org/10.1007/978-3-319-72914-5_13

MacKinnon, L. (2012). The neurosequential model of therapeutics: An interview with Bruce Perry. *Australian and New Zealand Journal of Family Therapy, 33*(3), 210–218. https://doi.org/10.1017/aft.2012.26

Martin, C. P., Russo, J., Goldenthal, H., Holley, C., Gouze, K. R., & Williford, A. (2021). Supporting young children exposed to potentially traumatic events: Implications for early care and education policy. *Policy Insights from the Behavioral and Brain Sciences, 8*(2), 119–126. https://doi.org/10.1177/23727322211033880

Nijhof, S. L., Vinkers, C. H., van Geelen, S. M., Duijff, S. N., Achterberg, E. J. M., van der Net, J., … Lesscher, H. M. (2018). Healthy play, better coping: The importance of play for the development of children in health and disease. *Neuroscience and Biobehavioral Reviews, 95*, 421–429. https://doi.org/10.1016/j.neubiorev.2018.09.024

Ogden, P., Minton, K., & Pain, C. (2006). *Trauma and the body: A sensorimotor approach to psychotherapy*. W.W. Norton & Company Inc.

Parker, M. M., Hergenrather, K., Smelser, Q., & Kelly, C. T. (2020). Exploring child-centered play therapy and trauma: A systematic review of literature. *International Journal of Play Therapy, 30*(1), 2–13. https://doi.org/10.1037/pla0000136

Perry, B. D., & Hambrick, E. P. (2008). The neurosequential model of therapeutics. *Reclaiming Children and Youth, 17*(3), 38–43.

Price, M., Higa-McMillan, C., Kim, S., & Frueh, B. C. (2013). Trauma experience in children and adolescents: An assessment of the effects of trauma type and role of interpersonal proximity. *Journal of anxiety disorders, 27*(7), 652–660.

Ray, D. C., Burgin, E., Gutierrez, D., Ceballos, P., & Lindo, N. (2022). Child-centered play therapy and adverse childhood experiences: A randomized controlled trial. *Journal of Counselling and Development, 100*(2), 134–145. https://doi.org/10.1002/jcad.12412

Ryan, K., Lane, S. J., & Powers, D. (2017). A multidisciplinary model for treating complex trauma in early childhood. *International Journal of Play Therapy, 26*(2), 111–123. https://doi.org/10.1037/pla0000044

Stegelin, D. A. (2005). Making the case for play policy: Research-based reasons to support play-based environments. *YC Young Children, 60*(2), 76–85.

Stenman, K., Christofferson, J., Alderfer, M. A., Pierce, J., Kelly, C., Schifano, E., … Kazak, A. E. (2019). Integrating play in trauma-informed care: Multidisciplinary pediatric healthcare provider perspectives. *Psychological Services, 16*(1), 7–15. https://doi.org/10.1037/ser0000294

Stevens-Smith, D. A., & Stegelin, D. A. (2015). Making connections between play and healthy development: Reasons to promote play-based learning environments. *The International Journal of Early Childhood Learning, 23*(2), 1–13. https://doi.org/10.18848/2327-7939/cgp/v23i02/48454

Sutapa, P., Pratama, K. W., Rosly, M. M., Ali, S. K. S., & Karakauki, M. (2021). Improving motor skills in early childhood through goal-oriented play activity. *Children, 8*(11), 994. https://doi.org/10.3390/children8110994

Tandon, P. S., Saelens, B. E., & Christakis, D. A. (2015). Active play opportunities at child care. *Pediatrics, 135*(6), e1425–e1431.https://doi.org/10.1542/peds.2014-2750

Truelove, S., Vanderloo, L. M., & Tucker, P. (2017). Defining and measuring active play among young children: A systematic review. *Journal of Physical Activity and Health*, *14*(2), 155–166. https://doi.org/10.1123/jpah.2016-0195

Vericat, R., & Ruitenberg, C. W. (2019). Trauma-informed practices in early childhood education: Contributions, limitations and ethical considerations. *Global Studies of Childhood*, *9*(2), 132–144. https://doi.org/10.1177/2043610619846319

Wolan, T., Delaney, M. A., & Weller, A. (2015). Group work with children who have experienced trauma using a sensorimotor framework. *Children Australia*, *40*, 205–208. https://doi.org/10.1017/cha.2015.16

12

An Ecological Approach to Measurement

Trauma-Informed Schools

Andrew Orapallo, Govind Krishnamoorthy, Cassandra Lobley, and Courtney N. Baker

Introduction

The increasing adoption of trauma-informed practice in schools over the past few decades is promising, as both school leaders continue to recognize the widespread impact of trauma and secondary traumatic stress on students, school staff, families/caregivers, and communities (Downey & Greco, 2023). This movement was largely driven in the United States by the Substance Abuse and Mental Health Services Administration's (SAMHSA, 2014) four seminal pillars underlying trauma-informed systems: (1) realizing the widespread prevalence of trauma exposure; (2) recognizing the signs of traumatic exposure among students, school staff, and families; (3) responding to trauma exposure using evidence-based frameworks; and (4) resisting re-traumatization. Since then, organizations including the National Child Traumatic Stress Network (NCTSN, 2017), the University of Maryland's National Center for School Mental Health Program (NCSMH, 2024), and the SAMHSA National Center for Trauma-Informed Care (SAMHSA, 2014) have greatly expanded their access in providing expert implementation guidance and resources for programmatic success of trauma-informed schools (TIS).

The Ecological Theory (Bronfenbrenner, 2009) can provide a framework for understanding how trauma exposure and impact as well as responses can be affected by multiple domains. These include the individual (student) at the center of the system, microsystem (e.g., peers, families/carers, school educators and leaders), mesosystem (interaction between the microsystems), exosystem (e.g., local governments, parent's friends), macrosystem (e.g., social

DOI: 10.4324/9781003436034-12

norms, policy) and the chronosystem (time in a child's life). By applying the ecological framework in relation to trauma and school settings, it is clear that federal and state policies, such as those related to discipline practices, need to be considered in creating trauma-informed environments. This is particularly relevant to policies such as exclusion policies related to student behaviors, which can be create re-traumatization (American Psychological Association, 2008). Addressing the negative impacts of trauma across domains has shown to result in positive outcomes on school climate and culture (Cole et al., 2013), teacher and staff attitudes toward trauma-informed care (Loomis & Felt, 2020), student achievement and behavior (Mendelson et al., 2015), as well as community and family sense of connectedness (Holmes et al., 2015).

When applying an ecological framework in creating TIS, data-based decision making at each domain can be a key component. Until relatively recently, the scope of understanding and evaluating the impacts of trauma exposure on a child or adolescent in schools was primarily limited to individual-level trauma screening and symptom checklists used to inform student treatment planning (Champine et al., 2019; Eklund et al., 2018). However, ensuring ongoing assessment (e.g., review of practices and policies) at the macro and micro levels is equally important (Downey & Greco, 2023). This process can seem daunting to schools, which are typically tasked with addressing the rising needs of students while advancing academic achievement. Specifically, educators and school leaders may benefit from guidance in *identifying* the needs of the students and school at each level (e.g., what are the areas of strength and where is there opportunity for growth?), *selecting* culturally responsive measures that address the identified goal at each level (e.g., what measures are available to evaluate the schools' policies and practices? What measures are available to assess teacher well-being?) and *disseminating* the findings into actionable plans that encourage sustainment of trauma-informed practices (e.g., how do school teams use findings to create organizational change?).

This chapter is intended to offer practical considerations and guidance to measurement at different domains of a trauma-informed school, including the school itself, teachers and other support staff, families/caregivers, as well as students. In addition, brief descriptions of several (not exhaustive) evidence-informed tools for use by educators and school staff are included at each level. At the end of the chapter, a case example is provided to illustrate a real-world exemplar for how educators and school teams can use data-based decision-making processes to strengthen the entire school and promote a school culture healing for all students, staff, and families.

Schools

Tools to Assess Trauma-Informed School Environments

A supportive, safe, and nurturing environment can have a positive impact on the entire school community, and importantly, protect against the negative impacts of trauma exposure on students, educators, and school staff (Berger, 2019). However, shifting the culture (also known as climate) and identity of the school to one that is trauma-informed is a multi-phased process which requires a whole-school effort. For example, school leaders or designated champions of school trauma-informed practice (e.g., teachers, school mental health staff) may lead efforts for reviewing existing practices and policies to ensure alignment with the guiding trauma-informed principles of SAMHSA (2014). This could include; creating a culture and climate that promotes positive interactions amongst school staff and students; empowering students, educators, and other staff members to have an active voice in decisions; viewing student behavior and classroom management strategies through the lens of potential trauma; providing opportunities for professional development and staff training in trauma-informed care; actively engage and collaborate with community members and families; and creating systems that are sustainable over time (Carello & Butler, 2015; Crosby, 2015). Despite these numerous areas to be explored within the context of a trauma-informed education system or school, few assessment tools and guides are available to support educators and school leaders in the process of delivering trauma-informed supports. A systematic review by Champine et al. (2019) revealed a scarcity of systems-level instruments specifically designed to assess trauma-informed practices. This gap is especially evident within school and other educational settings. The instruments outlined below represent some of the tools currently available for school teams to evaluate the impact of trauma-informed practices.

The TIS Organizational Readiness Assessment (McGlynn-Wright et al., 2021), is a free instrument designed to assist school teams to assess their readiness to adopt a trauma-informed approach. Proposed members of a school team typically include administrators, teachers, school mental health professionals, as well as other key staff. Involvement and feedback from caregivers, students, and community members are also encouraged, which may be most helpful for programmatic success. While the psychometric properties of this measure are not yet established, the instrument was developed through an extensive review of the literature on trauma-informed care and expert consultation with researchers, mental health providers, and school teams. The TIS Organizational Readiness Assessment consists of 16 items across three domains: general capacity of the school to implement trauma-informed practices (e.g., "the school is adequately staffed with teachers, administrators, social workers, Special Education coordinators, etc."), specific capacity of the school to carry out trauma-informed practice (e.g., "the school assesses climate at least quarterly"), and overall level of motivation for implementation (e.g., "the school conveys a unique rationale for why it is urgent to become a trauma-informed school now").

The Trauma Responsive Schools Implementation Assessment (TRS-IA, 2017) is another readily available and free instrument included in the School Health Assessment and Performance Evaluation System (SHAPE, 2024) database. The TRS-IA is an evidence-informed questionnaire completed by school teams to identify trauma responsive programming, areas of strength and priority areas across six key domains: targeted intervention for trauma (e.g., does the school offer TF-CBT or other evidence-based interventions?), early interventions for trauma (e.g., are trauma symptom items included in mental health assessments and screening tools?), classroom based strategies (e.g., do teachers provide trauma-sensitive behavioral supports to students in the classroom?), whole-school trauma programming (e.g., are discipline policies sensitive to trauma exposed students?), whole-school safety and prevention planning/staff support (e.g., is there an ongoing assessment of school climate? Are there on-site resources for staff in working with trauma exposed students?) and community and family supports (e.g., do partnerships with community organizations exist?).

After completing a school-wide assessment such as the two shared above, schools can create action plans to help guide their teams to address priority areas while sustaining areas of strength. For example, action plans should include 1–2 target areas that will be addressed over the course of the school year. Ideally, plans will outline available strategies and resources to be used in addition to identifying team leads. The TIS Organizational Readiness Assessment (McGlynn-Wright et al., 2021) offers a template for this process after school teams complete the assessment. Additionally, a template action plan is available from the Trauma-Sensitive Schools Training package (Guarino & Chagnon, 2018) that may be used after completing the online training module. The action plan provides a multi-phased roadmap to adopting a trauma-informed approach. School teams will similarly create key goals, outline available resources and activities to meet those established goals, and identify implementation champions to lead school-wide change initiatives.

Finally, the Thoughtful Schools Program (https://thoughtfulschools.org.au/) offers comprehensive assessment and action planning resources that are free for schools. The program was designed based on the recently published International Trauma-Informed Practice Principles for Schools (ITIPPS) (Martin et al., 2023). The ITIPPS were created using research methodology which included consensus for final Principles by international experts (Martin et al., 2023). In addition to the ITIPPS, program resources include a checklist to assist schools to measure their status in relation to each Principle, an action plan template for schools to generate priorities and targeted actions, and a guidebook (Martin et al., 2021), which offers evidence-informed strategies related to each Principle that schools can implement. The developers encourage schools to use a cyclical and reflexive process in which the trauma-informed environment is examined, planned, and revised annually.

Teachers, Leaders, and Other School Staff

Tools to Assess Trauma-Informed Attitudes, Knowledge, and Behaviors

Teachers and other school staff are key to the successful implementation of trauma-informed strategies in schools (Casimir & Baker, 2023). School staff typically learn new knowledge, shift their attitudes to be more trauma-informed, and change their behaviors (Overstreet & Baker, 2022; von der Embse et al., 2019). Best practice professional development for teachers and school staff includes both didactic training and implementation supports (e.g., coaching or support from champions (Fixsen et al., 2009)). It is through the day-to-day and moment-to-moment behaviors of teachers and other school staff that the goals of trauma-informed practices are likely to be achieved. The first goal, contextualized within the classroom, is to *prevent* students from experiencing additional trauma or stressful experiences. This includes attempting to eliminate punitive and coercive interactions such as suspensions and expulsions/exclusions, addressing bullying, and eradicating discrimination and microaggressions (Casimir & Baker, 2023). The second is to *intervene* upon stressors that have already been experienced by creating safe, predictable, and supportive places for students to learn skills which may be challenging, such as emotion regulation and relationship skills (Casimir & Baker, 2023; Greene & Ablon, 2006; Shonkoff, 2016). Additionally, educators who understand trauma and value TIS can help students get the services they may need by completing school-based social, emotional, and behavioral screenings, making referrals, and accommodating students' participation in school-based mental health services when appropriate. Finally, trauma-informed practices have the potential to protect the workforce by reducing burnout, re-engaging educators, and reducing staff turnover, thus preventing the negative impacts of understaffed classrooms and disrupted child-caregiver relationships (Casimir & Baker, 2023). Additionally, most schools partner with outside agencies to provide evidence-based treatment for students with identified traumatic stress reactions (Cole et al., 2013). These outside providers are also well positioned to understand how to implement trauma-informed practices from the perspectives of their disciplines, which are typically school social work, school counseling, or school or child clinical psychology.

Data-based decision-making plays a key role in evaluating educator education in, and implementation of trauma-informed practice. Scales have been developed to target the different outcomes of professional training completed by educators. These scales are generally combined into a questionnaire which is administered to participants before and after trauma education to help assess impact. First, school staff *attitudes* favorable to trauma-informed practice are often evaluated using the Attitudes Related to Trauma-Informed Care scale (ARTIC; Baker et al., 2016; Baker et al., 2021). Respondents rate items along a seven-point bipolar Likert scale containing statements favorable to trauma-informed practice on one end and unfavorable on the other end. A ten-item short form exists, as well as 35- and 45-item versions which provide additional nuance. An example item asks raters to choose between the unfavorable attitude, "the children I work with could act better if they really wanted to," and the favorable attitude, "the children I work with are doing the best they can with the skills they have." The ARTIC has adequate reliability, construct validity, and predictive validity (Baker et al., 2016, 2021; Bellamy et al., 2022). Second, educator *knowledge* about trauma-informed practice is often evaluated using a 12- to

15-item quiz (i.e., McIntyre et al., 2019). The quiz is typically written to reflect the content of the professional development session that was delivered. An example item might be, "What are the three brain regions that are most affected by chronic stress and trauma?," with answer options being a. amygdala, hippocampus, prefrontal cortex; b. temporal lobe, hippocampus, hypothalamus; c. cerebellum, amygdala, hypothalamus; d. prefrontal cortex, hippocampus, occipital lob; and e. do not know. Items are scored as correct or incorrect, with "do not know" scored as incorrect. This results in a percent correct summary score. Evaluations using knowledge quizzes have demonstrated that their scores are valid (Baker et al., 2021; McIntyre et al., 2019). Third, educator *behavior* favorable to trauma-informed practice is frequently evaluated using the TICOMETER scale (Bassuk et al., 2017; Unick et al., 2019). The TICOMETER is a 35-item scale that taps into non-specific behaviors favorable to trauma-informed practices, such as establishing trusting relationships and promoting trauma-informed policies and practices. The scale has demonstrated adequate psychometric properties (Bassuk et al., 2017; Unick et al., 2019). An example item is "Ongoing training on trauma is required for all staff and administrators (including clinical and non-clinical staff, peer support staff, and volunteers)." For schools that want to add an observational tool to their portfolio, any structured observation that taps into positive interactions (including between staff and students, between students, and between staff), socioemotional learning, and/or teacher-student relationships will provide valuable additional perspectives, with the bonus being that these observations can be used to drive goal setting in one-on-one teacher coaching. Finally, climate indicators, discussed in the school systems section of this chapter, can also be utilized to provide an aggregated snapshot of school staff perspectives and practices.

Tools to Assess Staff Professional Well-Being

In addition to attitudes, knowledge, and behaviors, staff *professional well-being* can also be evaluated. This construct when applied to staff in helping professions includes compassion satisfaction (the pleasure derived from doing one's work), burnout (the feelings of hopelessness and challenges managing work), and secondary traumatic stress (the experiences that result from working with individuals with trauma histories) (Stamm, 2005). The Professional Quality of Life measure (ProQOL; Stamm, 2005) includes 30 items that are rated on a five-point Likert scale. An example item includes "I feel worn out because of my work as a helper" with response options ranging from never (1) to very often (5). The ProQOL has strong internal consistency and construct validity (Baker et al., 2021; Stamm, 2005). Although it is clear that educators also experience compassion fatigue (Fleckman et al., 2022), the ProQOL is written for mental health providers and may not feel like a strong fit with educators. Alternatives include measuring burnout via the Maslach Burnout Inventory (Maslach et al., 1997) and/or vicarious traumatization and coping via one of the ARTIC subscales (Baker et al., 2016, 2021).

Tools to Assess the Process of Implementing Trauma-Informed Practices

Finally, the process of learning about, adopting, and implementing trauma-informed practices can also be assessed in a formative evaluation. Schools might opt to gather educator perspectives on satisfaction, feasibility, acceptability, and personal support for trauma-informed practices. A generic satisfaction scale can be used (see McIntyre et al., 2019). The Usage Rating Profile-Intervention Revised (URP-IR; Briesch et al., 2013) can evaluate feasibility and acceptability. The ARTIC (Baker et al., 2016, 2021) includes an indicator of personal support. Finally, self-efficacy, the belief that one is capable of successfully completing a task, is also important in creating trauma-informed practices and thus also relevant to measure (Wittich et al. 2020). For this reason, an indicator of self-efficacy with regard to trauma-informed practices is also included in the ARTIC (Baker et al., 2016, 2021).

Parents/Caregivers

Knowledge and Perspectives about Trauma and Trauma-Informed Practice

A school-wide trauma-informed environment requires an understanding of key social determinants impacting a student's capacity to learn (Ayre & Krishnamoorthy, 2020). Parents, caregivers, and families are an important part of the school community. A student's perception of the safety, trust, and empowerment within a school environment is significantly influenced by their early experiences with significant attachment figures in their families. Family and caregiver perceptions of school, and the child's wellbeing needs and functioning at school, can influence how responsive a student will be to trauma-informed supports provided (Plumb et al., 2016). Building a strong working alliance with families requires schools to regularly seek and act on feedback from parents and caregivers (Holmes et al., 2015). Such feedback also informs the robust evaluation of trauma-informed school practices and programs by assessing for any incidental gains experienced by families in the home environment, as well as any unintended negative consequences of such practices on families and caregivers (Bartlett et al., 2017). Indeed, certain trauma-informed programs implemented in school settings may include components that are directed toward families and caregivers of students. For example, Trauma Smart (Holmes et al., 2015) is a trauma-informed organizational change model implemented in preschools, and K-12 schools that includes caregiver education sessions in addition to staff professional development trainings and classroom consultation. The program intentionally involves caregivers and family members in training sessions and routinely seeks their feedback, which is critical to successful trauma-informed system change (Bartlett et al., 2017).

Despite the importance of seeking feedback from parents and caregivers, systematic reviews of parent or caregiver-rated measures revealed a limited number of validated measures (Traumatic Stress Institute, 2020). For example, Trauma-Informed Practice Scales (Goodman et al., 2016), captures information about domestic violence survivors', including caregivers', trauma-related knowledge, and competencies as well as their perceptions of the extent to which domestic violence program staff are skilled in responding to survivors' feelings and coping skills and engage them as partners in service delivery. The other measures identified related to psychometric instruments used as part of trauma-focused interventions, such as trauma-focused CBT. An example of such a parent-rated measure is the Parent Trauma Response Questionnaire (PTRQ); another validated measure of parental responses following child trauma exposure (Williamson et al., 2018). Overall, there is a need for empirically validated caregiver-rated measures of trauma-informed practice (Hanson & Lang, 2016).

Students

Studies have utilized measures that assess student views on the ecological context of the school to evaluate the impact of trauma-informed practices, highlighting the critical role of student input (Berardi & Morton, 2019; Stratford et al., 2022). Student voice refers to the active participation of students in the decision-making processes in educational environments. In the context of TIS, student voice refers to the involvement of students in the development and implementation of practices that understand the impact of trauma, which are culturally responsive and relevant to their experiences. The Trauma-Informed Care Grade (TIC Grade; Boucher et al., 2022) is one psychometrically valid and reliable youth-report instrument used to assess the quality of trauma-informed care they received. While the TIC Grade is not exclusively designed for use within schools, it was developed based on the National Center for Trauma-Informed Care principles – with an emphasis on safety, trustworthiness, collaboration, empowerment, and cultural competence, which are foundational for creating school environments that support healing and resilience in students impacted by trauma (Boucher et al., 2022). Despite the promise of the TIC Grade in school settings, it is noteworthy that no additional measures are available to school teams to further engage student participation and voice (Wassink-de Stigter et al., 2024). Given the importance of honoring and empowering students within the TIS approach, this is a notable omission. Similar to family and caregiver-rated measures, most measures reviewed in the literature are those used to measure aspects of a child's functioning at school, including their attendance, academic performance, rates of behavioral problems, and disciplinary sanctions (Bartlett et al., 2017; Bellamy et al., 2022).

School climate refers to the quality and character of school life, based on patterns of students', parents', and school personnel's experience of school life and reflects norms, goals, values, interpersonal relationships, teaching and learning practices, and organizational structures (Aldridge & Blackstock, 2024). A broad, multifaceted concept, school climate impacts and incorporates many aspects of the student's educational experience. While there is limited consensus about what school climate dimensions are essential to assess, the National School Climate Council (2007; NSCC) in the United States of America suggests that there are five major areas that school climate assessment needs to include: Safety, Interpersonal Relationships, Social Media, Teaching and Learning. Some schools and school districts assess how students feel about their school environment by using instruments such as the Elementary and Middle School Climate Survey, the School Climate Survey-Revised, and the Elementary School Environment Scale (Marraccini et al., 2020; Lenz et al., 2021). The data gathered through this measure provides educational leaders insights directly from students and can guide improvements into the implementation of TIS.

Trauma Exposure and Impact Measures

With regard to validated measures, universal screeners and child-rated measures assessing posttraumatic stress symptoms in children and adolescents are also available. At the school-wide or classroom level, schools have utilized screeners that assess for risks of behavioral and academic challenges due to traumatic stress exposure. One example of a validated universal screener is the Social, Academic, and Emotional Behavior Risk Screener (SAEBRS) (Kilgus et al., 2014). SAEBER is a brief instrument designed to screen all students, to identify students at risk of social-emotional and behavioral (SBL) challenges. This screen is among the few universal SEB screening instruments crafted to evaluate both the lack of problematic behaviors and symptoms (such as internalizing and externalizing behaviors) and the presence of positive attributes and skills (such as social-emotional competencies; Kilgus & Eklund, 2016) which acknowledges and adheres to a strengths-based approach to working with students impact by trauma. The identification of at-risk students, and a further assessment of their needs, informs a multi-tiered systems of support (MTSS) – in which schools allocate and implement trauma-informed practice-related resources to different segments of the student population.

It is essential to approach screening with care and sensitivity. Schools must ensure that any screening activities are conducted with appropriate permission from guardians, and most importantly, adequate supports must be in place to address identified needs. This includes having qualified professionals available to provide interventions and support for children, as well as clear protocols for responding to disclosures of trauma or abuse (Raja et al., 2021). Any indication of abuse must be reported and addressed in accordance with mandated reporting laws, ensuring timely and adequate responses to protect children.

Validated screening measures for posttraumatic stress in children include the Child and Adolescent Trauma Screen (CATS; Sachser et al., 2017), which is a brief, self-report measure that assesses exposure to traumatic events and symptoms of PTSD. Broadband measures assess a range of symptoms related to trauma exposure, such as anxiety, depression, and behavioral problems. One example of a broadband measure is the Trauma Symptom Checklist for Children (TSCC; Briere, 1996), which assesses a range of symptoms related to trauma exposure. PTSD-specific measures assess symptoms specific to PTSD. One example of a PTSD-specific measure is the Child PTSD Symptom Scale (CPSS; Foa et al., 2001), which assesses symptoms of PTSD in children and adolescents.

An important aspect of creating TIS is that students are involved in the development and implementation of appropriate strategies, not only does this acknowledge their central role in the schools but also their input can help ensure that practices are culturally responsive and relevant to their experiences (Donisch et al., 2016). Additionally, community mental health providers and other external agencies are also vital to this process, as schools typically rely on these partners to complete additional screening and provide more intensive individualized trauma interventions as needed (Cole et al., 2013).

Case Study

School ABC has been working to create a trauma-informed environment for five years. Schools newer to this work will have fewer components in place and a slimmer evaluation plan. The implementation has included all-staff trauma education and ongoing educator professional development focused on bridging the gap between understanding the importance of trauma-informed practice in schools and actually embedding them every day in the classroom. New staff are trained as they come on board, more seasoned staff receive boosters, and all staff are supported by coaching and peer support specialists who serve as informal champions of the work. A piece of the staff training has focused on understanding vicarious traumatization and self-care to prevent burnout and the disengagement of the school workforce. Alongside this intensive staff education and support, a TIS committee, which is comprised of key administrators, school-based mental health providers, peer support specialists, and a parent/caregiver representative, has reviewed the policies, practices, and procedures at the school to align them with trauma-informed practices. This has included a close look at the discipline policy, efforts to improve the safety of the physical environment, and the adoption and ongoing support of school-wide initiatives to promote student resilience and address risk factors. Examples of these initiatives include the following:

- a socioemotional learning program,
- a bullying prevention program,

- universal social, emotional, and behavioral (SEB) screening,
- multi-tiered systems of support for SEB needs,
- team-level review of disaggregated data to detect and address biased discipline and referral patterns by sociodemographic group and disability status,
- development of mental health agency partnerships to provide clinical services to students experiencing psychological distress including traumatic stress,
- and strong parent/caregiver engagement mechanisms.

School ABC's trauma-informed action plan incorporated the careful roll-out of these practices over time. The plan identified not only the key personnel responsible for the initiative, but also evaluation mechanisms to ensure fidelity, measure outcomes, and make changes as needed. At the organizational level, School ABC began with an organizational readiness assessment completed by the TIS committee, which guided the decision about when to begin the journey of adopting trauma-informed practices. After implementation began, the committee shifted to using an annual survey focused on quality improvement during ongoing implementation. Together, these two types of tools have provided a profile of strengths and areas of growth to guide the annual action planning process that has facilitated the adoption of trauma-informed practices. Additionally, the school monitors the implementation fidelity of any school-wide initiatives. An example is confirming that teachers delivered at least 80% of the socioemotional learning program annually, along with a classroom observation to confirm that it was being implemented at high quality and provide coaching to achieve fidelity if required. At the school staff level, the school has adopted a program evaluation model in which staff complete the same set of measures before and after the all staff trauma education and again at the end of the school year. This group of measures includes indicators of knowledge, attitudes, behaviors, and professional quality of life. The design allows the school to compare the information they gathered from their staff from before and education. The end-of-year timepoint helps the school check that knowledge and attitude growth is sustained and also spot changes in behavior and professional quality of life, which typically take longer to impact. Finally, the school also gathers the recommended process data after the training and again at the end of the year, including satisfaction, feasibility, acceptability, personal support of the initiative, and self-efficacy. Checking these process indicators is important because even the most powerful interventions will not have impacts if the staff needing to implement them are not supportive. Next, at the parent/caregiver level, School ABC delivered trauma education sessions to parents/caregivers and opted to gather feedback from them through post-session questionnaires, including quantitative items focused on their satisfaction with the session and qualitative items asking them about strengths and areas of growth for the session. Finally, at the student level, School ABC gathers annual school climate surveys, completed by both students and school staff, to understand how everyone in the school perceives school safety, student-teacher relationships, and other constructs key to trauma-informed practice. In addition, one month after school starts and again a few months after the mid-year break, the school collects universal SEB screening data from all the students. Screenings are completed using passive consent, in which caregivers are provided with information about the screening and offered the ability to opt out. When students have either a positive screen on the universal measure or are referred by a teacher or caregiver, the student proceeds through the second gate of screening, which can include screening for traumatic stress when indicated. During screening activities, school-based mental health providers or similarly trained providers should be a part of the process or at least on campus in the event that a student reports crisis-level distress on a screener. Positive screens for traumatic stress result in an initiation of the appropriate level of service within the MTSS team, which coordinates service delivery with agency partners and monitors outcomes to ensure that students are correctly identified and receive the supports they need to help enhance their wellbeing. Initiation of any services requires an active consent from the caregiver, which is usually obtained in the context of a conversation between school-based mental health providers or similarly trained professionals and the caregiver.

Recommendations

Based on the current research related to measuring trauma's impact and trauma-informed practice in schools, the following recommendations are provided:

Involve students, families/carers and educators in understanding trauma impact and trauma-informed practice measurement processes. With appropriate supports in place, utilize tools that seek information from students, their parents/carers, and educators about their experiences and needs. This provides relevant and meaningful information to inform the school community about trauma and effective implementation of trauma-informed practice. Students, their families/carers, and educators may each require the use of a different standardized tool, based on the context of the school community.

Communicate clearly about the purpose and process of data collection and ensure those participating provide their consent. Provide students, families/carers, and staff with clear expectations about how data will be used to support well-being. Transparency helps reduce anxiety and builds trust in the measurement process.

Create supportive, trauma-informed environments for data collection. Ensure data collection spaces are comfortable and non-threatening (e.g., quiet rooms, clear instructions, supportive staff). Positive interactions, consistent routines, and clarity around expectations promote a safe environment that minimizes stress during assessments.

Provide professional development for educators on trauma-informed measurement. Teachers and staff involved in data collection should be trained to recognize potential triggers and respond appropriately. Training helps staff administer assessments with empathy, reducing the risk of re-traumatization and fostering positive experiences for students.

Ensure appropriate expert supports are available for all school community members. This is required during the data collection as well as interpretation of the data. Schools can often link with sector or external services to ensure adequate response and follow up is required and to minimize risk of vicarious trauma.

Conclusion

Trauma-informed practices in schools offer a promising strategy to address the impacts of trauma on students as well as their teachers, families, and the community. The ecological theory (Bronfenbrenner, 2009) offers a framework for considering the transactional impacts of trauma across the levels of the system. Additionally, the same theory can be used to guide not only the adoption of trauma-informed practices across the system but also the targeted use of data-based decision-making during its implementation. The goals of data-based decision-making are to ensure fidelity of implementation, evaluate the effectiveness of initiatives, and make quality improvements when needed. Additionally, having a clear evaluation plan can serve to systematize and sustain the implementation effort. This is especially important for schools, which must accomplish both their academic missions and meet the rising social, emotional, and behavioral health needs of their students.

This chapter reviewed evidence-informed tools at each ecological systems level, including the school, the educators, the parents and families, and the students. The most commonly used tools were described in terms of their purposes and their psychometric properties. Overall, there is a dearth of validated instruments, which is a gap in the literature that urgently needs to be addressed by future research. When integrated into a thoughtful plan of action by schools, these tools can be used to identify strengths and areas for growth. Information gathered by these tools can provide an ecological perspective on the implementation of TIS across the system. In this way, school can make evidence-informed progress toward the goal of adopting, implementing, and sustaining trauma-informed practices in schools.

References

Aldridge, J. M., & Blackstock, M. J. (2024). Assessing students' perceptions of school climate in primary schools. *Learning Environments Research*. https://doi.org/10.1007/s10984-024-09492-2.

American Psychological Association Zero Tolerance Task Force. (2008). Are zero tolerance policies effective in the schools?: An evidentiary review and recommendations. *American Psychologist, 63*(9), 852–862.

Ayre, K., & Krishnamoorthy, G. (2020) *Trauma informed behaviour support*. Toowoomba: University of Southern Queensland. https://open.umn.edu/opentextbooks/textbooks/936

Baker, C. N., Brown, S. M., Overstreet, S., Wilcox, P. D., & the New Orleans Trauma-Informed Schools Learning Collaborative. (2021). Validation of the Attitudes Related to Trauma-Informed Care (ARTIC) scale. *Psychological Trauma: Theory, Research, Practice, and Policy, 13*(5), 505–513.

Baker, C. N., Brown, S. M., Wilcox, P. D., Overstreet, S., & Arora, P. (2016). Development and psychometric evaluation of the Attitudes Related to Trauma-Informed Care (ARTIC) scale. *School Mental Health, 8*, 61–76.

Bartlett, J. D., Barto, B., Griffin, J. L., Fraser, J. G., Hodgdon, H., & Bodian, R. (2017). Trauma-informed practices through whole school education. *Journal of Classroom Interaction, 52*(1), 34–46.

Bassuk, E. L., Unick, G. J., Paquette, K., & Richard, M. K. (2017). Developing an instrument to measure organizational trauma-informed care in human services: The TICOMETER. *Psychology of Violence, 7*(1), 150–157.

Bellamy, T., Krishnamoorthy, G., Ayre, K., Berger, E., Machin, T., & Rees, B. E. (2022). Trauma-informed school programming: A partnership approach to culturally responsive behaviour support. *Sustainability, 14*(7), 3997.

Berardi, A., & Morton, B. M. (2019). Trauma-informed practices in schools across two decades: An interdisciplinary review of research. *Frontiers in Psychology, 10*. https://doi.org/10.3389/fpsyg.2019.02806.

Berger, E. (2019). Multi-tiered approaches to trauma-informed care in schools: A systematic review. *School Mental Health, 11*(4), 650–664. https://doi.org/10.1007/s12310-019-09326-0.

Boucher, N., Darling-Fisher, C. S., Sinko, L., Beck, D., Granner, J., & Seng, J. (2022). Psychometric evaluation of the TIC Grade, a self-report measure to assess youth perceptions of the quality of trauma-informed care they received. *Journal of the American Psychiatric Nurses Association, 28*(4), 319–325. https://doi.org/10.1177/1078390320953896.

Briere, J. (1996). *Trauma Symptom Checklist for Children (TSCC), Professional Manual*. Odessa, FL: Psychological Assessment Resources.

Briesch, A. M., Chafouleas, S. M., Neugebauer, S. R., & Riley-Tillman, T. C. (2013). Assessing influences on intervention use: Revision of the usage rating profile-intervention. *Journal of School Psychology, 51*, 81–96.

Bronfenbrenner, U. (2009). *The ecology of human development*. Cambridge, MA: Harvard University Press.

Carello, J., & Butler, L. (2015). Practicing what we teach: Trauma-informed educational practice. *Journal of Teaching in Social Work, 35*(3), 262–278.

Casimir, A. E., & Baker, C. N. (2023). *Trauma-responsive pedagogy: Teaching for healing and transformation*. Portsmouth, NH: Heinemann.

Champine, R. B., Lang, J. M., Nelson, A. M., Hanson, R. F., & Tebes, J. K. (2019). Systems measures of a trauma-informed approach: A systematic review. *American Journal of Community Psychology, 64*(3–4), 418–437. https://doi.org/10.1002/ajcp.12388

Cole, S. F., Eisner, A., Gregory, M., & Ristuccia, J. (2013). *Helping traumatized children learn: Safe, supportive learning environments that benefit all children*. Boston, MA: Massachusetts Advocates for Children Trauma and Learning Policy Initiative.

Donisch, K., Bray, C., & Gewirtz, A. (2016). Child welfare, juvenile justice, mental health, and education providers' conceptualizations of trauma-informed practice. *Child Maltreatment, 21*(2), 125–134. https://doi.org/10.1177/1077559516633304.

Downey, J., & Greco, J. (2023). Trauma sensitive schools: A comprehensive guide for the assessment planning and implementation of trauma informed frameworks. *Children and Youth Services Review, 149*. https://doi.org/10.1016/j.childyouth.2023.106930.

Eklund, K., Rossen, E., Koriakin, T., Chafouleas, S. M., & Resnick, C. (2018). A systematic review of trauma screening measures for children and adolescents. *School Psychology Quarterly, 33*(1), 30–43. https://doi.org/10.1037/spq0000244.

Fixsen, D. L., Blase, K. A., Naoom, S. F., & Wallace, F. (2009). Core implementation components. *Research on Social Work Practice, 19*(5), 531–540.

Fleckman, J. M., Petrovic, L., Simon, K., Peele, H., Baker, C. N., Overstreet, S., & the New Orleans Trauma-Informed Schools Learning Collaborative. (2022). Compassion satisfaction, secondary traumatic stress, and burnout: A mixed methods analysis in a sample of public-school educators working in marginalized communities. *School Mental Health, 14*, 933–950.

Foa, E. B., Johnson, K. M., Feeny, N. C., & Treadwell, K. R. (2001). The child PTSD symptom scale: A preliminary examination of its psychometric properties. *Journal of Clinical Child Psychology, 30*(3), 376–384. https://doi.org/10.1207/S15374424JCCP3003_9

Goodman, L. A., Sullivan, C. M., Serrador, J., Perilla, J., Wilson, J. M., Fauci, J. E., & Shetterly, J. (2016). Development and validation of the trauma-informed practice scales. *Journal of Interpersonal Violence, 31*(14), 2467–2494.

Guarino, K., & Chagnon, E. (2018). *Trauma-sensitive schools training package*. Washington, DC: National Center on Safe Supportive Learning Environments.

Hanson, R. F., & Lang, J. (2016). A critical look at trauma-informed care among agencies and systems serving maltreated youth and their families. *Child Maltreatment, 21*(2), 95–100.

Holmes, C., Levy, M., Smith, A., Pinne, S., & Neese, P. (2015). A model for creating a supportive trauma-informed culture for children in preschool settings. *Journal of Child and Family Studies, 24*(6), 1650–1659. https://doi.org/10.1007/s10826-014-9968-6

Kilgus, S. P., Chafouleas, S. M., & Riley-Tillman, T. C. (2014). Development and initial validation of the social and academic behavior risk screener for elementary grades. *School Psychology Quarterly, 29*(3), 210–226. https://doi.org/10.1037/spq0000065

Kilgus, S. P., & Eklund, K. R. (2016). Consideration of base rates within universal screening for behavioral and emotional risk: A novel procedural framework. *School Psychology Forum, 10*(1), 120–130.

Lenz, A. S., Rocha, L., & Aras, Y. (2020). Measuring school climate: A systematic review of initial development and validation studies. *International Journal for the Advancement of Counselling, 42*(4), 431–451. https://doi.org/10.1007/s10447-020-09415-9

Loomis, A., & Felt, F. (2020). Knowledge, skills, and self-reflection: Linking trauma training content to trauma-informed attitudes and stress in preschool teachers and staff. *School Mental Health, 1*, 101–113. https://doi.org/10.1007/s12310-020-09394-7.

Marraccini, M. E., Fang, Y., Levine, S. P., Chin, A. J., & Pittleman, C. (2019). Measuring student perceptions of school climate: A systematic review and ecological content analysis. *School Mental Health, 12*(2), 195–221. https://doi.org/10.1007/s12310-019-09348-8

Martin, K., Dobson, M., Fitzgerald, K., Ford, M., Lund, S., Egeberg, H., Walker, R., Milroy, H., Wheeler, K., Kasten-Lee, A., Bayly, L., Gazey, A., Falconer, S., Platell, M., & Berger, E. (2023). International Trauma-Informed Practice Principles for Schools (ITIPPS): Expert consensus of best-practice principles. *Australian Educational Researcher, 51*, 1445–1468. https://doi.org/10.1007/s13384-023-00648-2

Martin, K. E., Ford, M., Fitzgerald, K., Falconer, S., Kasten-Lee, A., Egeberg, H., Walker, R., Dobson, M., Lund, S., Gazey, A., Parker, R., Berger, E., & Wheeler, K. (2021). *The Thoughtful Schools Program guidebook: A guide to using the trauma-informed practice principles* (Version 3). The University of Western Australia. https://thoughtfulschools.org.au/

McGlynn-Wright, T., Orapallo, A., Reyes, L., Overstreet, S., Baker, C. N., & the New Orleans Trauma-Informed Schools Learning Collaborative (2021). *Trauma-informed schools organizational readiness assessment*. Unpublished instrument. Retrieved from https://safeschoolsnola.tulane.edu/trauma-informed-schools-organizational-readiness-assessment/

McIntyre, E. M., Baker, C. N., Overstreet, S., & the New Orleans Trauma-Informed Schools Learning Collaborative. (2019). Evaluating foundational professional development training for trauma-informed approaches in schools. *Psychological Services, 16*, 95–102.

Mendelson, T., Tandon, S. D., O'Brennan, L., Leaf, P. J., & Ialongo, N. S. (2015). Brief report: Moving prevention into schools: The impact of a trauma-informed school-based intervention. *Journal of Adolescence, 43*, 142–147. https://doi.org/10.1016/j.adolescence.2015.05.017

National Center for School Mental Health. (2024). *School mental health quality guide: Impact*. Retrieved from schoolmentalhealth.org.

National Child Traumatic Stress Network, Schools Committee. (2017). *Creating, supporting, and sustaining trauma-informed schools: A system framework*. Los Angeles, CA, and Durham, NC: National Center for Child Traumatic Stress

National School Climate Council. (2007). *The School Climate Challenge: Narrowing the gap between school climate research and school climate policy, practice guidelines and teacher education policy*. Retrieved from https://schoolclimate.org/wp-content/uploads/2021/05/school-climate-challenge-web.pdf

Overstreet, S., & Baker, C. N. (2022). *Trauma-informed approaches to improve school safety*. Retrieved from https://www.ojp.gov/pdffiles1/nij/grants/305489.pdf

Plumb, J. L., Bush, K. A., & Kersevich, S. E. (2016). Trauma-sensitive schools: An evidence-based approach. *School Social Work Journal, 40*(2), 37–60.

Raja, S., Rabinowitz, E. P., & Gray, M. J. (2021). Universal screening and trauma informed care: Current concerns and future directions. *Families, Systems, & Health, 39*(3), 526.

Sachser, C., Berliner, L., Holt, T., Jensen, T. K., Jungbluth, N., Risch, E., … Goldbeck, L. (2017). International development and psychometric properties of the Child and Adolescent Trauma Screen (CATS). *Journal of Affective Disorders, 210*, 189–195. https://doi.org/10.1016/j.jad.2016.12.040.

The School Health Assessment and Evaluation System. (2024). Retrieved from https://theshapesystem.com/

Shonkoff, J. P. (2016). Capitalizing on advances in science to reduce the health consequences of early childhood adversity. *JAMA Pediatrics, 170*(10), 1003–1007.

Stamm, B. H. (2005). *Professional Quality of Life Measure (ProQOL 5.0)*. Retrieved from https://survey.alchemer.com/s3/6727286/Professional-Quality-of-Life-Measure-ProQOL-5-0

Stratford, B., Cook, E., Hanneke, R., Katz, E., Seok, D., Steed, H., Fulks, E., Lessans, A.. & Temkin, D. (2020). A scoping review of school-based efforts to support students who have experienced trauma. *School Mental Health, 12*, 442–477 (2020). https://doi.org/10.1007/s12310-020-09368-9

The Substance Abuse and Mental Health Service Administration. (2014, April 25). *Trauma-informed approach and trauma-specific interventions*. Retrieved from https://www.samhsa.gov/nctic/trauma-interventions.

Trauma Responsive School Implementation Assessment. (2017). *Treatment and services adaptation center for resilience, hope, and wellness in Schools and the Center for School Mental Health*. Retrieved from https://traumaawareschools.org/resources-materials/3162/TRS-IA+1-25-18.pdf?1516971845.

Traumatic Stress Institute. (2020, February). *Measuring trauma-informed care series* (Monograph). https://traumaticstressinstitute.org/wp-content/uploads/2020/05/Measuring-Trauma-Informed-Care-Series-Final-02.2020.pdf

Unick, G. J., Bassuk, E. L., Richard, M. K., & Paquette, K. (2019). Organizational trauma-informed care: Associations with individual and agency factors. *Psychological Services, 16*(1), 134–142.

von der Embse, N., Rutherford, L., Mankin, A., & Jenkins, A. (2019). Demonstration of a trauma-informed assessment to intervention model in a large urban school district. *School Mental Health, 11*, 276–289.

de Stigter, R. W., Nelen, W., Delsing, M., de Berk, A., Kooijmans, R., Offerman, E., Asselman, M., Nijhof, K., Lindauer, R., & Helmond, P. (2024). Implementing a school-wide trauma-informed education approach: An evaluation of student-outcomes during the first year of implementation. *Journal of child & adolescent trauma, 18*(1), 71–85. https://doi.org/10.1007/s40653-024-00663-0

Williamson, V., Hiller, R. M., Meiser-Stedman, R., Creswell, C., Dalgleish, T., Fearon, P., Goodall, B., McKinnon, A., Smith, P., Wright, I., & Halligan, S. L. (2018). The Parent Trauma Response Questionnaire (PTRQ): Development and preliminary validation. *European Journal of Psychotraumatology, 9*(1), 1478583. https://doi.org/10.1080/20008198.2018.1478583

Wittich, C., Rupp, C., Overstreet, S., Baker, C. N., & the New Orleans Trauma-Informed Schools Learning Collaborative. (2020). Barriers and facilitators of the implementation of trauma-informed schools. *Research and Practice in the Schools, 7*, 33–48.

13

Conclusion and Future Directions

Emily Berger, Shantel D. Crosby, and Karen E. Martin

Introduction

The chapters within this book have highlighted the role of trauma-informed practice as one of the most important interventions for schools to manage the multiple and complex needs of students and families experiencing trauma. The importance of a whole-school approach to trauma-informed practice also clearly emerges as a theme. However, also noted throughout this book are the challenges that leaders, teachers, and schools face in implementing trauma-informed approaches into everyday practices, policies, and processes. In addition, the need to incorporate social justice learning, advocacy, and practice change has emerged. The additional focusing on effective strategies to support marginalized and high-risk groups, largely excluded from the trauma-informed literature to-date, has also emerged. This chapter summarizes gaps in policy and practice, and possible future research directions, and provides key recommendations for designing, delivering, and evaluating trauma-informed practice in schools and education sectors worldwide.

Whole-School Trauma-Informed Practice

The World Health Organisation (WHO) defines whole-school health programs as those that comprise healthy school policies, curricula, environments, communities, and health services (World Health Organization, 2023). Further, WHO highlights that a health-promoting education system is one that "through intentional, planned actions, institutionalizes health promotion in all its functions, i.e. governance of the educational process

DOI: 10.4324/9781003436034-13

and its content, resource allocation, educators' professional development, information systems and performance management" (p. 1).

Creating trauma-informed practice and policies school-wide, whilst ideal, is challenging. As highlighted throughout the chapters within this book, mental health-related whole-school programs can have a positive effect on students' social and emotional adjustment, behaviour, and internalizing symptoms (e.g., anxiety and depression). However, there is mixed evidence for the effectiveness of whole-school programs on students' learning. A number of barriers have been identified in incorporating school-wide approaches, including: (1) limited consistency on key components of whole-school programs, (2) inadequate emphasis on effective implementation of whole-school programs in schools to improve the quality and sustainability of programs, (3) lack of ongoing professional development of school staff to deliver whole-school programs, (4) limited evaluation of whole-school programs for continual improvement, (5) school infrastructure and systems which do not support whole-school implementation of programs, (6) lack of school leadership commitment and department planning support, and (7) limited engagement of families and community groups to support whole-school delivery of interventions (Goldberg et al., 2019).

Based on the current evidence, a whole-school approach to trauma-informed practice is required to improve effective and sustained delivery of a trauma-informed culture. However, consistent with observations made by Goldberg et al. (2019), whole-school trauma-informed programs require significant investment and commitment by school staff and educational leaders to ensure all components of this approach are implemented. Evidence presented in the chapters of this book demonstrate that successful whole-school integration of trauma-informed practice requires several key components. Chapter 4 discussed the importance of school policies, supportive classroom environments, professional development for teachers, approaches to support the wellbeing of teachers, and improved relationships and collaboration between educators, parents, and other support services for students. Chapter 5 discussed frameworks designed to support teacher wellbeing and recommended that approaches to promote teacher wellbeing, as well as support from school leaders, school policies, and supportive collegial relationships should be considered key components of a whole-school approach to trauma-informed practice. Chapter 7 detailed the importance of whole-school approaches, including support from school leaders and school policies, to improve trauma-informed practice for Black students attending urban schools in the United States of America. The next section of this chapter will focus on outlining the key components of a whole-school trauma-informed approach based on the available evidence.

Multi-Tiered Systems of Support

Multi-Tiered Systems of Support (MTSS) has been discussed within the chapters of this book and shown to be an effective model of practice to support students impacted by trauma. Chapter 4 outlined evidence from the Healthy Environments and Response to Trauma in Schools (HEARTS) model (Dorado et al., 2016), which is a multi-tiered approach to trauma-informed practice in schools. The following is an example, based on the HEARTS model, of how the MTSS framework can be applied in the context of supporting students exposed to trauma:

- Universal support: All students participate in social-emotional, resilience, and coping programs to prepare them in the event they experience a traumatic event
- Secondary support: Students exposed to a single incident trauma or experiencing moderate challenges in response to trauma receive additional support
- Tertiary support: Students exposed to repeated trauma or experiencing more severe challenges associated with their trauma exposure, receive more intensive support.

Evaluation of the HEARTS model has shown success in improving student's wellbeing, learning, and school engagement (Dorado et al., 2016). A review by Berger (2019), which evaluated multi-tiered trauma-informed programs in schools, also demonstrated the benefits of this approach for improving student's mental health and school outcomes. Berger (2019) and Dorado et al. (2016) have also advocated for multi-tiered trauma-informed support for school staff, including appropriate levels of training and mental health support for school staff based on their level of exposure to students who have experienced trauma.

Leadership Commitment and Support

School and district leaders (e.g., school principals, coordinators, education department staff) need to be committed to whole-school integration of trauma-informed practice, such as supporting ongoing professional learning of teachers and overseeing implementation of effective trauma-informed policies and practices. Commitment of school leaders is essential because evidence shows that school leaders are often responsible for selecting and promoting mental health and wellbeing interventions that will be delivered in their school community (Turan & Bektas, 2013). However, growing studies have identified that school leaders lack adequate knowledge and confidence to support the implementation of trauma-informed programs in schools (Berger et al., 2020). Therefore, it is important that schools have appropriate resources, policies, and staff professional development to support school leaders when implementing trauma-informed programs.

Trauma-Informed Professional Development

All school staff, including teachers, school leaders, administrative staff, and school support and wellbeing staff (e.g., teachers' aides, school nurses, counselors, and psychologists) should receive ongoing professional development and coaching to support implementation of trauma-informed practice. As highlighted in previous chapters, teachers lack knowledge, confidence, and skills to deliver trauma-informed support to students and their parents. Recent evidence has also shown that school support and wellbeing staff, including school counsellors and psychologists, also lack trauma-informed knowledge and skills, and require more training to better support teachers and school leaders when implementing trauma-informed approaches. Research about the effectiveness of trauma-informed professional development for teachers has shown that such training improves teachers' knowledge, confidence, and reduces the psychological impact on teachers of working with traumatized students (Berger & Nott, 2024). Therefore, trauma-informed training programs in schools should be designed to target all members of school staff, including members of school wellbeing teams. Professional development for school staff should follow the MTSS model of intervention based on the different roles and responsibilities of staff members, including more specialized training for school wellbeing staff (Berger, 2019).

Embedded Trauma-Informed Approaches

Trauma-informed practice should be embedded across the school curriculum, teaching and learning activities, and interactions between school staff, students, and parents and caregivers. Early evidence as presented throughout this book demonstrates the benefits of trauma-informed practice for teachers, students from diverse backgrounds, First Nations students, students with disability, and culturally and linguistically diverse students. As detailed in Chapters 10 and 11 of this book, research is also emerging about the benefits of trauma-informed approaches in music and physical activity classes in schools. However, ways to embed trauma-informed care into different areas of the school curriculum, and the benefits of such an approach, remain important areas for further research. Although Chapter 8 of this book highlights some of the available evidence supporting a trauma-informed approach with parents and caregivers of children exposed to trauma, research into the benefits of school trauma-informed programs for parents, caregivers, and families is another important area of future study.

Community Engagement

External services (e.g., mental health professionals, family violence services, and child protection) and parents and caregivers should be seen as important contributors to successful delivery of whole-school trauma-informed practice. It is often documented that schools do not have access to appropriately trained mental health providers (e.g., school psychologists) and therefore students exposed to trauma are often referred to mental health services outside of the school. Unfortunately, teachers, especially those in regional and rural locations, often have very limited mental health providers and health and wellbeing services available in their community (Berger et al., 2024). Therefore, timely access to appropriately trained professionals and mental health services is an ongoing challenge for some schools seeking to deliver whole-school support for students exposed to trauma. Chapter 8 of this book and existing evidence (e.g., Berger et al., 2023) has also highlighted that engaging with parents and caregivers is one of the most challenging aspects for teachers in response to students exposed to trauma. It is important that whole-school trauma-informed programs address this challenge, such as through trauma-informed education and policies to help teachers to manage their interactions with parents and families as well as education provision for parents.

Wellbeing Is Prioritized

Whole-school trauma-informed practice should ensure that the wellbeing of all school community members, including school leaders, teachers, support staff, parents and caregivers, and students is prioritized through policies, practices, and programs. Evidence presented in Chapters 5 and 8 of this book illustrates the significant impact that exposure to a traumatized student can have on teachers and their parents and caregivers, and how this can affect how successfully teachers and parents and caregivers can support students exposed to trauma. Chapters 5 and 8 also suggest that there is limited research and few trauma-informed interventions designed specifically to support the mental wellbeing of teachers and parents and caregivers. Therefore, through a whole-of-school approach, greater support and research is required to enable teachers and parents and caregivers to provide paramount care to students (and themselves) exposed to trauma.

School Values and Policies

School values and policies should be implemented to support and promote trauma-informed practice in schools, including a respectful relationships policy, mandatory reporting of suspected child maltreatment/abuse policy, teacher and student wellbeing policy, parent communication policy, and other policies relevant to successful delivery of trauma-informed practice. Such policies will also assist teachers and other school staff to understand their role and responsibilities in response to students exposed to trauma. Research finds that role confusion is a leading cause of burnout for teachers (Papastylianou et al., 2009) and therefore policies should be implemented to provide greater certainty for teachers regarding their role and responsibilities in response to traumatized students.

School Physical Environment

The school's physical, ambient, and aesthetic environment should support the principles of trauma-informed practice, including the layout of classrooms, quiet spaces in classrooms, and appropriate lighting, temperature, and noise control to limit distress among students exposed to trauma. Although this is a new area of trauma-informed practice in schools,

Chapter 6 of this book outlines the available evidence on designing appropriate school learning environments to support students exposed to trauma.

Contextually Aligned Programs

School trauma-informed practice should be aligned with the context of schools and school communities. For example, school psychologists in regional and rural areas with reduced access to external health and mental health services compared with metropolitan schools may need more training related to trauma. Lack of access to external health and mental health services may limit a school's capacity to deliver whole-school trauma-informed practice and this should be reflected in the school's policies and programs. Schools exposed to natural disasters also require different types of trauma-informed policies and programs compared to schools at lower risk of exposure to natural disasters. Chapters 7 and 9 of this book also discuss different approaches to delivery of trauma-informed practice with Black and Aboriginal and Torres Strait Islander students and families. Schools with higher proportions of students from marginalized and culturally diverse communities require trauma-informed school policies, practices, and programs that align with the support needs of students, staff, and parents and caregivers in their school community.

Culturally-Informed Trauma-Informed Practice

Trauma-informed policies and programs in schools should seek to be culturally safe and responsive to support students and families from culturally and linguistically diverse communities. Chapters 7 and 9 of this book provide evidence to support culturally aligned trauma-informed practices in schools. The authors demonstrate that providing culturally safe and responsive trauma-informed care to students and families is an area that is supported by the available literature. Examples include recognizing the impact of cultural and historical trauma on students and families, responding to students and families exposed to trauma using culturally sensitive practices, professional development for school staff to learn about culturally safe and responsive trauma-informed approaches, and representing different cultures through artwork, school events, and flags represented on school grounds. Chapters 7 and 9 of this book mention that trauma-informed approaches for Black and Aboriginal and Torres Strait Islander students and families should focus on systematic trauma as the root cause of individual trauma for these communities. It is suggested that a systematic, contextual, and cultural lens is required to deliver universal whole-school change for these students and families. Chapter 5 of this book which focuses on ways to promote teacher wellbeing in the context of trauma-informed practice also presents evidence showing that teachers from marginalized backgrounds, including Aboriginal and Torres Strait Islander teachers, teachers from culturally and linguistically diverse groups, teachers located in regional and rural areas, and LGBTQIA+ educators are at greater risk of discrimination in the workplace and mental ill-health compared to teachers not from these groups. Chapter 5 argues that teachers from marginalized groups should be the focus of wellbeing initiatives for teachers in schools.

Evaluation and Continual Improvement

Whole-school trauma-informed policies and programs should be continually evaluated by schools and education departments to ensure that the approaches are evidence-based. In addition, schools and education departments should ensure that they select trauma-informed programs that have been evaluated and shown to improve students (and potentially parent, caregiver, and school staff) wellbeing. Unfortunately, there are few evidence-based trauma-informed programs available, and limited randomized controlled trials have been conducted to evaluate current trauma-informed programs in schools. Continual collection and analysis of school data is also an integral component of a trauma-informed school, including measuring changes in students' academic, social-emotional, engagement, and behavioural outcomes as a result of delivery of an intervention, policy, or practice. Chapter 12 of this book discusses the importance of data collection and measurement in the context of MTSS and trauma-informed practice in schools, however, it also indicates that there is a lack of suitable measures available for schools.

Social Justice and Strengths-Based Approaches

An aspect of trauma-informed practice and discourse which needs to be strengthened is the importance of understanding the extent of the relationship between trauma and social injustice. Integrating an equity lens throughout the construction and implementation of trauma-informed practices is needed by schools and their communities. For example, specific strategies can include:

- Embedding flexible policies that can work in conjunction with the differences that may derive from diverse cultural beliefs and practices
- Co-creating approaches with community members that challenge oppressive systemic barriers
- Highlighting student and family strengths over deficits to ensure that practices do not further stigmatise or 'other' students and families, while still recognizing the impact of cultural and historical trauma.

Communities who are particularly vulnerable due to past or current injustice or disadvantage, for example, First Nations people (who are vulnerable to intergenerational trauma and school exclusion), students and farming families from regional and rural settings (experiencing impact from drought, disasters, and significant loss), LGBTQIA+ people, and people with disability. Thus, a trauma-informed school needs to be rooted in an equity framework with full understanding of the impact of adversity, inequity, and abuse on children and marginalized communities.

As highlighted above, schools need to move away from strategies which focus on reducing 'negative' behaviours and 'poor' emotional regulation which is often reported to be an important target for intervention in trauma-informed intervention. Coming from a strengths-based approach in which the needs of students and other members of the school community (including teachers) are understood is likely to enhance and create a positive and supportive culture for students, teachers, parents, and caregivers. Also required is an understanding that there are likely to be distinct limits schools have in impacting outcomes for some children – particularly those experiencing significant adversity. Learning, social-emotional, and behavioural goals therefore should be individualized for students, considering each student's unique needs, strengths, and trauma experiences.

O'Toole (2022) emphasizes that deficit-based language used in the childhood trauma and trauma-informed literature serves to reinforce negative stereotypes and stigmas associated with children and families exposed to trauma. O'Toole (2022) asserts that such language tends to overlook schools and school systems as contributors to childhood trauma, and marginalization of caregivers and communities. The trauma and trauma-informed literature have also historically been based on the outdated medical model, which emphasizes emotional distress as a symptom of mental illness, rather than a functional response to traumatic experiences. Illustrated in the chapters of this book is a more holistic understanding of childhood trauma and application of trauma-informed principles using socio-cultural frameworks in schools. Understanding the social and cultural determinants of health and wellbeing detailed in Chapters 7 and 9 of this book should be used in the future to design trauma-informed programs that centre a social justice and inclusion lens to trauma-informed responses in schools.

Call for More Research and Evidence-Based Trauma-Informed Programs

As indicated within this book and chapter, there is emerging research demonstrating the benefits of trauma-informed programs in schools. However, researchers continue to call for more evidence and higher quality research (e.g., randomized controlled trials) to evaluate the benefits, and potential risks, of trauma-informed programs in schools. The majority of research evaluating trauma-informed practice in schools has used quasi-experimental or qualitative research design. Currently, there are limited peer-reviewed, published randomized control trials of trauma-informed programs in schools large enough to avoid bias.

Several chapters in this book also identified a lack of research designed to evaluate and improve trauma-informed programs in schools. Chapter 4 discussed the need for more research to evaluate the benefits of trauma-informed programs for cultivating students' sense of belonging. Chapter 6 identified a lack of evidence addressing the significance of the built environment (e.g., classroom design, ambiance, and aesthetic) when implementing trauma-informed programs in schools. Chapter 5 recommended more research to evaluate the benefits of school trauma-informed programs to improve teachers' wellbeing. Several chapters in this book also identified the importance of evidence-based 'whole-school' approaches to implementing and sustaining trauma-informed practice. However, there is limited research which has evaluated the outcomes for students, parents/caregivers, and school staff following implementation of whole-school trauma-informed programs. It is therefore imperative that governments and funding bodies support implementation and research of whole-school trauma-informed programs.

An issue identified in this book is the importance of considering all children, teachers, and parents/caregivers when developing and implementing trauma-informed interventions. MTSS and whole-school approaches can be used to further advocate for the importance of addressing the needs of all members of the school community when designing and delivering trauma-informed models. This is discussed in Chapter 4 which covers the importance of building a sense of belonging and safe school climate for all children, and again in Chapter 6 when discussing that the school build environment can be used to provide the wellbeing of all students and, the 'entire school community', beyond just those exposed to trauma. Chapter 8 recommends that more needs to be done to incorporate and evaluate the benefits of parent/caregiver involvement in delivery of whole-school trauma-informed frameworks, including approaches to educate teachers about how best to communicate with and support parents of students exposed to trauma. Using MTSS and the whole-school components discussed in this final chapter will hopefully provide some guidance to schools and education departments seeking to ensure that all necessary elements of trauma-informed practice are embedded into school systems.

Conclusion

Development and delivery of school trauma-informed programs has increased significantly over the past ten years. And yet, there is limited evidence to support the design and delivery of these programs in schools. The intention of this book was to present the current evidence on trauma-informed approaches in schools, and the limitations and recommendations for further research in this field. This final chapter and the chapters within this book present evidence showing that trauma-informed school practice should be multifaceted, from approaches to support students exposed to trauma and their parents/caregivers, to provision of adequate professional learning and support for teachers and other school staff, and appropriate integration of trauma-informed practice into different areas of the school curriculum. The chapters in this book present clear evidence to support multi-tiered, whole-school trauma-informed practice in schools, but also demonstrate that there are several aspects of the current evidence which are lacking and require additional research to ensure that trauma-informed programs are effective, sustainable, and importantly do no harm to students exposed to trauma, parents and families, and the teachers who support them. Greater financial and government support for research into effective trauma-informed practice in schools is required to enhance current trauma-informed approaches and ensure that we mitigate any risks to students exposed to trauma.

References

Berger, E. (2019). Multi-tiered approaches to trauma-informed care in schools: A systematic review. *School Mental Health, 11*(4), 650–664. https://doi.org/10.1007/s12310-019-09326-0

Berger, E., Martin, K., & Phal, A. (2020). Dealing with student trauma: Exploring school leadership experiences and impact. *Leadership and Policy in Schools, 21*(4), 780–790. https://doi.org/10.1080/15700763.2020.1836231

Berger, E., & Nott, D. (2024). Predictors of compassion fatigue and compassion satisfaction among Australian teachers. *Psychological Trauma: Theory, Research, Practice, and Policy, 16*(8), 1309–1318. https://doi.org/10.1037/tra0001573

Berger, E., O'Donohue, K., La, C., Quiñones, G., & Barnes, M. (2023). Early childhood professionals' perspectives on dealing with trauma of children. *School Mental Health, 15*, 300–311. https://doi.org/10.1007/s12310-022-09551-0

Berger, E., Reupert, A., Stewart, S., Miko, A., Holford, T., & Stracey, L. (2024). School-based well-being programs for children living in regional and rural Australia: Stakeholder views. *Current Psychology, 43*, 220964–220975. https://doi.org/10.1007/s12144-024-05853-5

Dorado, J. S., Martinez, M., McArthur, L. E., & Leibovitz, T. (2016). Healthy Environments and Response to Trauma in Schools (HEARTS): A whole-school, multi-level, prevention and intervention program for creating trauma-informed, safe and supportive schools. *School Mental Health: A Multidisciplinary Research and Practice Journal, 8*(1), 163–176. https://doi.org/10.1007/s12310-016-9177-0

Goldberg, J. M., Sklad, M., Elfrink, T. R., Schreurs, K. M. G., Bohlmeijer, E. T., & Clarke, A. M. (2019). Effectiveness of interventions adopting a whole school approach to enhancing social and emotional development: A meta-analysis. *European Journal of Psychology of Education, 34*(4), 755–782. https://doi.org/10.1007/s10212-018-0406-9

O'Toole, C. (2022). When trauma comes to school: Toward a socially just trauma-informed praxis. *International Journal of School Social Work, 6*(2). https://doi.org/10.4148/2161-4148.1076

Papastylianou, A., Kaila, M., & Polychronopoulos, M. (2009). Teachers' burnout, depression, role ambiguity and conflict. *Social Psychology of Education: An International Journal, 12*(3), 295–314. https://doi.org/10.1007/s11218-008-9086-7

Turan, S., & Bektas, F. (2013). The relationship between school culture and leadership practices. *Eurasian Journal of Educational Research, 52,* 155–168.

World Health Organization. (2023). *How school systems can improve health and wellbeing. Topic brief: Mental health*. World Health Organization.

Index

Note: **Bold** page numbers refer to tables; *italic* page numbers refer to figures and page numbers followed by "n" denote endnotes.

For Product Safety Concerns and Information please contact our
EU representative GPSR@taylorandfrancis.com Taylor & Francis
Verlag GmbH, Kaufingerstraße 24, 80331 München, Germany